D0334844

Aberdeenshire Library and Information Service
www.aberdeenshire.gov.uk/libraries
Renewals Hotline 01224 661511

MERRITT, Stephanie

The devil
within

A L I S

2616610

The Devil Within

The Devil Within

Stephanie Merritt

Vermilion
LONDON

1 3 5 7 9 10 8 6 4 2

Published in 2008 by Vermilion, an imprint of Ebury Publishing

Ebury Publishing is a Random House Group company

The Random House Group Limited Reg. No. 954009

Addresses for companies within the Random House Group can be found at
www.rbooks.co.uk

A CIP catalogue record for this book is available from the British Library

The Random House Group Limited supports The Forest Stewardship
Council (FSC), the leading international forest certification organisation.
All our titles that are printed on Greenpeace approved FSC certified paper carry
the FSC logo. Our paper procurement policy can be found at
www.rbooks.co.uk/environment

Mixed Sources
Product group from well-managed
forests and other controlled sources
www.fsc.org Cert no. TT-COC-2139
© 1996 Forest Stewardship Council

FSC

Printed and bound in Great Britain by Clays of St Ives PLC

ISBN 9780091917456

The publishers have made every reasonable effort to contact the copyright owners of the
extracts reproduced in this book. In the few cases where they have been unsuccessful they
invite copyright holders to contact them direct and corrections can be made in reprints.

I did not hear the bird sounds.
They had left.
I did not see the speechless clouds,
I saw only the little white dish of my faith
breaking in the crater.
I kept saying:
I've got to have something to hold on to.

Anne Sexton, 'The Sickness Unto Death'

Introduction

The winter of 2003. January with its brief, bitter daylight, its forced frugality and sobriety. Less than a week apart, I have turned 29 and my son has turned one. Returning home from work one dark evening on my usual commuter train between London and Hampshire, I find myself alone in a small compartment. The train is the old-fashioned rolling stock, with some carriages partitioned into smaller sections along a narrow corridor for first-class passengers and the odd compartment on the end left for smoking or standard class. These have doors that open from the inside, with a silver spring-loaded catch. As I child I used to worry about these doors endlessly: what if you opened it while the train was moving? There was nothing to stop you. What if you got sucked out through the open door at high speed? The possibility produced a thrilling kind of frisson even then. Half-empty car parks, warehouses and gas cylinders blur past, stained orange in the tired light of street-lamps, and it comes to me with glittering clarity that now would be the time to do it.

For some time now, I have felt that I could not go on for much longer. For months – more than a year, since before my son was born – it is as if I have been incrementally crushed by a weight of despair that has left me unable to feel anything except a sense of complete failure, hopelessness and certainty that I am not up to whatever was being asked of me. I have pretended – quite successfully, it seems – to be coping, but the truth is that I am not coping; the act is exhausting and now I want everyone to leave me alone, to stop making demands, to allow me simply to disappear. I would like very much to be able to admit that I am a failure, that I believe myself to be worthless and think about dying most of the time, that I can't imagine a future in which I will not feel like this, but there are some things you can't say. I am supposed to be a high achiever. I have an enviable job as a literary journalist for a national newspaper, a beautiful healthy baby and, though I am a single parent, I am surrounded by loving, supportive family and friends. I am about to publish my first novel, something I have dreamed of since I first started writing stories in old notebooks as a child. Barely a day passes without someone in the office – usually a woman – stopping me to tell me how admirable I am to juggle all this successfully. When they say that, I shuffle and look at the floor and mumble something that I hope sounds grateful, because I am uncomfortable with praise at the best of times and a little part of me is tempted to tell them that beneath this apparently convincing veneer I am unravelling faster by the day, that I hate my life and spend most nights awake, working out the least inconvenient way to end it. But I don't say this, of course, because I have worked hard to create this illusion of competence, and it would be a shame to shatter their belief.

The train barrels on through the unpeopled stretch of track between the outskirts of London and the string of small country stations where it will begin to slow down. Nothing particularly terrible has happened on this day, no one final blow, but suddenly

I feel with a great sense of urgency that I do not want to go home, where my parents will have collected my son from his nursery and where I will have to make bright, cheery conversation with them about my day at work so that they, too, will be persuaded that I am fine before returning to their own house, leaving me to crouch on the floor in the sitting room in the dark on my own as I often do at night, as if that might make me disappear, as if keeping perfectly still and as small as possible might protect me from doing anything sudden or crazy. Then the baby will wake and need attention and I will have to be cheerful for him too, sing songs and make funny faces until I can once again deposit him gratefully at the nursery and leave him to someone more professional, after which I will drive on to the station, take the train back to London and fake competence in my office for another day, and suddenly I can't do it all over again, not like this, with no prospect of respite, not with this malevolent thing squatting on the back of my neck, pressing its leathery hands around my temples and around my throat. Enough.

Holding the door towards me with one hand, I turn the silver handle 90 degrees to the right with the other until I hear the catch disengage, so that, leaning back, my weight is all that keeps the door from smashing open. For a moment I wonder if it will trigger an alarm, if someone will come, what will happen if they do. But no one appears, and the train hurtles on at what speed I have no idea, but we are a good 15 minutes from the first station so it must be close to full tilt. Years ago, a boy at my school tried to kill himself by jumping in front of a train, but it was slowing into a station and he only lost a leg. I used to wonder, when I saw him limping along the corridors with his stick, if he was glad or sorry about that, but never quite found the courage to ask. But this train has warmed up to a fine speed; this is the time to do it. The landscape looks so sad in the winter dusk: the water treatment plant, the cemetery, the scrubby recreation grounds. These flashing frames are the last bits of the world I will look at; all that is needed is to drop the tension in my arm, allow the door to be torn from my hand and then fall forwards through the space, into the rush of air and slicing wheels and strobing tracks.

I am saved, on this occasion, partly by my own squeamishness, my cowardice in the face of pain. The desire for annihilation, for non-existence, remains real and present, but I find I can't do it so violently; I retain a kind of pitying concern for my physical body, even while I want to be rid of it. There is no need to smash it up altogether. It also occurs to me, as I appear to be frozen in position holding the unlocked door, that although my mother will be spared the initial horror of being the one who finds me, she will almost certainly be called upon to identify whatever can be scraped up off the tracks, and she doesn't deserve that. Then I think of my son, and I realise that I have not left him a note. Though I am still convinced that he and my parents would be better off without me, I feel a sudden compunction: I should not leave him with nothing of me. I am a writer; the least I can do is leave him some kind of account of who I was, how he came to be, not abandon him to other people's versions. One day he will want to know.

So the train slows, eventually, and I am still standing, my arm cramped from the effort of holding the door, still pulled between the urge to fall and the need to stay. I drive home, shaken, and no one knows how close I came to leaving them. But I am afraid, because the compulsion has not gone away; it tugs at me, urgent and tenacious, and I know that soon I will try again, and the next time I will plan it better. I don't feel I have any choice. I understand properly, for the first time, that I am in real danger. The next day, in a state of desperation, I go to the doctor and tell her that if she doesn't help me, I won't be here by the end of the week.

There are other things the people close to me don't know, because I don't tell them, because I am ashamed. They don't know that this is not the first time; these months since my son was born have been the worst, but this black weather has descended on me repeatedly, since the age of 17. They don't know that I have often felt this urge towards self-annihilation: sometimes it comes with a despair that sucks all power of movement from my limbs and renders me incapable of the smallest decisions, so that all I can do is lie down with the curtains closed, facing the wall, and pray to be left alone, but at others it rushes in with a kind of malign energy, like a sudden surge of voltage, a frenzied compulsion to run head-long into destruction. I had never told anyone about this for the simple reason that I felt it was a problem exclusive to me, a fault in my attitude, my character. These black moods never appeared out of nowhere; with me, they were always a response to events, some-times the most trivial, everyday occurrences that other people seemed able to accommodate and ride out with dignity. Minor heartbreak, disappointment, small failures would hurl me into raging seas of despair so wholly disproportionate to the reality of the situation and its consequences that I was often accused of being melodramatic or over-reacting, and so I came to believe that this was a fault of my character, an inability to behave with maturity and the temperate moods that responsible British adults are expected to exhibit. Uncontrollable mood swings are, after all, the hallmark of adolescence, and I feared that my failure to rein in my moods (I was also capable of unbounded, wildly careening hope and over-optimism, on the slightest of triggers) was indicative of a failure somehow to grow up, to fit in. It never occurred to me that it might have a medical name.

On that occasion, the doctor gave me antidepressants and sent me on my way. When, two years later, it returned with the same vigour, I wanted more than a prescription. I wanted to find out why I was so often prey to these moods, what caused them and whether I could find something beyond repeat prescriptions of pills that might treat the root cause, not just the symptoms. Eventually, at the age of 32, I was diagnosed by a psychiatrist as having a 'soft', that is, non-psychotic, form of bipolar disorder, or manic depression.

My reaction to this diagnosis was split: part of me wanted to disown it, to argue that it couldn't be anything like that. Manic depression was an illness I associated with artists such as Virginia Woolf or Vincent Van Gogh, people who, in my view, blazed brilliantly and as a corollary had properly crossed the border into the land of the crazy. I didn't belong in such company, in any sense. But another part of me wanted to hug the shrink and weep with relief. It wasn't my fault! Giving a name to it, discovering that it was a recognised illness, lifted some of the responsibility I felt for certain aspects of my behaviour over the years. Perhaps I was not a terrible person after all. Bipolar disorder, like unipolar depression, which doesn't have manic episodes, exists as a spectrum of moods. There is no test that will prove you positive or negative; people experience these mood disorders by degrees of severity. Though I had never experienced an episode of psychotic mania, I came to recognise that I had, since I first began to suffer episodes of depression, also lived through periods of what is called hypomania (from the Greek for 'little mania'), though I did not know enough to recognise them as such. The shrink explained to me that symptoms of hypomania can include excessive energy, decreased need for sleep, increased sociability, disinhibition and creativity, flights of over-optimism, reckless or impetuous behaviour and spending, and increased urges towards alcohol, drugs and promiscuity. He was describing the way I had lived for half of my twenties. Oh, I said. Well, that explains a lot.

Recently, at the Edinburgh Fringe, I listened to a debate about taboos in comedy. One of the participants was the comic André Vincent, who had created a critically acclaimed show about his experience of cancer. Vincent told the audience how, afterwards, a young woman had accosted him in the street in Edinburgh and pressed into his hand a flyer for her own one-woman show, insisting that he would appreciate it because it was similar to his own. It was a show about her depression, she explained.

'Depression?' Vincent exploded, his eyes fairly popping with incredulity. '*Depression?!!* I had fucking *cancer!*'

If we're honest, this is the response most of us would have. Cancer, we feel, is a proper, frightening illness that can kill; it's usually not your fault if you get it, and even if it is, no one would be so unfeeling as to say so. If you have cancer, you deserve the best medical treatment at any price, and there is national media outrage when the NHS refuses life-saving cancer treatments on the grounds of cost. Very few people, if diagnosed with cancer, would feel the need to hide the fact or go about their lives pretending, even to themselves, that nothing was wrong, nor would they be too ashamed to ask for medical help; neither would their friends dream of telling them to come for a drink, pull themselves together and think of all the people who were much worse off than themselves.

Depression, on the other hand, is one of those words, like 'schizophrenic' or 'fascist', whose meaning in our culture has become blunted by common misuse. 'God, I'm depressed,' we say, at the end of a long day, when we really mean disappointed or fed-up or frustrated, or just plain old sad, and anyone fortunate enough never to have experienced severe depression could be forgiven for imagining that those who claim it as an illness are merely overdramatising one of the above. But clinical depression is as far removed from sadness or disappointment as it is from joy; it exists outside the normal spectrum of light and shade that make up human emotion, like a flatlining of the self. The late William Styron called it 'a true wimp of a word for such a major illness'.

Perhaps this confusion over semantics is the reason for a perceived lack of sympathy about depression, and explains why many of us are reluctant to admit to it or to seek help. Everyone knows what it means to feel sad, bereaved, heartbroken, lonely, futile; we have all felt at some time that there was no good reason to get up in the morning, but we don't all demand time off work because of it. The most recent NICE guidelines for medical professionals, published in 2007, state that for a diagnosis of 'depression' the patient needs to have experienced a certain number of ten key symptoms every day for at least a month, but concedes, 'it is doubtful whether the severity of the depressive illness can realistically be captured in a single symptom count'. In my experience, the clearest distinction between the kind of low mood that occurs to everyone as part of our normal emotional language, and depression as an illness, is the loss of volition. Ordinary unhappiness can be alleviated, to a greater or lesser degree, by some effort on our part, or on the part of our friends, to do something proactive that will take our mind off it. Depression is a bleakness that has gone beyond your control: you can no longer climb out of it through any act of will or be jollied out of it by others or by a change of circumstance. In this state of mind, you believe that neither the best nor the worst news imaginable would make any measurable difference to the way you feel. You cannot take your mind off it, because it *is* your mind: bitter, relentless, despairing.

The stigma may have lessened in recent years, but still it remains. Even the phrase 'mental health problems' drags behind it all kinds of connotations that make me recoil from applying the words to myself. More than once while I was writing this book, whose aim is partly to lessen that stigma, when asked by people I didn't know well what I was working on, I would hear myself answer quickly, 'it's about psychology', in order to spare their embarrassment and mine. We are not comfortable talking about depression. Our culture insists on success and the pursuit of happiness; to own up to depression looks like an admission of failure at life.

At its heart, depression remains a knot of contradictions. It is an illness of the mind and the emotions which nevertheless produces (and can be produced by) demonstrable chemical changes in the brain and an array of crippling physical symptoms. It can grow stealthily from the most obvious and logical causes – abuse, trauma, grief, loss – or it can apparently crash unexpectedly into the midst of a life that outwardly contains all the ingredients for happiness. Some experts argue that its prevalence in modern, affluent societies is directly linked to a consumer culture dominated by advertising and obsessed with personal wealth, fame and success; others suggest it is linked to poor modern diet and an abundance of pollutants, or a by-product of our urbanised, atomised society, stripped of the support systems of extended family and cohesive communities with shared values; still others assert that we have too readily pathologised everyday anxieties or fluctuations of mood that our more stoical forebears would either not have had time to contemplate or simply endured without complaint as part of life. In 2006, The Depression Report, an extensive study by the Mental Health Policy Group at the London School of Economics, concluded that only a quarter of those suffering from depression in the UK were receiving treatment, while a year later, a report in the British Medical Journal stated that doctors are diagnosing 'depression' at too low a threshold and over-prescribing antidepressant medication, where 20 years ago they would simply have recommended a brisk walk or a holiday. No wonder there is such confusion about recognising and responding to this condition.

Yet, according to the most recent Psychiatric Morbidity Survey carried out in 2000 by the Office of National Statistics, between one in ten and one in six of us in the UK would be diagnosed as suffering from depression at any one time; in 2006, 31 million prescriptions for antidepressant medication were written in Britain, a rise of six per cent on the previous year. Statistics produced by the American Foundation for Suicide Prevention state that every 16 minutes someone in the US dies by suicide. According to the World Health Organization, depression is presently the second biggest killer worldwide for people in the 15–44 age range and by 2020 is predicted to be the second biggest killer, after heart disease, altogether. Approximately 850,000 people commit suicide every year as a result of depression. The WHO also states that 'barriers to effective care include the lack of resources, lack of trained providers, and the social stigma associated with mental disorders including depression'. This description is, shamefully, as true of the UK and the US as it is for parts of the developing world.

It is important to make clear that bipolar disorder and unipolar depression are not the same condition – the former is thought to have a stronger genetic basis and is experienced more equally between men and women, while depression without manic episodes is twice as common in women – and I do not wish to give the impression that the conditions are interchangeable. But the experience of depression has much in common in both conditions, including almost identical diagnostic criteria, and since it is through my depressive episodes that I finally understood the illness and was able to receive diagnosis and treatment, I hope that this book will be relevant to anyone who has suffered or wishes to understand depression, regardless of whether it comes accompanied by mania or hypomania. Professor Nick Craddock, who leads the Mood Disorders Research Team at the University of Cardiff, believes that there is a lot of evidence to suggest that bipolar disorders are vastly underdiagnosed, since many people only seek treatment during episodes of depression and may not even have recognised their hypomanic moments as such, which was certainly true in my case. Unfortunately, medication that proves effective for unipolar depression can cause additional problems for those with a bipolar tendency. 'There is increasing recognition among researchers that we have to get a lot better at picking out who has a bipolar type of depressed mood and who has unipolar so that you can be much safer in using antidepressants,' explains Professor Craddock, though he reiterates the difficulty for health-care professionals with limited time and resources in distinguishing and diagnosing from depressive symptoms alone.

If I had to summarise how depression feels from inside, I would call it the absence of hope. It is the sense that you will always be like this, that nothing can change, that there is nothing to look forward to and no reason to go on. To exist without hope is not only to be alienated from life, it is actively life-threatening; without hope, the logical conclusion is that there is no point, and after that comes nihilism. Rebecca Solnit, in her inspiring book about political activism, *Hope in the Dark*, writes: 'To hope is to give yourself to the future, and that commitment to the future makes the present inhabitable.' This remains as true on the individual level as it is on the global.

This was not a book I expected to write. 'Tell the truth, but tell it slant,' wrote Christina Rossetti, and I have always used the prism of fiction and drama to do that. In writing about my own experience I have had to reach for a kind of honesty that necessarily ripples out to the people whose lives have touched mine, and who have not asked to be written about. Therefore I have tried to be circumspect, and in particular have written very little about my immediate family out of a wish to protect their privacy as far as possible. While I have also changed some names, I have not fictionalised events or people.

Neither did I expect to find myself writing so much about faith, but I found I could not separate it from my experience. I grew up in an evangelical Christian church that furnished me as a child and teenager with membership of a close-knit, supportive community and, on a philosophical level, with definitive answers to the big existential questions and a high degree of security about the purpose of the universe and my place within it. In my late teens I could no longer convince myself of the truth of this belief system and left the church; the subsequent loss of that kind of certainty had a more profound effect on me than I realised at the time. In his recent book *Affluenza*, an international study of depression and anxiety and their relation to the dominant culture, the psychologist Oliver James remarks that 'wherever I went, I found that religion seemed to be a powerful vaccine'. The significantly lower incidences of these disorders among religious believers, he notes, 'is regardless of the kind of religion, or of the nationality, gender, age, social class or ethnic background of the believer'. For all its many faults, a widely practised and accepted religious culture used to provide people with a support system, shared values, moral certainties and the opportunity – through confession or prayer – for people to talk about their problems and concerns to someone whose job it was to listen and dispense advice. Now that, for most of us, these elements are not features of our lives, what we have gained in terms of intellectual and individual freedoms is countered by the fact that we are undoubtedly more isolated and perhaps less sure about what we should value. Though I had experienced depression before I lost my faith, these questions have remained inseparable. I have found it curious, too, how often religious imagery is used in descriptions of depression. In the Middle Ages this black melancholia was viewed – as were most psychological disturbances – as caused by demonic influence, something bad and sinful, the opposite of godly, and this image of possession by a malevolent, supernatural force remains one of the most powerful and frequent in contemporary writing about depression – with reason, for this is often how depression feels. On a more damaging level, the idea that depression is a sin or a fault of the sufferer has also persisted, with the result that many people feel terrible guilt about their depression, and this is a cultural perception that we really do need to change.

All my life I had looked in novels and plays for understanding of my own experience and emotions, but in the worst of my depressions, I found I could not read fiction, nor persuade myself that it mattered. The only glimmer of connection in those moments came to me through the accounts of others who had walked where I was then walking, without light or oxygen; brave and honest narratives of despair, and the other side of despair, by writers such as William Styron, Andrew Solomon, Lewis Wolpert, Richard Mabey, Kay Redfield Jamison and Elizabeth Wurtzel. They had put their agony into words so that I might feel less alone in mine, and I remain profoundly grateful for those books and the wisdom and empathy I found in them. I add my account, then, only as the story of one person's ongoing journey through the dark to the discovery that depression can be battled and hope imperfectly learned. If there are one or two thoughts here that might be useful or encouraging to those in similar circumstances, I would be glad.

1

The Devil Within

As the setting for an exorcism, the Morrisons' pleasant suburban sitting room with its floral three-piece suite was disappointingly lacking in atmosphere. Secretly, I would have preferred the odd theatrical flourish: incense, candles, Gothic architecture, priests in robes or at least a bit of Latin, and if my father had stayed true to his Irish Catholic upbringing, instead of converting to the evangelicals when he met my mother, I might now be enjoying all the solemn trappings of ecclesiastical ritual that the event ought to demand. The point of the Morrisons' sitting room, of course, was to emphasise the whole ethos of our church: that God didn't demand fancy architecture or the business of ceremony. He was present everywhere and anywhere. Besides, if we had been Catholic, I probably wouldn't be having the exorcism at all. I wasn't sure that the modern Catholic church still countenanced the casting out of evil spirits, though it was still their province in cinema and the popular imagination. But the popular imagination had not yet learned the truth about biblical signs and wonders, that they had apparently been rediscovered by the charismatic churches in the seventies and eighties, whose services often ended up in extemporaneous singing in tongues or healing the sick or with the entire congregation keeling over, lying on the floor and laughing hysterically. The early nineties was an exciting time to be a teenager in one of these churches; suddenly faith was something real and unpredictable. After all, didn't Jesus command his disciples to 'Heal the sick, raise the dead, cleanse those who have leprosy, drive out demons' (Matthew 10:8), and wasn't it precisely these manifestations of His Spirit at work that were attracting people towards the charismatic movement and away from the traditional churches, with their King James language, their staid prayer books, their ancient hymns and not an electric guitar in sight? It seemed so to me in my mid-teens, on the brink of a promised spiritual revival across the land. At least, it had seemed so in the days before all my enthusiasm was inexplicably snuffed out by this wasting despair that had brought me to the Morrisons' in the first place.

Sue handed me a cup of tea as I tipped back into their low-slung sofa, and offered a reassuring pat on the knee. Above me, Roger Morrison loomed enormously in his Pringle sweater, stroking his chin and measuring me up in silence, with the expression of someone trying to judge if his car would fit in a tricky parking space. I wondered if God was speaking to him at that moment, and if so, what exactly He might be divulging. Could Roger actually *see* the demons in me, or was it more of an inner sense? Through the windows that faced the lane, a pearly, hard-edged sky was visible above the scalloped net curtains; the winter of 1991 still resisting spring. I was 17, pale and too thin. Not so thin yet as to require medical intervention, but growing noticeably underweight for my height, thin enough to cause my parents increasing concern, though I still saw, if ever I was incautious enough to catch a glimpse of myself in a shop window, a monstrous lumbering bulk that demanded ever more stringent measures to keep it in check. I hated her, that fat girl in the window. It was my job to see her punished for being so ugly. In fact, much of the time I wished her dead.

There was no obvious reason for the change in me, for this darkness that had apparently descended out of nowhere and felt as if it were both inside my head trying to burst its way out and outside, clamped around my eyes and temples, squeezing inwards. My life so far had been notable for its absence of trauma, for its uneventful cosiness. I had grown up in a small village in the Home Counties, a comfortable and affluent part of England, safely cocooned in a loving family, my parents still married to each other and devoted to me and my little brother, seven years my junior. My parents both taught at a sixth-form college, but both were first-generation graduates from working-class homes where money had been very tight and they knew how to look after what they had, so I was never aware, growing up, that in relative terms we were not well off; my brother and I never missed out on holidays or school trips abroad through lack of resources. But we had a house full of classical records and books in three languages and were taken to the theatre, which was enough to qualify us as 'posh' in the eyes of some of my schoolmates. Beyond this, we were further nurtured by the extended family of the church, which was the centre of all our social life; most of our extra-curricular activities as children – drama, music, summer camps – was centred on the church and its various groups. Throughout my childhood, our church was a small and rather sedate, traditional kind of evangelical church, much like hundreds of others across the country. At Sunday School we were taught Bible stories, songs about Noah's Ark and learned verses by heart in return for sweets or coloured pencils. The church supported missionaries, who would appear at intervals to give talks with slide shows about the schools and churches they ran in Africa or India, where I saw brown-skinned children with dusty feet laughing into the camera, and felt glad that putting my ten pence into the collection purse meant that those children had the chance to learn about Jesus. Church was part of the fabric of my growing up, the structure of my weekly routine, and it never occurred to me to question it.

As I reached my teens, though, the church was changing. In subtle ways, at first; the hymns were replaced by more modern songs and the old organ was stripped out to make way for guitars and electric keyboards. During the songs, people would clap and raise their hands, and then dancing became commonplace, a form of worship borrowed from the gospel churches and giving rise to the 'happy-clappy' label. The congregation began to grow and to include more young people, twenty-somethings and young families; we could no longer fit everyone in the old chapel and instead began to meet in the local cinema, which seemed to aid a transition to greater informality.

But the real revolution was spiritual. Gradually our church had been caught up in the movement sometimes called 'charismatic renewal'. Though it was not specific to any Christian denomination, 'charismatic renewal' flourished in the less formal, low churches and grew from an interpretation of the Bible that put great emphasis on the account of the day of Pentecost in the Acts of the Apostles, when the Holy Spirit descended on the early church and gave the apostles supernatural gifts: the ability to heal the sick, cast out demons, speak in unknown spiritual languages – 'the gift of tongues' – and display powers of knowledge that appeared psychic. If God was unchanging, it was argued, then the power of God must be the same today as it was on the day of

Pentecost, and these same supernatural gifts must still be available to those who have faith. Though in format the church seemed to have grown more modern, it had certainly not grown liberal; evangelical theology depended on a fairly literal reading of the Bible and was ultra-conservative in its stance on issues such as marriage, homosexuality, other religions and the sanctity of life.

As our church transformed, my understanding of religious faith altered; from being something you learned about, it was transformed into something that you lived, and it was this sense of immediacy, this potential for drama, that attracted so many young people to the charismatic churches and upended their ideas about religion; that and the music. I heard people around me speaking in tongues; I knew people who claimed to have been healed miraculously and – most awesome of all – I had witnessed people being delivered from demons.

The first time was at the end of a meeting at one of the larger local churches our youth group sometimes visited, but I had observed it more ostentatiously at a Christian Bible Week in the Malvern Hills, where I had been volunteering as a children's drama leader. Satan and his demons in all their various manifestations had received a great deal of attention at the Malvern camp because of our situation, both geographically and historically. The gently swelling green and pleasant hills that hugged the festival site, home to Elgar and mineral water, were, according to the people who knew about such things, situated on a significant ley line and magnetised a dramatic amount of occult activity. There were even, said the people who knew, covens of *witches* who met in the hills. Boldly convening a festival of Christian worship in the midst of such a satanic stronghold was therefore an act of aggression in the spiritual realm, like poking a wasps' nest, and we could expect quite a stirring of demonic activity. This prospect was thrilling to most of the young people, who were secretly quite excited about witnessing real demons; it added a cinematic frisson to our faith.

Walking back to my tent late one evening, I passed one of the marquees where the aftermath of an evening meeting could be glimpsed through the rolled-up canvas side. Scattered about the tent were individuals, mostly on the floor, shaking, convulsing, crying, shouting and in some cases producing odd, guttural screams. Gathered about these individuals were clusters of people standing or kneeling and praying aloud, largely in tongues. Each of these groups seemed to have one authority figure doing the actual deliverance, which was effected (and here life was not so different from films) by shouting at the demon in the person, commanding it to come out in the name of Jesus. In gaping fascination I drew closer, like a bystander at a medical emergency. According to both folklore and charismatic Christian teaching, demons come out through the mouth. From the people on the ground rose a cacophony of hissing, choking and retching, and as the prone figures began to make these noises, the voice of the person casting out the demon grew correspondingly sterner and louder, until eventually the demonised person appeared to slump and lie quite still, as if exhausted by an epileptic fit, whereupon the group would begin to offer prayers and songs of thanks to God.

My curiosity as I hovered in the shadows of the marquee, watching, was forensic, but I was not afraid. My faith, then, was ardent and sincere enough to accept that, in the grand scheme of things, Satan was not only real but was already defeated by the resurrection of Christ, as the demons well knew, so that all this was mere sound and fury. I knew this with the same certainty that I knew, on first reading *The Lion, The Witch and The Wardrobe* or

Lord of the Rings, that Aslan and Gandalf would come back to life – because the story demanded a trust in the triumph of Good. But although the end result was guaranteed, the drama still had to be played out, like a rigged fight, until the final bell, and this was known as Spiritual Warfare.

Spiritual Warfare was a prominent activity of these charismatic churches at the end of the twentieth century. According to the Bible, from the fall of Lucifer to the Apocalypse, the Earth has been and will be the battleground for a cosmic conflict between angels and demons, played out in human souls, but we were far from passive chess pieces – through prayer, Christians could affect the outcome of struggles in the heavenly realms and reclaim territory on Earth for the Lord. Most mainstream variants of Christianity believe this, but, since we graduated from the age of burning witches, most had accepted it as metaphor. Now, with the advent of charismatic renewal, the role of demons had been re-evaluated, and many evangelicals were being taught that they were neither medieval folklore nor symbolic, but an unseen reality. Some Christians believed that the influence of demons was to blame for every malady from migraines to alcoholism, but most especially when it came to disorders of the mind. We were spiritual beings, and if your relationship with God were out of kilter, this allowed room for demons, which would in turn affect your emotions, your self-image, your ability to relate to others. I had never heard of anyone seeing a psychotherapist; why would you? Applying a secular remedy to a spiritual problem could never find and heal its root.

Instead, the church offered its own support system in the form of counsellors, women (they were almost always women) who had taken a short course in Christian counselling but generally had no formal training or qualifications in psychology, and whose role was largely to provide tea, sympathy and prayer for those in the church who needed an ear and a kind word.

At 17, when I became 'difficult', I was sent to one of these counsellors; a compromise made under duress once it became clear to my parents that what had begun as faddy eating and teenage sulks had shifted into deliberate starvation and a filthy black mood that infected the whole house with dank self-loathing. It was not that I didn't get on with my parents – by 17 I was over the worst of my early experiments in teenage rebellion and not yet winding up for the full-throttle leap into hedonism that came with leaving home, so most of the time our relations were quite cordial – but some things were simply too vast and too volatile to be unleashed within a family. Things that would shake its very foundation and alter its shape irreparably; how, for example, were you supposed to tell your own mother that every waking moment you thought about killing yourself? It seemed ungrateful, to say the least.

My poor parents, who had never come into contact with eating disorders or depression, both of which were far less openly discussed then, were at a loss. At first my mother had generously tried to accommodate my increasingly peculiar dietary requirements into family meals and my father had attempted to jolt me out of this silliness with humour ('Pull up a couple of chairs,' he would say jovially, the point being that he would never say such a thing to a real fat person). But when we reached the point where I would consume only black coffee and apples, get up to cycle ten miles every morning before college and experienced panic attacks if asked to try a piece of toast, they decided that I had gone beyond self-indulgent, and that firmer measures were required. Their approach was to treat my behaviour as if it were any other wilful act of teenage rebellion, with a combination of coercion and bribery. It must have looked whimsical to them; wilful attention-seeking. To me it had become a matter of mortal terror. I was afraid of food, afraid of my reflection, afraid of being in company. Sometimes, when I caught sight of myself in a glass door or shop window, it would set off an explosion inside my skull, glittering black fireworks that left me shaking with the compulsion to some act of blind self-harm. There were moments when I thought I was losing my mind, but I couldn't explain the way it had taken me over, so it went on looking as if I were being simply perverse. I was not fat by anyone's standards, I was told, surely I must see that; why was I being so ridiculous? My parents offered me the choice between counselling and the doctor. I was not an idiot: the doctor would make me eat, and that would make me *fat* (or fat*ter*).

My counsellor was called Ruth; she was a handsome, well-spoken woman in her fifties with a silver-blonde bob and a rare mystique. Ruth approached counselling with experience of a different kind of life from that of the Christians I knew; she had come to faith after many picaresque years of exotic travel and worldly adventures, darkly hinted-at. On Sunday mornings, after church, she actually *smoked* in the car park outside the hall, and no one ever told her she mustn't, although all the Christians I knew frowned on smoking; she seemed to have a special dispensation. Ruth was one of the few adults I knew who had really *lived*, so I grudgingly tolerated these visits and secretly liked listening to her rich tarry voice, which sounded as if it had been marinating for years in a basement blues bar.

Gradually, her kindness and cups of tea, together with the tobacco-edged aura of expensive perfume and the gentle clinking of her silver bracelets, softened me a little and unbuttoned my resistance, though it was painstaking archaeological work for her; I was unused to talking to anyone about my intimate thoughts, and every tiny admission had to be coaxed out and carefully examined. Whatever she saw in me must have daunted her, though, because on our second or third session she announced that she felt I needed special prayer, and that instead of coming to see her the following week, she would make an appointment for me to see Roger Morrison.

I knew what this meant, of course; everyone in our church knew the shorthand. Roger Morrison was one of the senior church leaders, whose spiritual stature matched his physical enormity; he was known as a figure of great faith and authority who had a surprisingly gentle voice and tiny round glasses that seemed too small for him and perched on the end of his nose like a womble's. But he was recognised in our church as having a special gift from God for the discernment and deliverance of demons. If Ruth was suggesting a visit to Roger – and his wife Sue, of course, since it was inappropriate for any male leader to pray with a woman alone, which was why so many married couples went into ministry together – she must think I have demons, I concluded, as if demons were a sort of virus. I did not question her judgement. Over the past few months it had come to feel very much as if some evil gargoyle had perched on my shoulders and spread its leathery wings over my eyes; I had no reasonable explanation for this tide of misery that had recently engulfed me and which I could not seem to shake through any effort of will. It felt alien, imposed on me from outside. In the absence of any knowledge or understanding of depressive illness I was quite willing to try out a diagnosis of demons.

After much tilting of head and stroking of chin, Roger

Morrison sat on the other side of me and clasped his hands together. Before he began to pray, he explained, there were a few things I needed to know about demons. As a born-again Christian – I nodded fervently, anxious that there should be no doubt on that point – I could not be possessed by demons, but I could be *oppressed* by them if I had unwittingly left a door open in my life through sin. Demons, it seemed, were less like a virus than an infestation of mice; they needed to be flushed out and their point of entry firmly boarded up.

Had I been dabbling in the occult? Roger asked, gently but with terrible sternness.

I most certainly had not! I was certain of my purity on that point, since I was genuinely terrified of such things – my memory was so photographically vivid and my imagination so lurid that I had never managed to sit through a single horror film from start to finish because I knew the subsequent nightmares and sleepless nights of terror were not worth it; I had always run away to another room when friends brought out R18 videos at sleepovers. Once, one of the most popular girls at school, whom I had desperately wanted to impress, had brought out a ouija board when a group of us were gathered at her house on a wet afternoon; I had declared, with mortifying embarrassment, that my religion would not permit me to take part, and so I left, enduring their mockery and jeering with tight throat and pricking eyes, rather than dare run the risk of contacting dark powers. Growing up in the church, the reality of Satan and his better-known wiles had been so impressed upon me that I could never treat any form of divination – even a sideshow fortune teller or *Jackie* magazine's horoscope – as a harmless game.

Was I then, Roger continued, guilty of sexual immorality?

This one required more sophistry. Technically, sexual immorality included everything except *doing it* with a person of the opposite sex to whom you were legally married, and even then you had to be wary of certain more exotic practices. I had not yet *done it* with anyone, not for lack of interest but for much the same reasons that I fled from the ouija board: I was terrified of the metaphysical consequences. This was before the age of formalised virginity pledges and the Silver Ring Thing so popular among evangelical youth in the US, but it had been impressed upon us at our youth group meetings that virginity was a gift you could only give once, and how would we feel explaining to our future husband or wife that this precious commodity we should have saved for them alone had already been squandered elsewhere? (It was simply assumed that we would all achieve a husband or wife at some point, and that we would all want one.) So I had not been *doing it*, but I did have a boyfriend and a couple of brief experimental encounters and I suspected that I might, in the course of these explorations, have passed the limit of what Jesus would tolerate. What exactly constituted appropriate physical expression for Christian youth was the subject of much debate; I heard one Christian leader encapsulate it charmingly with the maxim 'Don't touch anything you haven't got yourself'. The more legalistic among us instantly found exploitable loopholes in this, but it seemed unlikely that my inexpert fumblings had been egregious enough to invite in demons. But then who was I to judge? Nor did I want to discuss this in detail with Roger and Sue, but I was nervous about Words of Knowledge – the gift of the Holy Spirit whereby God gave a person specific supernatural information about another person for the purposes of prayer, healing or encouragement. I suspected Roger got these regularly; he struck me as the sort of person God would confide in.

There were other possible points of entry for the demons, Roger explained, false religion and the generational curse. I knew about the spectre of Catholicism in my father's family, with all its idolatry of the Holy Mother and unbiblical ideas of Purgatory and Limbo; worse still, what my Nana practised was working-class northern Irish Catholicism, nurtured in the Bogside and, for her generation of uneducated women, inseparably entwined with ancient folklore and pagan superstition. Beyond that, I had no idea what unholy shenanigans my ancestors might have got up to. I was told that I should seek God's guidance to reveal the demons' path into my life so that I could renounce it and be forgiven; the deliverance required active engagement of my will as well. Obediently, I closed my eyes and prayed, partly afraid of what might happen next, but knowing too that I would be frantically disappointed if nothing did. Like Doubting Thomas, I itched for some irrefutable proof that the object of my faith was real. I was not keen on the idea that I might have demons in me, but at least it would mean that this darkness was not strictly my fault.

*L*ate teens to early twenties is the most frequent age of onset for bipolar disorders, but at the time I had no idea that I was suffering an episode of depression, or even what depression was, or that there was anything at all unusual or illogical about my behaviour. In common with many other teenage girls, I simply thought I was too fat, and that being too fat was the root cause of all my unhappiness and poor self-esteem; if I could become thin, I believed, it would automatically follow that I would be prettier, more popular and instantly happier. According to Ulrike Schmidt, Professor in Eating Disorders at London's Institute of Psychiatry, there is some overlap between depression and eating disorders in terms of genetic predisposition and childhood risk factors, but additional factors are present in the development of eating disorders – usually family issues with food and weight or prolonged criticism about weight or appearance. 'So this is something that affects young women who might otherwise have developed depression,' she explains, 'but because weight has always mattered they have been pushed in that direction rather than just depression. If you ask people with bulimia about depression many have had episodes before developing bulimia, and once you have an eating disorder, you can develop symptoms of depression such as feeling exhausted, feeling bad about what you're doing, so that it becomes difficult to distinguish between the two.' A study carried out in the US in 2005 showed that people with bipolar disorder have a much higher incidence of eating disorders than the general population and concluded that the two are related.

A friend once claimed that he'd nailed the secret of success with women: tell pretty girls that they're clever, and clever girls they're pretty. There is a brutal logic behind the joke; we are all insecure about those qualities we imagine ourselves to lack. I was one of the clever girls who had never bothered much about being pretty as a child, but by the time I reached my mid-teens, I was fully convinced that I was hideous to look at; after all, I had been told so almost relentlessly since the beginning of secondary school by a group of girls who devoted hours of creative ingenuity to harassing me. As a child, being top of the class was something I had been encouraged to feel proud of, though privately I never regarded being good at reading as any kind of special talent, it was just something you did, like washing or eating. It was not until I arrived at secondary school that I discovered it might in fact be something to hide.

At the age of 11, I had looked forward to going up to my comprehensive and had taken great care and pride, as August faded towards autumn, in assembling for the new term an exemplary collection of stationery and folders and different coloured pens for different subjects, because I liked to be methodical and orderly. I had a new uniform: grey shoes with a coppery buckle and a crisp bottle-green blazer with the school crest, a silver deer, embroidered on the breast pocket. Neatly parcelled in my buttoned-up uniform, I entered that school on the first day of term a happy, outgoing child who for the preceding 11 years had been loved and praised and had no reason to dislike herself.

Almost immediately I discovered that I was all wrong. Not that I had got things wrong; I simply *was* wrong, everything about me was wrong, from my hair to my bag to my shoes to my music (mainly my dad's extensive album collection from the sixties – Beatles, Beach Boys, Hollies, Small Faces, Simon and Garfunkel, Dylan – and a woeful amount of Christian rock) to my vocabulary – my first nickname, bestowed on me by Joe Burgess, the class rebel with the Flock of Seagulls haircut, was 'Granny', on the grounds that only really *old* people used long words.

The hard-faced kids from the estates generally took against the children of the middle-class lefties, with their piano lessons and their trips to the Science Museum, but within this crude schism were curious sub-cults, factions and unlikely alliances, none of which seemed to include me. I had no knack for joining groups; I just didn't know how it was done, though everyone else seemed to have the secret and I longed to share it. These little cliques that sprang into being, fully formed, in our new tutor group – how had they done it? I began to worry that I had missed some kind of orientation day on which all these supposedly new, lost people like me had bonded in my absence. I had been a solitary child by preference; now I was solitary by default. Everyone seemed to have filled up their quota of friends before I got there, though I made a few attempts. Inevitably, though, my untethered status, together with my terminally uncool appearance and my shameless pursuit of top grades, were an invitation to demolition.

'Merritt, you fat bitch.'

'Oi, Merritt, who cuts your hair – your blind nan?'

'Where did you get your jumper, Merritt – *Oxfam*?'

'Why have you got a *boy's* bag, Merritt – are you a lezzer?'

'She must be, cause no one would ever fancy her except another fat *lezzer*.'

'Oi, Merritt – did your *mum* buy your shoes?'

Of course my mum bought my shoes, I thought. Then I realised that she was implying my mum had *chosen* my shoes, and that was dismaying, because in fact *I* had chosen my shoes because I'd thought they were unusual and a bit daring, with the buckle and everything, and they were more than my mum had wanted to pay for school shoes but I'd pleaded because this was secondary school and it was essential to have the right ones, except that it now appeared these were not the right shoes at all, not by a long way. I had been so thrilled to carry them home and had worn them around the house at every opportunity, and now Melanie Cleaver, with her pre-teen sexual bravado and her corkscrew perm, and her sidekick Louise Jones, who skulked behind a peroxide fringe, were sneering at my shoes because they were ugly, and I saw that in fact they *were* ugly, and began to hate them, feeling guilty and ungrateful as I did so.

'*Lezzer* shoes.'

It continued in this relentless but uninspired vein, which remained largely ignorable until the werewolf day. School Meeting took place every Friday afternoon, all eleven hundred pupils packed into the sports hall for the usual miscellany of vaguely religious sentiment, awards and notices and usually a recital from a string quartet. The fifth years slouched on chairs at the back, leggy and laconic, while the rest of us had to sit on the concrete floor, shifting and fidgeting endlessly with knees pulled up to our chests. One such Friday afternoon I was minding my own business as the Head delivered an anodyne homily about community spirit, when I became oddly aware that the boy next to me was staring fiercely. I glanced sideways at him and he looked away, but the minute my profile turned again to the front I could feel his eyes on me again. It was a very determined stare, with undertones of incredulity; then he turned to the boy on his right and whispered something, and this boy leaned round, stared at me, and then giggled and whispered to the person on his right. The whispering and laughter began to spread virally outwards from me; people in other rows were turning to see the spectacle, and two rows in front, a fourth-year boy called Craig, who was icily supercilious and even then magnificently camp, scooted a quick backward glance at me and whispered to the girl next to him, 'Oh. My. *God*. You *have* to look.'

At first I tried to tell myself that it wasn't actually me that was the focus of all this attention; when this was no longer convincing, I silently asked Jesus to help me not to cry, and He more or less obliged. I went on staring ahead as the Head held forth about tolerance and respect (it was always about tolerance and respect, and fuck all good it did too), biting the insides of my cheeks as the outsides grew deeper and deeper scarlet, and tried to work out what it was about me that had occasioned such derision. Was it the shoes? I looked down to examine them once more and it was at that point that I heard the word, borne to me on a current of whispers, and finally understood.

'*Werewolf!*'

I had been a committed tomboy throughout my childhood and had not yet outgrown it; at 11, I was still very young in many ways, compared to the knowing girls who had older sisters and were already experimenting with boys. I had not yet developed any interest in lipstick, mascara, exfoliating, waxing, varnishing, buffing, tanning, dyeing, perming, crimping or primping, and I couldn't remember the last time I had even taken any notice of my legs, other than to count the impressive collection of trophy scars and bruises I had achieved from trying to jump ditches on my BMX. It had certainly never occurred to me to worry about the hairs on them, but now that I looked afresh, with the eyes of my peers, I could see that I did seem to be hairier than was strictly acceptable.

At the end of the meeting, as we processed back to our classrooms, I was carried along by a marvelling human stream, which I tried stoically to ignore.

'Merritt's a *bloke!*'

'*Cave*man, more like.'

'No, man, she's a fucking *gorilla.*'

'Oi, Merritt, show us your arms!'

'No,' I said, folding them tightly.

'Show us your fucking *arms*,' and two boys grabbed me and forcibly pulled up the sleeves of my blazer.

'Oh my God! You're a fucking *werewolf!*'

That evening, my mother found me perched on the edge of the bath with my dad's razor and a bar of Imperial Leather, blood coursing through my fingers from deep gashes the length of my shins. I was not actually self-harming, just trying to shave. Self-harming was a phenomenon unknown to my mother at that time in any case, so she was more perplexed than panicked.

'I'm shaving my legs,' I explained.

'You're 11,' she said.

'But I look like a werewolf.'

'No, you don't. I can't even see any hairs on your legs.'

She'd gone too far with that; now I knew she was lying to be kind.

'You're setting yourself up for a lifetime of misery if you start shaving now,' she went on, and I pointed out that I was all set for a lifetime of misery anyway if I went back to school on Monday without doing something about this, in fact I refused to set foot in the place again unless I could do so with smooth and gleaming limbs and, furthermore, I announced grandly, I would rather kill myself.

I was not, in fact, planning to kill myself, but having said so aloud, I found that the idea suggested itself as a fascinating possibility. What if I really did try to kill myself? I realised then, for the first time, that I actually had a choice. It was entirely up to me. If life became unbearable, I could always decide not to carry on. This realisation was violently at odds with the teachings of my faith, and I was immediately doused in guilt for having allowed such a thought, when the correct response would be to ask Jesus for strength to endure my unhappiness. But that weekend, even after my mother had helped me make a passable job of de-fuzzing my shins, I sat up late into the night on my windowsill, looking out over the dark garden, terrified of going back to school, wildly dreaming up ways to avoid it. I could feign a major illness, perhaps; if that failed, I could choose not to go through the gates, just keep walking, hide somewhere, go home at four as if nothing had happened. But where would I go? The village was tiny; I was sure to run into someone who knew my mother, and all the obvious places to loiter, behind the cricket pavilion or the copse by the old hospital, would already be full of the hard kids, the habitual truants. Besides, the school would find out. I never did run away, but the urge to retreat, to bury myself, to avoid pain by removing myself from the world was planted in that moment, and always, shut away carefully in a secret place in my mind, was the thought of that other possibility, that permanent way out.

I shaved my legs to placate my classmates, but by Monday they had found something else. There was always something else; my physical imperfections were an unending source of sport. Every morning I trudged through the door of the Portakabin that housed our form room, braced against misery, coldly dreading which of my flaws would be put under the microscope today – would it be my freckles, my nose, my hair, my paleness, my lack of breasts or something more conceptual, like the fact that I was not allowed to have my ears pierced or watch *EastEnders*? Melanie Cleaver and her friends led the assaults, but kids are quick to sniff out victims; some joined in for something to do or for the approval of the rest, but I imagine half the kids who goaded me with their witless insults did so not through malice but mainly out of relief that it was not them.

For a while I did find a real place to hide. The school sports fields backed on to farmland; at the furthest border was a neglected copse with a stream half-heartedly running through it, edged by a series of solemn oak trees. If you pushed through the fence and hid among these trees you were far enough from the school buildings to be forgotten; in summer, the fifth years would go there to smoke and their old dog ends, Coke cans and chocolate wrappers strewed the banks, but on cold days it was too far and too damp, and they made do with the back of the sports shed instead. If I was quick enough out of my morning lessons, I could run across the field unseen and burrow with my book and my sandwiches between the roots of one of these oaks and there read undisturbed for the whole of the lunch hour. Often, though, I did not read; I crouched, shivering, against the damp bark and wondered what I had done to make them hate me so much, why I seemed made not to fit. My mother said they were just jealous, but this, I felt, was just a thing that mothers are obliged to say. What did she imagine that Melanie Cleaver and her entourage, with their pixie boots and lip gloss and third-year boyfriends, could possibly find to envy about me? Eventually, of course, the mystery of where Merritt went at lunchtime became too intriguing and I was followed. When it was discovered that my enigmatic disappearances consisted merely of hiding in a ditch there was great mirth all round, and that was the end of my little refuge. At home I begged to be allowed to move schools, but for one reason or another it was deemed to be impractical; my father wanted instead to complain to the school, and to avoid the inevitable fall-out of being seen to have grassed to my parents, I had to pretend that the situation was suddenly resolved and that school was great. At this time, I began to fantasise about how sorry and bad they would all feel if I really did kill myself.

In these fantasies, I was always somehow invisibly present to observe and enjoy the remorse my sad end had occasioned in Melanie Cleaver and her troupe, and in my parents and teachers for not realising how miserable I had been and letting me move; usually in these imaginings I survived miraculously, like Sylvia Plath the first time around, and everyone was left contrite and reformed by the recognition of how they had almost lost me. But the misery was real enough to make me long constantly to be else-where, and being dead, in my mind, became just another means of getting away from them.

All this barely counts as bullying by the standards of today's news reports, where kids seem to be routinely knifed, sexually assaulted and filmed as they are beaten up by their peers, and phones and the internet have given persecutors a seemingly limit-less reach into the lives of their victims; still, it was a war of attrition on my self-esteem over three relentless years and its effects were lasting. I was always looking over my shoulder; every day some item of mine would go missing, or a cruel piece of graffiti would appear on the wall of the changing rooms. There was no point in complaining to any member of staff; one of the barbs often thrown at me was that the only people who liked me were the teachers. For my thirteenth birthday, Melanie Cleaver and Louise Jones made me a chocolate cake and even got the whole class singing Happy Birthday. I was so overwhelmed by this gesture, so pathetically touched by the idea that they wanted to be my friends after all, that I rushed to share it with the whole class at break time. By the time I had finished doling out cake there was none left for me to have a slice myself, but I didn't mind; I was too busy relish-ing the novelty of everyone having forgotten momentarily to hate me. It was only when everyone else was struck down by chronic stomach cramps and diarrhoea after lunch that Melanie and Louise confessed that they had made the cake with eight bars of laxative chocolate. They were sent to the Head – one especially skinny boy who had eaten three slices had to be taken to the doctor. Since I had not had any cake, I was unaffected, but I felt as if my stomach had dropped out anyway. Not for the first time, they had made a pretence of friendship as a means to entertain themselves further at my expense. The cruellest thing was that it was not merely a practical joke involving laxatives, which could potentially seem funny when you're 13; the real trick had been to make me think they liked me. So it went on for three years. I became withdrawn and introverted, fearful and self-critical, where once I had been confident and enthusiastic, but I learned how to hide the worst of it from everyone – from the kids at school, so they didn't have the satisfaction of making me cry, and from my parents at home, so they wouldn't have to be upset and feel helpless.

Teenagers are expected to be moody and sullen, to shut themselves away and fester in dark bedrooms, hating the world, hating their parents, wishing they'd never been born; all this is part of the script, and so teenage depression often goes unrecognised, dismissed as a phase. According to Liz Carnell, founder of the UK charity Bullying Online, between 16 and 20 teenage suicides every year in the UK are directly related to school bullying, though the real figure may be much higher because coroners are often reluctant to record a verdict of suicide on teenagers. The charity's helpline is contacted by up to four children a day who say they are thinking of killing themselves and many more describing clear symptoms of depression. Carnell also says that, purely from anecdotal evidence based on calls to their helpline, it would be very difficult to obtain official statistics on the number of adolescents suffering from depression directly related to bullying because a majority avoid seeking treatment or asking for help from parents or schools. One 16-year-old told Carnell that she would certainly have tried to kill herself if not for the helpline where she could be anonymous. Depression in teenagers frequently finds physical expression, especially in girls, in self-harm or eating disorders, because these can be a means of expressing distress without having to articulate it, but these things are also often done in secret, as a private source of shame. Certainly, when I was at my lowest during those three years between 11 and 14, I didn't have the knowledge to match my misery to any recognised template, nor did I have the vocabulary for it; I had a vague idea that something called 'depression' existed because I had read about Sylvia Plath and Virginia Woolf, but the word remained something grand and dramatic, applied to dead literary heroines, not to teenage girls who merely dreaded walking into their classroom in the mornings. I thought my unhappiness was too ordinary to qualify. It was only years later, in my twenties, when I saw a news bulletin about a 15-year-old girl who had hanged herself because of almost exactly the kind of protracted, low-level psychological bullying that I had experienced, that I realised with a cold shock how nearly that could have been me.

There came an end to it, perhaps because most of us simply grew up a little. Walking to school one October morning, at 14, I stopped suddenly in the drizzle at the top of the road that led to the school, and it was as if I'd been granted a larger perspective than I had been capable of before. I realised that in less than two years I would never have to go to that school or see any of them again. When I considered the irritations of school in the light of my possible future, I saw that they were simply not worth the attention. If you can't join them, I decided, then beat them. They wanted long words, I would show them long words. They thought I was too clever – well, then, I would show them how fucking clever I could be.

I developed a withering brand of sarcasm borrowed largely from *Blackadder*, and an arcane vocabulary borrowed from *Saturday Night Fry*, my hero Stephen Fry's late-night Radio 4 show, which I would tape and play over and over until I had memorised every episode. As a means of self-defence, this attempt at wit, coupled with a brittle air of superiority, seemed to work. When they came at me with their old and tired insults, I volleyed back ingenious put-downs that left them wrong-footed and perplexed and to which they could only retort, 'Yeah, well, fuck off then,' as others laughed, uncomfortably suspecting that it was they who had been left looking stupid. After a while, they stopped bothering, and for the first time at that school, I was left to get on with my life. Instead of a ditch, I hid myself in a frenzy of school plays, school newspapers, student council committees, bands and literary societies; I threw myself into overachieving and for the final two years of school became a prominent member of the student body. I was not necessarily popular, but at least they didn't bother to harass me.

I adopted an eccentric style of dress to go with my new, fuck-'em personality: part Edwardian dandy, part Robert Smith of the Cure – a little bit Russell Brand before the fact. There were cravats involved, and frock coats and a great deal of backcombing and hairspray. It was a look that said: *I'm deliberately not trying to be attractive, and have thereby cleverly pre-empted failure.* All my affectations – the compulsive achievements, the amateur dramatics, the ridiculous clothes – were a series of fragile barricades built around a badly bruised ego. I left with the highest exam results in the school and my self-esteem shredded; not all the A-grades in the world could repair the damage done in those first three miserable years. I had no coherent sense of self; I only existed as a series of awards strung together. Everyone had commended my acting; they didn't realise that every day I determinedly played the part of someone who liked herself, who was at home in her own skin, who greeted life with a spring in her step, because I carried it off quite convincingly. Only I knew that the version of myself I presented to the world was a fake.

Since I have come to recognise and understand the symptoms of my depression and, in conversations with psychiatrists and therapists, followed its course backwards, I have often wondered if my experiences at school between 11 and 14 were in some way the 'cause' of my depression. Those years of isolation and the fear of always being on the outside, together with an exaggerated and disproportionate sense of unattractiveness, almost irreparably undermined my ability to like myself. Before I had even approached the threshold of puberty, I had already learned to scrutinise my body for imperfections and had grown impossibly critical of the way I looked. I was never going to be a prom queen beauty, but photographic evidence testifies that although I looked young for my age, there was nothing especially freakish about my appearance to have provoked their attention, no crooked teeth, glasses or garish birthmarks. Though I was not good at team sports, I loved walking and cycling and was not overweight. But I drew unwelcome attention because I did well at school and was literate beyond my years, and I have no doubt that at the beginning I carried a kind of arrogance along with those abilities that must have been intensely unappealing. But though they sometimes called me 'brainbox' or 'creep', it is not much of an insult to tell someone they're clever, so what they fixed on was 'ugly' and 'fat'. After a while, this becomes a self-fulfilling prophecy: once you become known as the girl so ugly she will never get a boyfriend, no boy with any care for his social standing will even talk to you, and so you start to believe it.

But none of this is unusual; countless books and indie films document the loneliness of the bookish kid who doesn't fit in with the popular crowd, because this is the commonplace experience of the people who go on to become writers and film-makers, artists, musicians, and often actors and models or people who have been successful in business. Very few of us were lucky enough to be the best-looking or most popular kid in school, and though teenage misery can leave a mark, it is often just as effective in galvanising people to prove themselves and achieve in other ways. Not everyone who was bullied or found themselves the unwelcome target of adolescent cruelty goes on to develop severe depression, yet I can't help wondering if my experience at school had been a little milder, if I had asserted myself earlier and survived adolescence with a little more self-confidence, would I have been more resistant to my first attack of real depression and incipient anorexia at 17, which did seem to grow out of a sense of chronic insecurity? Or would it have come anyway, an inbuilt shift of brain chemistry that even the firmest self-regard could not have withstood?

Psychologists are generally agreed that there is no single 'cause' of depression but that it is usually triggered by a combination of biological, psychological and social factors. While it would be simplistic to say that depression is hereditary, a number of studies of identical twins have shown that certain types of depression, particularly bipolar disorders, have a strong genetic link. Some people do seem to be genetically predisposed to problems with the brain chemistry that governs mood, and it is thought that genes determine our threshold of coping with stress and everything the men in white lump together under the term 'life events'. Though she had never heard the term 'bipolar' before, years later when I pressed my mother for what she knew of the family psychiatric history she identified close relatives on both sides of my family who had been treated for 'nervous' illnesses but whose symptoms would seem so precisely to fit a description of bipolar disorder that it seems likely I carried the blueprint for it without knowing. Among other biological components, fluctuations in hormone levels can also significantly affect brain chemistry, making pregnant and menopausal women and new mothers extremely vulnerable to depressive states, while long-term illness, stress, poor diet and substance misuse can all contribute significantly to depleted levels of serotonin, the neurotransmitter in the brain that plays a central role in regulating mood, appetite, sleep and aggression. Low levels of serotonin are closely associated with depression, anxiety, bipolar disorder and a number of mood-related conditions; the most common antidepressant medication works on the basic principle of increasing concentrations of serotonin in the brain.

Psychological factors include all the experiences that forge our view of the world and our place in it, and in our earliest years these are indivisible from biological factors, since the development of the infant brain is physically affected by social input and emotional experiences. Recurrent depression is very common among people who lost a parent, particularly their mother, at a young age, and among those who suffered childhood abuse or emotional deprivation, and research suggests that those early experiences have long-term implications for the development of those areas of the brain associated with mood. There will be physical differences in the brain of a child who grows up surrounded by love and encouragement, and one who grows up knowing neglect or abuse. Though I was incredibly fortunate in that I could not have been more loved or supported by my family as a child, and the security of that environment provided a sure foundation for my sense of self, that confidence that I was loved and valued was profoundly shaken by the experience of being ostracised at school. At 12 or 13, you don't have the maturity to conclude that bullying is a manifestation of the bullies' own insecurities; all you know is that you are told relentlessly that you are fat and ugly and everyone hates you, and since everyone is saying it, you conclude that it must be true, until eventually you absorb it, and it becomes a kind of self-bullying. Sometimes psychological influences can be less obvious; contrary to accepted belief, high achievers, rather than being protected by confidence in their successes, are frequently vulnerable to depression because often their sense of self has rested on those achievements and is bound up with perfectionism, a sense of never being good enough and a chronic fear of failure.

Social factors include the influences that surround us in the present and affect our sense of our own status and self-worth. Freud famously identified love and work as 'the cornerstones of our humanness', and certainly unemployment, poverty and isolation contribute significantly to the likelihood of suffering depression. Comparing ourselves unfavourably to others can also have an impact; in *Affluenza*, Oliver James argues that the high levels of depression and anxiety in Britain and the US stem from the exaggerated inequality of our societies (in comparison with some European countries) and a media culture that holds up wealth, fame and physical beauty as the only attributes worth aspiring to or celebrating.

At 16, I left school with a profound sense of relief and moved to the sixth-form college where my father taught, across the county border, so that I left behind everyone who had known me as the werewolf and was granted the chance to begin in a new place, with no history. This college, renowned for its good results and strong record of Oxbridge entrance, took a significant proportion of its students from the surrounding Surrey private schools, and here I learned about the aristocracy of beauty.

There had been pretty girls at school, of course, but those who commanded attention, whom the boys pursued and the girls tried to emulate, were girls like Melanie Cleaver and Louise Jones – a riot of cheap jewellery, hairspray, puffball skirts and pixie boots. The private-school girls were another race altogether. They had thoroughbred qualities: tall and willowy, with long, coltish limbs, sheer falls of naturally white-blonde hair, year-round tans from their Caribbean holidays or their mothers' sun-beds. In their cashmere and their leather they carried themselves with effortless grace and an air of entitlement. Many of them seemed to have mothers who had once been models in Europe, and these Lucies and Sophias had been groomed since birth to be beautiful women, presumably so that they could go on to win a rich husband and breed the next generation of beautiful, rich girls. They had flats in London, homes in France or Spain, parents who were glamorously divorced and remarried and they would fly off to spend Christmas with their fathers in New York or their stepsisters in St Lucia. They seemed constantly to be going skiing. Their clothes were casually scattered with real designer labels, where I had thought 'designer' meant a jumper from Benetton rather than Tesco. They owned cocktail dresses that had been made for them especially. I could not imagine any occasion in my life that might require a cocktail dress; not even the church Christmas social, which was the nearest I came to a party. As they began to turn 17 and pass their driving tests over the course of our first term, many of them acquired jaunty little

Suzuki jeeps in shades of raspberry or mint, which they drove wearing big sunglasses and smoking Marlboro Lights. They all seemed to be interconnected, too; their fathers knew one another from business or the golf club, their mothers from the tennis club, they had been out with each other's brothers and cousins and seemed to be on familiar terms with all the equally perfect models from the boys' schools.

Every Monday they would debrief eagerly in the canteen, assessing the weekend's parties and who had got off with Myles or Charlie on Friday night at The Castle, a pub where sixth formers might hope to get away with offering up fake ID. I hovered on the fringes of these conversations, experiencing a social life vicariously; the downside of starting afresh was that I knew no one, I couldn't drive and lived too far out to get to The Castle. Besides, I would never have been allowed to go, as I was still underage and my father was a strict stickler for the letter of the law.

I longed to be invited to the rich girls' parties, but it never happened. They did not exclude me out of spite, as had been the case at school; it was simply that I did not appear on their radar. They were friendly and pleasant to me at college, but it would no more have occurred to them to invite me to a party than it occurs to most people to invite the waitress to join you for a drink when you go out for dinner. Instead, I concentrated my social life on the church's youth group, where, fortunately, people were not allowed to judge you by your appearance because the Lord looked at the heart, even if you did have Robert Smith hair and wear men's dinner jackets from Oxfam that smelled of neglect and mothballs.

Being surrounded every day by such expensive beauty made me uncomfortably aware that my idiosyncratic style was no longer working. I didn't look quirky and eccentric, like a bohemian artist,

I just looked like someone who had had a selection of her dead grandfather's clothes thrown at her. Alongside the posh girls I felt increasingly gauche, lumpen and clumsy; all the school-bred self-criticism of the way I looked came rushing back. Perhaps if I renounced my strange motley and adopted their uniform of 501s, Timberland deck shoes and lambswool sweaters from Jigsaw, I might feel less unattractive, more like them. And then I was struck by a novel idea: before I embarked on this makeover, it would be a good idea if I lost a bit of weight.

At first I was galvanised by my new goal; I borrowed from my mother a 28-day diet plan by a well-known weight-loss guru and applied myself to the business of losing weight as if it were an exam course I could pass or fail. The diet itself was low fat but not extreme, based largely and sensibly around fish, poultry and vegetables, and I stuck to it obsessively, producing long and detailed lists of foodstuffs for my mother to add to the weekly shop, appropriating the cooker for my special recipes while she tried to make a meal for the rest of the family. She didn't complain or try to dissuade me, assuming perhaps that this was all part of the self-absorption of adolescence, and for the first three weeks or so my diet became a full-time occupation. I had always had a tendency to be all-or-nothing about my interests ('Stephanie is a rather obsessive child,' said my first ever school report, at the age of five), and I gave this diet book more attention and close-reading than any of my A-level texts; I spent very little time actually eating the recommended foods compared to the time I spent reading and thinking about them, or explaining knowledgably to my parents over dinner, with all the irksome zeal of a new convert, what their shepherd's pie was doing to their arteries. I almost began to forget that the diet was supposed to be a means to an end, rather than a new kind of religion.

At the same time I bought a second-hand exercise bike from the local paper, which I rode for half an hour every evening in the kitchen and followed with some furious sit-ups, which I calculated would burn off approximately two to three hundred calories and thus I would be in credit by an extra muesli bar.

At the end of the 28 days, I examined the results in a full-length mirror and concluded that it was a bit of a disappointment. I had lost half a stone and was certainly fitter, but in my reflection I saw no resemblance to the slender, insouciant pedigree blondes at college. For someone who had by now read a substantial number of books about nutrition and weight loss, I had a very eccentric grasp of the science; I really believed that it was possible, with enough self-discipline, to make myself into someone with the figure of a Russian catwalk model, just as I believed that if I stayed in the sun long enough, my freckled Irish skin would eventually turn a deep golden brown like that of Natasha, who sat opposite me in my English class and whose effortless beauty always left me feeling profoundly defeated. Perhaps it was more that I could not bear very much reality. Perhaps it was because I had grown up to be a frighteningly demanding perfectionist. Now I was training these impossible standards on my body and finding that I had fallen very short indeed; still I was unwilling to accept that there was anything in the world I couldn't change simply by applying myself. It never occurred to me that this way of thinking bore any relation to an eating disorder, partly because I knew very little about anorexia and did not think I was prone to such things, and partly because taking control of my diet, deciding to change the way I looked, made me feel positive and assertive. I later learned that these thought processes are common to people who develop eating disorders. Anorexia involves different risk factors from bulimia, the cycle of binging and purges. While bulimia is more common among women who have had a difficult or abusive childhood, anorexia – self-starving – is more often related to obsessive-compulsive traits and often occurs among high achievers, people driven to perfectionism, often those prone to high levels of anxiety. Imposing rigid controls on what they eat in a sense makes them feel safer, because they can live within a construct of self-imposed rules.

My failure to be as thin as I had dreamed of being at the end of the month was, I concluded, the fault of the diet guru; she had been too lenient, too generous in her portions and her ingredients. I needed to undertake the whole enterprise again, but this time the rules needed to be more stringent. There would be no snacks, none of the little treats the regime allowed once a week or so to make sure you didn't become demoralised. I would halve the amounts she recommended in the recipes. That ought to do the job. At the same time, I would increase my time on the bike to at least an hour a day. Satisfied with my new plan, I marked the date in my diary, certain that after a further 28 days I would have the figure I wanted, and *then* I would be happy.

I don't know the precise moment in which my weather changed, I can't pinpoint what might now be called the tipping point; there was no one decisive instant in which dissatisfaction with myself turned into a destructive self-hatred. I only know that a change took place, gradual and insidious; one day I was a slightly troubled but otherwise relatively enthusiastic 16-year-old with a sensible, even laudable, regard for health and fitness, and on a different day, I was crushed beneath a weight of hopelessness that astonished me with its totality. The diet – though the word had become redundant, I was no longer dieting but quite deliberately starving myself – had ceased to be about getting in shape, making myself more attractive, fitting into a particular pair of jeans. It had twisted into an outward sign of the darkness brewing in me. I no longer looked forward to reaching my target weight, the moment when I would wake to find myself a perfect ten and thereby be liberated to achieve all my dreams, because there was no target weight any more, no realistic goal, and I could no longer imagine myself feeling happy, even in the unlikely event of that day dawning. Thin, I would still be me, and what I loathed and wanted to punish was not this rebellious body that so defiantly refused to look like a picture in a magazine, but the me that was inside it, the essence of who I believed myself to be – someone who would always be standing on the outside looking in. But I didn't know how to express this hatred except by inflicting damage on what was visible. Something had descended on me, and I could not explain it; it had entered through my ears and nostrils like vapour and wrapped itself around my brain; it clouded my vision and made me retreat into myself, fearful of company and the sound of my own voice. Incapable of eating or making small talk, I refused to sit down to dinner with my family, saying I would eat something later; if I did, it was a green apple or a fat-free yogurt, and at first there was a kind of satisfaction in forcing this deprivation on myself, in feeling the consequent cramps and hunger pangs and dizziness, as if these pains were somehow purifying, but after a while even that small and perverse pleasure faded and I reached a point where I was no longer proactive in the business of deprivation, no longer exercising self-control or inflicting punishment. I reached a point where I no longer felt in control at all.

The thoughts that raged endlessly inside my head like trapped wasps grew increasingly morbid, untethered from reason and realism. I developed a dread of mirrors and reflective surfaces and quickly averted my eyes to avoid them; my mind had grown so distorted that when I glimpsed myself I saw something monstrous and repellant, Caliban-like, someone who would never walk down the street with a sense of entitlement or open the door to a future in which things might be vaguely all right, never mind sunny. I would never be one of those girls who drove an open-topped jeep full of friends to the beach and laughed and whisked their hair in the sunshine and if I couldn't be that, if I was always going to feel like this, what was the point of carrying on? This dread of mirrors quickly blossomed into a full-grown phobia, complete with anxiety attacks; a fleeting sideways glance in a glass door could trigger flickering light-headedness, palpitations and constricted breathing and tremors. All sense of the bright possibilities I might escape to had evaporated; there had been so much I had wanted to do with my life, so many things I wanted to create and places I wanted to see and books I wanted to write, and now I was indifferent to all of it. Exhausted by hunger, I was still unable to sleep, and I would sit up long into the night reading, taut with unfocused anxiety, in search of distractions from myself. One night I came across Keats's 'Ode to a Nightingale' and read the lines, 'Now more than ever seems it rich to die/To cease upon the midnight with no pain.' Couldn't have put it better myself, I thought. That was it, so perfectly articulated, precisely what I craved: a gentle but definitive end. I wanted to cease. Death again became a kind of alternative fantasy, but this time it was not the gleeful act of revenge that it had been when I used to imagine Melanie Cleaver weeping with remorse over my coffin; now it was death as another means of being elsewhere, of removing myself from the reality of my life and my own responsibility for it. I was not, at this point, close enough to the edge to seriously consider taking my own life, but I was frightened by how insistent the thoughts became; they seemed to return over and over, wilful and unbidden. Even as I entertained these voices, a small flame of reason burned with the knowledge that sitting up all night reading the Romantic poets and wallowing in your own misery was a pitiful cliché of hormonal adolescent *Sturm und Drang*, and I so hated the idea of being a cliché. If I wasn't careful I'd be writing poetry next. I *knew* I had everything out of proportion, that I had become ridiculous, that I only needed to snap out of it; it was just that I couldn't seem to summon the will. But what was happening to my mind was quite different from the dull enduring misery of my early teens; now it rushed in with a violent, glittering energy, as if something had taken hold of me, and was stronger than I was.

The worst of it was the guilt I felt about my state of mind. I ought to be happy; objectively, my life was better than it had been at any time since childhood, and I was ashamed to be so ungrateful for all my blessings. *Why* could I not be happy? I loved my A-level courses; all the subjects that had blighted my school timetable – maths, science, PE – were things of the past, and it seemed to me almost immoral that I should be allowed to go to college and study exclusively the things that mattered – literature, languages and drama – without some payment being exacted. I also had, for the first time, a real boyfriend. Paul was good-looking and kind; he was also ten years older than me and had a motorbike, which in different circumstances would have given my parents an embolism, but in this case it was acceptable because Paul was from the church and the relationship was infuriatingly chaste. Having a boyfriend at last should have ramped up my self-esteem, but as my mood darkened over the course of that winter, I began to wonder more and more what Paul could possibly see in someone as fat and ugly as I believed myself to be; paradoxically, this made me suspicious of Paul. If he was genuinely interested in me, went my Groucho Marx reasoning, there must be something wrong with him, and I was not sure that I wanted to be with someone whose judgement was so self-evidently faulty. But I kept up appearances, an ability I had honed at school and which I found effective in keeping people at a distance for almost two decades. I did not tell Paul, or anyone else, despite all the exhortations to openness and honesty that arose from the weekly youth group Bible studies and discussions, how empty and wretched I felt. I was afraid they would be horrified: I was *saved*, for goodness' sake, I had been baptised by immersion and baptised in the Holy Spirit, I went to meetings and prayed with and for my friends, I taught music and drama in the Sunday School, took part in street evangelism and spoke in tongues; I was, as far as anyone could see, an enthusiastic young Christian eager to serve the Lord. I was supposed to be filled with joy; the fact that I was saturated instead with despair would have looked like gross spiritual failure, and it was better if no one knew about that.

In January, on my seventeenth birthday, Paul took me out for dinner. It was a local pub tucked away up a remote lane in the hills, the restaurant so tiny that there were only a handful of tables and aficionados were always trying to play down its reputation for fear of its being overrun. It was not a chic place, but it was more expensive than anywhere we usually ate and I knew it was more than Paul could afford, but this was a special occasion: we were celebrating the arrival of my provisional licence. Paul had been teaching me the basics of driving on some disused army tracks and I was already picturing the vistas that would open up once I had a set of wheels. For a start, it would mean an end to my dad picking me up every time I went out – always arriving too early, then sitting outside huffing and tutting in the car or, infinitely worse, coming into wherever it might be to find me, tapping his watch with pantomime gestures. It would mean the beginnings of independence, of getting out of that town. I should have been happy: I was 17 and I had a grown-up boyfriend who was taking me out to a grown-up restaurant. And yet I was not happy – I could barely remember how it felt to be happy – and I hated myself with increasing vigour for lacking the backbone or moral fibre or force of character or whatever was needed to shake off this worsening mood. When I had been unhappy at school, I had tried to block it out by focusing on my plans for the future; half my life so far had been a dream of arriving, of getting beyond the next horizon. I was always projecting myself forward into a time when I would be thinner/prettier/independent/more successful/better liked, and that would be my real life; the present was only ever a prologue. But now I had even lost the ability to imagine a better future.

I could still pretend when it mattered, though, so I put on some make up and sat down opposite Paul in the restaurant with a smile that I hoped gave the appearance of being grateful. He was chatting away about his work but his voice was distant, like a radio in another room, because I was reading the menu and already my heart had begun to drill against my ribs. I felt raw, exposed to the gaze of the other diners, always convinced that every time I stepped out of the house the world was staring in disgust and thinking, 'Look at the fat girl – how could she bear to walk around looking like that?' Every adolescent lives with this aggrandised sense of a tracking spotlight – one of the cruellest and most liberating lessons of adulthood is the discovery that you're not nearly as important as you imagined and that on any given occasion barely anyone will have noticed what you wore or said – but to me even the most casual eye contact with a stranger in the street was confirmation of a freak-show hideousness. Mealtimes had reached the level of an ordeal; not an inconvenience, or the ground for a battle of wills with my parents, or even an opportunity to display my iron self-control or to punish my body, but a truly distressing ordeal. I was frightened by the prospect of eating; whenever I was expected to do so, my entire body would clench against it, my throat would tighten and close, my stomach contort and I would begin to experience what I now know to be the symptoms of a panic attack.

Through my rictus grin I ordered chicken; of all the dishes on the menu, I thought it would hold the least terrors in terms of fat or calories. Paul asked for a beer and carried on talking cheerfully over the rattling of glassware as the table shuddered to the frantic jigging of my leg from too much Diet Coke. I wasn't drinking alcohol, I could have told you the precise number of calories in one sip of beer. Instead, a thin girl at college had informed me knowledgably that caffeine boosted the metabolism, so I now lived on Diet Coke and coffee in the belief that this was actively making me thinner rather than just unbearably fidgety.

Then the waiter arrived, and the world shattered in slow motion. There was chicken on my plate, but it was in a sauce, and the sauce was made with butter. Slick yellow platelets of grease floated on its surface, colliding and pooling into wide, mocking puddles of *pure fat* that had seeped into every crevice of the meat. I stared at it for a moment, aghast and utterly betrayed – it hadn't said anything about butter on the menu! I imagined that fat sliding down my throat, sliming its way through my innards, I imagined the gleeful havoc it would wreak on my thighs and hips and my throat seized up, accompanied by a faint nausea. Paul smiled encouragingly. 'Yours looks nice,' he said. Something twanged in my head, everything turned purple for a moment, I had lost the rhythm of my breathing and couldn't now seem to remember how to get it back, I knew only that I could not put that chicken in my mouth, I couldn't even stand to look at it, and my only option was to flee.

Blurting an excuse, I careened blindly through the restaurant until I could crash through the door of the ladies' and lock myself in a cubicle, where I turned round and round in a growing frenzy, like an animal forcibly herded into a stall, feeling the Formica walls with my hands as I spun as if to keep myself upright. By this time I was properly hyperventilating, but I was also crying, which made breathing all the more difficult, and at the same time I was aware of and incredulous at my own absurdity, as if I were looking down at this ragged mess clinging to the wall of a pub toilet from over the top of the partition. Who would countenance it? Poor Paul – how could I possibly make him understand, when I didn't understand myself, what on earth was wrong with me? It was my birthday dinner, my boyfriend was trying to give me something special to make me happy, and I was shut in a toilet in a state of hysteria, as if I were being pursued by a homicidal psychopath – *why couldn't I just be normal??*

There was no way I could go back out there and eat that chicken; I was shaking and gulping down splinters of air, and at that moment I felt very clearly that I wanted to die. It was a very precise sense that I could not stand another minute, never mind a lifetime, of being trapped inside this mind and this body. I looked around wildly and snatched at my belt, but there was no apparatus to help me; the only possibility was to hang the belt off the coat hook on the back of the door, but one glance told me it would never hold. I slumped to the floor and crouched there, back against the door, for some time. When I could gather myself enough to return to the table, I told Paul I felt sick and needed to go home; he was gracious but I could see that he was hurt and disappointed. I don't remember what he said, but it was not the first time I had claimed to be ill when confronted with food, though I had never had such an extreme reaction before. Paul was a straightforward, logical sort of person and I think my strangeness was outside his experience, so he explained it to himself by way of hormones, or the fact that I was 'arty'; besides, I deliberately obscured the worst of myself precisely so that people around me would not see how badly wrong I was. I wouldn't have dreamed of telling Paul, or my parents, or any of my friends, that I had wanted to kill myself in a pub toilet because there was butter on my chicken, because it sounded insane. Perhaps I *was* insane, I thought, which seemed all the more reason not to tell them. But I was not getting better, and gradually those who cared about me began to notice, even if they didn't have a name for it. Shortly after the chicken incident I had my first appointment with Ruth the counsellor, and found myself referred to the Morrisons, as the only people deemed capable of handling my demons.

*D*id I really believe in the demons as more than metaphor? The simple answer is that I did, or I thought at the time that I did; at least, I believed in them to the same degree that I believed in the Holy Trinity and in the notion that I had been born again, which is to say that I accepted on the surface all the beliefs and doctrines that I had grown up with because they were the framework that supported my understanding of the world. It had always been

The Devil Within

impressed upon us at church that if we made the choice to follow Christ we were to accept His word wholeheartedly, even those parts that made us uncomfortable; it was not for us to pick and choose the bits of God's message to mankind that suited our desires – that way liberal theology lay. We were encouraged to question, and to express doubt when doubts presented themselves, but it always seemed to me that doubt was only really acceptable if the doubter followed the example of the man who said to Jesus, 'Lord, I do believe; help me overcome my unbelief.' Doubt was natural, but the proper way of dealing with it was to confess it and hand it to the Lord, and ask him to strengthen our faith. I could not imagine any situation in which doubt might lead the doubter to conclude that they were in fact on the side of reason and should declare themselves an atheist – at least, we were never told of any such examples.

It may have been a lack of courage that kept me from acting on the doubt I had begun to feel in my teens, or an unwillingness to upset my parents, or another fear entirely, the fear that if I were to reject the faith I had always known, I would for once have to work out by myself what I really thought about the world, and formulate my own morals and values rather than accepting the off-the-peg package presented by a religious creed. But having doubted, and allowed myself to imagine life through a very different lens, I retreated hurriedly from the possibility of atheism and made an effort to shore up my faith in God and Christ; effectively, this meant accommodating the tension between my intellect and my desire to please, and pretending to everyone, including myself, for the next few years until I arrived at university.

Some might find the practice of telling a vulnerable teenager almost paralysed by depression that she is under the influence of demons somewhat unsophisticated, and it would be easy for me now, as a professed secular humanist looking back half a lifetime, to regard with cynicism the people who wielded such beliefs. But that would be to underestimate the force of the beliefs I had grown up with and the security of an utterly certain and complete system of thought. I willingly colluded because I wanted to be healed, but also because I trusted that their intervention was kindly meant and the right thing to do. Unlike the rebellious teenager Adrian in *Tongues of Flame*, Tim Parks' satirical novel about the charismatic church, I was not exorcised against my will; I made myself believe, because I wanted to believe.

The more crucial question, perhaps, is did it *work*? This is harder to ascertain. Certainly that afternoon at the Morrisons' was pivotal, but there was no sudden and visible transformation, no miraculous emergence into light and joy; rather, returning home, I felt almost embarrassed about what had happened, ashamed to have this darkness in me, and I said very little about it to my family.

In the weeks that followed, I began a laborious but steady ascent from that nadir, suicidal in a pub toilet on my seventeenth birthday. I continued my weekly visits to Ruth, and in time my fragile trust grew in proportion to her patience. Slowly, I learned to engage with the world again; I felt less desperate, less fearful of my reflection and of food; I carefully retooled my defences, concentrated on my studies, put on a little weight without hating myself for it, and returned to regarding the future with some optimism. In *The Noonday Demon*, Andrew Solomon remarks in a chapter on alternative therapies, 'Frankly, I think that the best treatment for depression is belief, which is in itself far more essential than what you believe in.' Did I get better, on this occasion, because I believed that I had been freed from the demons that were causing my misery, self-loathing and fear of food? Did I simply emerge from the depression as part of its natural cycle, or did I actively will myself out of it because I believed that I *ought* to have been cured by the exorcism, that it was my duty to have been cured, and that a failure to display signs of being better would indicate one of two possibilities – that the demons were still there, or that they had never been there in the first place, neither of which was the 'correct' response? I don't know. I do know that belief is an exceptionally powerful force, and that many Christians, including a number of intelligent and educated people I know well, will testify to first-hand experience of personal 'miracles' – healing from seemingly incurable illnesses, children born after diagnosis of untreatable infertility, extraordinary recoveries from addictions. Those who believe in the supernatural call these things miracles; those who do not explain them in terms of auto-suggestion and psychosomatic influence (or simply chance and coincidence). But in the long history of writing about depressive illness, even now that the chemistry of the brain and its aberrations has begun to be mapped and quantified, the most persistent metaphor for the experience of depression remains the image of a demon. For years after I stopped believing in God, I could not shake off this idea that my black weather came from a place of darkness and was in itself something bad and shameful, an indication of evil in me.

2

The Road of Excess

When extreme moods seem to be a part of your temperament, when you (and those around you) have grown used to the idea that you are prone to overly dramatic emotional responses to everyday events, it can take a long time to recognise those moods as evidence of illness. People with bipolar disorder may have been mercurial as children or adolescents, typically experience a marked episode of either depression, mania or hypomania in their late teens or early twenties, and are often not diagnosed until their thirties. Studies in the UK suggest that it can take on average ten years to receive a correct diagnosis. This may be because, in its milder forms, hypomania doesn't feel like an illness at all – it can make you feel invincible, as if you are beyond the limits of ordinary experience. There are moments when you almost believe you could fly.

I began again at Cambridge. The distance from home and church and everyone who knew the person I had been at school, at college, at the youth fellowship, was far greater than could be measured on the map. Like every university town, it was full of young people trying out new versions of themselves, tasting the liberty of reinventing themselves as they hoped others would see them. Some people came out for the first time. Others changed the way they dressed, the way they spoke. I became something I had never dared dream I might aspire to: one of the party crowd.

The Christianity I had grown up with pivoted on the moment of being 'born again', when your past life was rendered obsolete by faith in Christ, and you were given the chance to begin as a different person. I was 'born again' at the age of seven, when there was little cause for remorse and shame in my past, so I didn't fully appreciate the powerful lure of that possibility of reinvention until I got to university. Here, I felt that for the first time in my life I could stop acting. I was no longer an oddity; it was as if I had stumbled upon a little colony of misfits, all of us delighted and surprised to have wandered in and discovered that there were other people like us in the world, others who lived largely in books and tried confidently to wield ideas that we didn't necessarily quite understand. Uncertain and chronically awkward at first, I was amazed to find that people wanted to talk to me. They invited me to parties and to brunches, when I didn't even know what a brunch was. I seemed to have become part of a group without even trying, and I was launched at last into the life I had been waiting to step into. And everything we did revolved around drinking.

It was a talent I had never had the chance to develop, since I had only ever been invited to parties associated with the church youth group, and it was remarkable to discover in what high regard the ability to put away drink was held here, amid the cloisters and half-timbering. Perhaps for many of us it was a way to offset a fear of our own nerdhood, or perhaps the commitment to excess was just part of the drive to do everything to the maximum. Perhaps it was also that the collegiate system seemed perfectly tailored to favour heavy drinking with minimal need to take responsibility for oneself. Locked into our colleges at two every morning (trying to skulk back any later entailed scaling nine-foot iron railings topped with barbaric spikes; legends flowered of hapless souls impaled or disembowelled attempting it in ballgowns), with a subsidised bar, we never even needed to worry about how we would get home, since home involved negotiating only a staircase or a small bridge; consequently there was no reason to hold on to the merest shred of sobriety or consciousness. Perhaps this is just what most British students do. I started drinking to excess on my first day of college and kept it up more or less for the next 12 years.

But I drank convivially and exuberantly at the beginning; it chimed with a new zest and excitement welling up in those first weeks, a newly piqued appetite for everything that fear and guilt and the unavoidable presence of parental and ecclesiastical author-ity had kept beyond my reach until that glorious moment when my parents, having hefted my boxes and pot plants up four flights of stairs and stayed, agonisingly, for lunch in the college canteen, finally drove away moist-eyed and left me free to sit in a slant of sunlight, among a spill of books, and watch the blue smoke twist-ing from a cigarette, thinking 'here, I will be somebody different'. I was chasing the horizon; I wanted to see what lay beyond reason, sobriety and diligence. What would it be like to abandon all three? Was there really a wildness straining in me, or was that just wish-ful thinking?

In fact, I was not leaving home for the first time. I had first endured, and eventually enjoyed, a gap year in Spain, but it had been heavily mortgaged with ties to home. I had gone there to work for a Christian charity and was partially subsidised by my church, which entailed certain responsibilities – not to sleep with boys or declare myself an atheist chief among them. The church at home had connections to the people I worked alongside in Spain, so that the freedom of another country was compromised by the certain knowledge that everything I did would somehow find its way back to my parents.

These tensions between the desire to feel my way into a new, unfettered adult self and the need to be a good girl and not let anyone down created an ongoing inner turbulence over that year, added to the overwhelming moments of loneliness and dislocation that come of being in a strange country and the discovery that, no matter how proficient, you can never quite be yourself in a second language, especially if you exist principally through words. It all lent a sense of melancholy to the early months of my year in Spain. Melancholy, yes, and loneliness, but of a yearning, romantic kind that could be savoured by an over-earnest young person with poetic aspirations. I fell in love with Ernesto Sabato's 1948 novel *El Túnel*, a short, bleak existentialist work, and carried it everywhere in my pocket, taking it out importantly to underline passages as I sat in cafés with my cortados and my little notebook, self-consciously fancying myself a writer. I was particularly pleased with its central metaphor, the idea that we are all proceeding through life along a series of parallel tunnels, essentially alone; romantic fallacy persuades us to hope one day that our tunnel might merge with someone else's, or open up to reveal sea and sky and a distant horizon, but after the narrator, Castel, is disappointed by love, he concludes, 'the whole story of these tunnels was a ridiculous invention of mine, and in any case, there was only one tunnel, dark and solitary: my own.' *That's me!* I thought. Alone in a tunnel, looking blindly for someone; it was perfect. It was not an image that sat well with the notion of being part of the body of

Christ and the church community, but that was partly why I liked it; flirting with existentialism felt a bit transgressive.

This self-indulgent melancholy was quite enjoyable, because I knew that I was the one in control of it. There had not been a return of the unanswerable, encompassing misery of two years earlier, and to recall it left me puzzled, as if I didn't recognise the memory. But there was one incident in Spain that troubled me because I could not explain it, though I sensed that it might be connected to that previous experience.

I don't remember what precipitated the episode, except that I could not blame drink or drugs, as I did in later years, because I had nothing to do with either at that time. I remember only this: that one night, a growing agitation had bloomed into a kind of frenzy that manifested itself in a need for urgent flight, as if there was a force in me that could not be contained but had to be given its head. I found myself running frantically through the streets of Salamanca in the early hours of the morning, across the town from the bullring and through the narrow medieval streets of the university barrio, past the historic buildings of pale stone with their elaborate carvings and wrought windows, into streets I didn't know, residential streets, still furiously running, almost blindly, blood roiling, because it was the only thing I could think to do with this unnatural energy. Though thinking was barely involved; it made no sense, and yet to go on running was the only possibility that did make sense. When, eventually, I collapsed on the pavement, snatching jagged mouthfuls of night air as I crouched by a low wall outside an apartment building in a part of the city that was entirely unfamiliar, my first thought was *I must never tell anyone about this*. I was not sure how long the frenzy had lasted, but I knew, even in its immediate aftermath, that it had felt like nothing so much as being driven by a sudden extraordinary surge of voltage. A couple of days later, when I tried to recall what had provoked it, I just felt silly, so I shrugged it away and forgot.

Part of the difficulty with diagnosing manic depression is that, unless the episodes are identified at the time, by the time they are recalled in the light of a possible diagnosis they have become blurred by memory and distorted by subjectivity, and the very act of mooting a diagnosis of bipolar disorder is likely to influence recollection anyway. This moment is my first clear memory of a concentrated experience of a hypomanic episode, though I had exhibited other symptoms through my teens: the over-optimism, the unrealistic proliferating plans, the furious involvement in too many activities. But these had always seemed like part of what my father called my 'all-or-nothingness'; that night, running through Spanish streets, I experienced for the first time the sensation that has returned periodically in the years since, that there was a force inside me threatening to explode out through my skull. At the time, I decided it was probably something to do with PMT. Perhaps this is not altogether erroneous; according to Dr Ian Jones, a specialist in mood disorders in relation to childbirth with the Mood Disorders Research Group at the University of Cardiff, some women with bipolar disorder can be extremely vulnerable at times when hormones are fluctuating rapidly – during pregnancy and birth, in relation to the menstrual cycle or the menopause.

'With women who have had severe episodes [of mania or depression] in relation to childbirth, if you do experiments where you artificially manipulate the hormone levels they can show the development of mood symptoms, whereas in women who have not had these episodes in relation to childbirth you don't have that effect,' he explains. 'Contrary to what most people would think, it's not that the hormonal changes are any different – they don't have higher levels of oestrogen or the drop isn't greater, but there are other factors that make some women higher risk around those hormonal fluctuations, and this is an area that needs to be explored further.' It seems that the extreme mood swings I often dismissed as 'hormonal' when I was younger may have been indicative of bipolar disorder, but precipitated and so disguised by times when I might have been expected to be moody and irrational anyway, so that neither I nor the people close to me recognised any real cause for alarm.

By the beginning of my second term at university I had passed through two rites of passage almost simultaneously: my first bereavement and my first heartbreak. Both were significant not so much for the degree of attachment to the people concerned, but – with the self-obsession of youth – for the capacity and intensity of emotion that the events created in me, depths I hadn't previously known I owned. But then, falling in love is usually an act of vanity, being concentrated on how it makes *me* feel, and the death of a contemporary inevitably refers us back to ourselves: the first funeral of someone your own age is an unavoidable *memento mori*. I had been lucky, up to that point; though I had lost a grandfather at the age of eight and various hamsters along the way, my child-hood had been funeral-free, and now I was hungry for every kind of life experience *in extremis* so that I would have something to write about. I was capable of plenty of darkness inside my own head, I knew that, but it had no objective correlative; I felt, as I had felt during my first skirmish with the demons, that it wasn't legiti-mate. I wasn't entitled to be depressed, because I hadn't really suffered by any real standards. So I welcomed these new pains of love and death because they were real and I believed importantly that they were giving me substance.

I lived most of that first year in a state of heightened emotion and rapidly swinging moods, but this was only part of college life; everyone I knew was intense, given to sudden enthusiasms, prone to staying up working for several nights on end if they had a project or an essay due, constantly falling in or out of love with a Shakespearian flourish. It was an intensely pressurised existence: eight-week terms living and working in the same enclosed environment; a fierce academic workload and competition many of us had not been used to; expectations both self-imposed and from parents and tutors. Most people wigged out at some point; you could not use any bathroom around the university without being confronted with an advert for the university's counselling service greeting you from the back of the cubicle door. The vulnerability of students to depression is widely acknowledged now – the British Association for Counselling and Psychotherapy carries out an annual study of student mental health which has shown problems of depression worsening in recent years – but resources for treating it are still scant. Recent web-based projects such as the American Foundation for the Prevention of Suicide's College and University Screening Project or Students Against Depression, a web information service founded by the Charlie Waller Memorial Trust, have shown that through the anonymity of the Internet many students were prepared to admit to depressed or suicidal feelings which they would not have been willing to discuss with their friends or tutors for fear of confidentiality, parents being notified or even sanctions from the college.

There had been a suicide in my college only the year before

I arrived; these things were talked of almost casually, as if we could all be expected to empathise. In recognising the pressures of the university environment and endeavouring to provide accessible support systems within it, Cambridge was then, and remains, highly progressive in the services it offered, perhaps from bitter necessity – one study of Cambridge students between 1970–1996 showed that statistically there were two suicides a year. In terms of discussion of mental health problems and easily available help, it was the most open environment I had experienced and the most conducive to seeking help, yet it never occurred to me to go near the counselling service. I thought I was fine: I had friends now, and if something troubled me, I went to find them in the bar.

Whether I was elated or despondent, drinking gave it the edge. Constitutionally, if not psychologically, I found that I was blessed with natural advantages. I had the ability to get riotously drunk, behave outrageously and go on doing so for a considerable time without spoiling it by passing out too early. This stamina attracted admiration from my new friends, many of whom were equally gifted in endurance, and came as something of a relief since, after the initial joy of being among like-minded people, I'd realised the negative side of blending into the background. Here, my exam results no longer made me special, and an alarming number of my fellow students seemed to have already built a skyscraper with Norman Foster or performed with the Royal Shakespeare Company or taken part in the Olympics. The old insecurities began slithering back; there was nothing I was good at except read- ing, and here *everyone* was good at reading. I was hopeless at sport, compared to all these county champions (though I gamely took up rowing because at least nobody else knew how to do that either). I had once thought I was good at drama, but my first audition for a

Cambridge production was so intimidating that it was also my last: here were people who had written, directed and starred in their own *films*! For someone whose self-confidence depended so entirely on measurable achievements, it was disconcerting to find that I was no longer remarkable, and I became afraid again that I was not worth anyone's notice. So when it was pronounced by those who seemed to be the arbiters of such things that I could drink, I gladly claimed the consensus as a prize, or at least a passport to a social life.

Black academic gowns flapping behind us like a coven of witches, my college drinking society, defiantly underdressed against the East Anglian winds that came scything in from the Urals, would set out into the night, a bottle of wine in each hand, our heels jack-knifing between the cobbles, to Formal Hall at one or other college at the invitation of a men's drinking society. In this arena, I tried on and strutted about in my new self, and found it fitted very well. I took to drinking with conviction because I preferred the personality it lent me. Suddenly I, who had been so cowed in the presence of popular girls, was revealed to be funny, outspoken, flirty, daring. It also made me maudlin or confrontational on occasion, but more often a bottle or several ignited a boldness and self-confidence that had never come to me naturally, except, occasionally, in school plays. In the world outside the college, ladette culture was in full-throated roar; young women now felt 'empowered' by the right to drink, throw up and fight like men, and perhaps there was an element of that confused attempt at liberation in our cloistered little world too – still in a minority, still condescended to by some of the older male dons, perhaps on some unconscious level we were trying to show that we could fit right into the bullish, swaggering traditions of the university. But for the most part we drank the way we did because it was fun, because it was intrinsic to the riotous, hectic way we lived, because it broke down inhibitions and gave us so much to laugh about. I drank like this not because I was unhappy, but because I was swept up in the current of feeling, for once, right at the heart of things, and because sometimes it seemed to click with a mood that came over me, a fierce drive towards speed, towards wildness and disinhibition that here, away from my family and the church, I could finally allow its head.

The demons came back the summer I graduated, as if they had been waiting patiently all this time behind the painted backdrop of spires and poplars. I sensed the clouds gathering at the edges of the wide June sky on graduation day, even before they began to cast a shadow; already I felt the intimation of a slow falling. Knots of students – no longer students, but proud graduates poised to step into the rest of their lives – gathered on the striped lawn of the Senate House after the ceremony, buoyant with adrenalin, laughing and shrieking, huddling for photographs, running to jump in the frame of another group photo, gowns streaming out behind them as parents trotted behind with video cameras. I laughed with them, but a fist of panic bunched in my throat. They were going to make me leave. It had only been three years, and that was not long enough to have become someone else; they couldn't make me leave yet! I knew it was not real life, all this soft blond stone and high Gothic arches, these bridges and lawns and cobbles; I knew, too, from observing some of the dons, what became of those who never left its magical cloisters and rejoined the world, and that should have been deterrent enough, but for three years I had been allowed

to feel that I belonged, and the thought of being turned away terrified me.

The previous few weeks had been more turbulent than usual, as
if I had been trying to pre-empt a catastrophe, or create one. While
I should have been revising for finals, I abandoned the two-year
relationship on which all my plans for the following year depended
in favour of a new, recklessly inappropriate fling, and while reading Marlowe's *Edward II* was struck with an idea for a novel which
became instantly far more urgent than the reading I was supposed
to be doing for my exams. The man I had left was working in the
City; the plan had been that I would live with him in his well-
appointed Kensington flat after graduation while I began the
wearying round of unpaid work experience, pleading letters and
rejections that might some day lay a foundation for a menial position in the arts. His financial and emotional support would have
smoothed all the rough edges from the life of an arts graduate with
no money, connections or experience in the capital, yet as the term
wound itself up towards finals I found myself increasingly agitated
and restless at the thought that I was about to launch myself into
the rest of my life, and it had all been already mapped out. I was
not ready to yoke my future so tightly to someone else's, so in the
name of adventure I ripped the map into confetti, took up with
someone who offered plenty of drama but no future, royally sabo-
taged my exams and found myself, on graduation day, with no job,
no money and nowhere to live.

There was no going home. Too much distance had opened up
between me and my family, a metaphysical gulf now existed – in
my mind at least – since I had let go of any pretence to faith. It had
not been a triumphant declaration of atheism, a kind of intellectual 'coming out', but rather a shame-faced confession, in my

second term, that I no longer went to church. Nor had there been much confrontation over it – one or two heated arguments with my mother, a series of kind, anxious letters from the church pastor offering to help me through this time of doubt – but when it became clear that this lost sheep had no intention of returning to the fold, and was in fact merrily gambolling through the fields with not so much as a backward glance at the fold, the arguments stopped. Instead, they were replaced by what I perceived as a pervasive disappointment in me, a kind of severance that would not be easily mended. We had not fallen out, but in my perception we were now on different sides of an unbridgeable divide. Everyone I knew and loved at home viewed the world in the context of eternity, while my perspective was suddenly foreshortened, and I was almost frantic with the need to wring every last drop of experience out of life before the deadline. They disapproved of my lifestyle, naturally, though they only guessed at much of it and preferred not to look too closely, so that when we met there were vast plains of conversation that were permanently fenced off if we wanted to preserve the peace. But it was on an elemental level that I had hurt them and let them down; I understood that for them, the failure of my faith was a rejection of the most important part of their life, the force that shaped and sustained them. It was not just a rejection of custom, or tradition, or philosophy, but a rejection of *who they were*. How could they not take it personally, and how could I not be miserably conscious every time I saw them that, whatever else I might achieve, in this regard I would always feel a failure?

This paranoia was largely imagined, but it made it impossible for me to think of going home; not because I would not have been welcomed, but because I would, and my parents' kindness would have occasioned such guilt that I feared I would slip back into the old routines of the double life to spare their feelings. The new self I had constructed depended on all the props, the drink and the cigarettes, the sexual bravado, and the thought of returning to the confines of that life – their little village, my old bedroom, the silence and isolation – terrified me. I feared that my transformation would prove to be only temporary, that the new, expansive life I had discovered would be crushed if I set foot in my home town, that I would be instantly sucked back in and reduced. Martin Amis calls this 'tramp dread': the unshakeable sense that, whatever you achieve, you might still find yourself the next day rooting through bins. Tramp dread was not quite what possessed me. To lose everything, to end up literally scavenging, would at least have something heroic about it; that would be failure on a grand scale. Rather, I was afraid of a small life, of ending up like one of the faceless characters in Larkin's poetry that had so reminded me of the suburban flatlands in which I grew up. Square-edged estates of new brick, washing on the line, long after-noon shadows, children pulling at your coat, endless days that looked the same as the one before and the ones to come. Unfulfilled hopes. I was bound to the swings of the pendulum but I preferred it that way, believing that in these pitches of mood, at the extremes its own momentum would eventually carry it back in the other direction. Infinitely worse, I thought, would be for the pendulum to settle gently somewhere in the middle and hang there, becalmed. What would I be then?

Instead I took a summer job on the river, punting tourists along the Backs, parroting histories of the colleges in three languages and inventing increasingly outré details for the more credulous Americans ('And this bridge was originally built by Henry the Eighth entirely out of cocktail sticks.' '*No!* Did you hear that,

Dwight?'), and moved into a five-bedroom detached house belonging to the owner of the punting company and shared by a number of his employees, all of us former students who couldn't quite manage to leave.

By September, the air was dry and cold and the coachloads of tourists clotting the narrow streets had thinned to a trickle; some days you could stand on the empty bridge in the wind, touting for trippers as the curling leaves scuttled around your feet, and go home having made a loss, if there was no business and you'd had to fork out for warm drinks and cigarettes to pass the time. My rent in the punting house was minimal, but I was earning so little that some weeks I could not afford to pay it. I had applied half-heartedly for a Master's degree in Medieval and Renaissance Literature, which would have been as useful as cutting off both hands when it came to getting a job, but would at least have bought me another year in the cloisters, hiding from the world. But my application missed the deadline, and my predicted First had slipped through my fingers somewhere in the shambles of my last term, so the university did not offer me a place, and I discovered that there is a very particular flavour of bitterness in being rejected by something (or someone) that you weren't even sure you really wanted. There were those with a sense of entitlement, for whom Oxbridge was always a given, one more step along a well-established trail, but to me it had been a kind of Narnia that I couldn't quite believe I had been allowed to glimpse and I still regarded it as hallowed; it had saved me as surely as I once believed Jesus had. I didn't know who I was outside the university; I wasn't sure that I could find anything to value in myself without its imprimatur, and now it didn't want me. My parents suggested again that I come home and live with them while I looked for jobs in London, but pride and fear dictated that I could not. I hated the thought of asking them for money, partly because they had supported me through college and I felt that the least I could do in return was to use this degree to pay my own rent, but mainly because I felt so guilty about what I had turned into and how far it was from what they had wanted. I wrote to every bookshop in Cambridge to see if they had any part-time work; they all wrote back politely saying they felt I was overqualified. I made desultory applications for other local jobs I had no interest in, and eventually turned to waitressing and bar work, but it was always the same answer: I was underequipped for a real job in any of the things I really wanted, and too burdened with qualifications for the minimum wage. It was not worth their while taking on new graduates, one bar manager explained, because it was obvious I would soon be moving on.

It was no longer obvious from where I stood. Too stubborn to go home, I decided that the only way to stay in Cambridge, while I trudged around London literary establishments soliciting unpaid work, was to sign on. In a different frame of mind I might have enjoyed the vaguely decadent overtones of drawing the dole while I tried to write my Edward the Second novel, but in the shallows of a new depression I felt no stick-it-to-the-man buzz of counter-cultural solidarity as I queued for 40 pounds a week in a squat municipal building with damply peeling paint, just half a mile from the centre of town but a universe away from the vaulted ceilings and oak-panelled rooms of the world I had only recently left. I had been sneaking into my old college computer room to print out job application letters since I could not afford a computer of my own; one morning, in mid-September, I found that my password no longer worked, and I understood that my name had been deleted from the college register.

In the same month, with gleefully malevolent timing, all four of my wisdom teeth exploded in the wrong directions in a firework display of pain. They required surgery, I was told, which could not be done on the NHS for a further ten months, and since there was no money for any other option, the best I could hope for was to manage the problem with painkillers and antibiotics each time they became inflamed or infected, which turned out to be at least once a week. With a lower jaw the shape and colour of an exotic fruit more days than not, I became less enthusiastic about applying for jobs; it was pointless anyway, since every newspaper, publisher and literary agency that agreed to see me seemed more interested in how many words I could type in a minute than in whether I had read *Don Quixote* in the original. This unexpected and wholly unreasonable demand that I exhibit some practical skills beyond being able to pronounce *Sir Gawain and the Green Knight* in a plausible fourteenth-century accent had come out of left-field to me; at what point in my rarefied tutorials had it ever been suggested that I would need a secretarial course as well as a working knowledge of Jung? We had been led to believe that doors would open at the mere mention of a Cambridge degree; now it appeared they were all firmly shut in my face, except the reinforced glass door to the Job Centre, with its welcome mat of dog ends and discarded hopes.

At my father's urging, I submitted to a typing course on an industrial estate, fuming at my own incompetence; once in possession of a secretarial certificate, I spent less and less time at the careers office, less and less time working on the novel (which, unaccountably, was now largely in italics and had started to sound like a bad pastiche of Borges), and long, formless hours lying in my room in the punting house with the curtains closed. It was furnished only with a single mattress on the floor and my books, forlornly heaped against every inch of wall space, but this barely mattered, since I could lie for the best part of a day staring at the same spot on the wall. I slid into a grey state of anomie; getting dressed seemed a Herculean effort I couldn't summon the strength to attempt; presenting myself as a chirpy and self-motivated individual eager for a filing job at a publishing house was as likely as spontaneously running a marathon. I cancelled the few interviews I was offered, because I felt incapable of fielding any more rejection. If it hadn't been forbidden to smoke in the house I could have stayed motionless on that mattress for days; even the decision to get as far as shivering in the garden with my spitty little roll-ups could take the best part of an hour. I ate rarely; hauling myself to the shops, choosing what to buy and then lugging it home and cooking it to a consistency that wouldn't offend my wounded jaw struck me as dauntingly complicated and in any case I had no appetite. On the plus side, I had become quite effortlessly very skinny. On the increasingly infrequent occasions when I saw my girlfriends, they congratulated me enviously and wanted to know my secret.

'Pterodactyls?' enquired my housemate Freddy on the occasions when we coincided in the kitchen. The pterodactyls, Freddy's shorthand for depression, were his equivalent of my demons; you could hear them beating their leathery wings as they circled around your head, he claimed. I would nod, often unable to speak for the riot of inflammation in my gums, and he would make me a cup of tea. We were all adrift in that house, in our different ways, but these small acts of kindness made it feel sometimes like an improvised patchwork family.

Under duress I went to a party, given by the wealthy boyfriend of a friend at his mother's colonnaded townhouse in south-west

London. This was the Brideshead set, the trustafarians, the crowd I had never really encountered at Cambridge (meritocracy had its boundaries) and I had resisted the invitation, but the girls had persuaded me that I needed to be cheered up by a night out. Though a number of my good friends were still at the university, finishing fourth years or starting graduate work, which had been one of the attractions of staying in Cambridge, I had barely seen them lately because I was too sharply reminded of my failings in their presence. They still belonged; I did not, and I was embarrassed by their insistence on subsidising me for drinks and by my inability to stand a round in my turn. Their concerns were still the concerns of students; they were busy and although they knew I was down about not having a job, I didn't elaborate and there was little they could say beyond blithe reassurances that something would turn up. I found my own company wearing, hunkered down into my melancholy and sense of worthlessness; I felt I brought nothing but pain and the whiff of failure to any gathering and I wanted to pre-empt their tiring of me. It was still so new to me, this fact of being liked, being part of a group, that I didn't trust my luck to continue now that I was reverting to my old, dismal self. My friends' response to seeing me more Eeyorish than usual was to try and lift me out of it by inviting me to parties or the pub with groups of friends from their courses, social occasions among large numbers of strangers that terrified me in this present state of mind. And at heart I was afraid that they were only continuing to invite me out through pity and a sense of obligation, and more than anything I could not bear to be pitied. But they bought my train ticket, so I had to go.

It was not until I attempted to renovate my exterior for the party that I realised how fragile I had become. I had been out of the house occasionally, though only to the Job Centre or the university library, where I had been doing some cash-in-hand research work for an American academic, but I had not been out socially for a while, certainly not in London, and I was experiencing a wholly disproportionate panic. On the Tube, I felt overwhelmed by the noise and the mass of other people and held myself carefully against the walls as we walked along, certain that if anyone bumped into me I would cry. At the imposing front door I almost turned and ran but couldn't think how I would explain it to my friends, who were smiling encouragement at me like a medical team watching for signs of improvement.

I drank at the party, because it was there and it was free, and I vaguely hoped there was a chance I might find some shred of my lost personality in a bottle – I had been drinking very little since the summer ended, mainly because I had no money and also because of the industrial quantities of painkillers and antibiotics I was taking for my teeth – but now the drink seemed to have abandoned me; with every glass I just felt tired and faintly nauseous. I skimmed the party: here was money, the young and beautiful and privileged with advantage smoothly stretching out before them like sunlit lawns in a Merchant Ivory film. I was young too, but beside the sleek girls in their little black dresses I felt suddenly a terrible weight of age and experience that I had not asked for; I heard their laughter and it seemed distant, as if the sound were travelling to me across water. Next to them I looked exhausted, used-up. My skull appeared to be pressing inwards, constricting, and I wanted desperately to cry and knew at the same time that I could not, it would be like dry heaving because I was scoured inside, scraped out, empty and brittle.

'And what do *you* do?' asked an affable older man, someone's uncle, perhaps, who was nursing a bottle of champagne in the crook of his arm like an infant. I thought about the answers he would already have heard: law, banking, consulting, finance. Proper professions. Or those still at college, studying for proper professions. In a different mood I might have said that I reviewed books for *The Times* and the *Daily Telegraph*, which was true, or that I was a historical researcher, which was also true, or that I was writing my first novel, which was true-ish, but I was not in a different mood.

'Nothing.'

'Nothing?' He raised a polite eyebrow. I presumed it was not unusual in his circles for young people blithely to do nothing. 'You were at Cambridge with Caspar?'

I nodded.

'Well, then. Good to have a bit of time out, I say.'

'I'm on the dole. I can't get a job.'

He did not miss the controlled violence in my voice, and a flicker of disquiet registered in his eyes, the anxiety that a line may be about to be crossed, that someone may be about to breach the English protocol and present you with unwanted real and painful details about their life. I spared him the awkwardness of facing my despair head-on and left. For a while I scuffed through the streets around Victoria Station. Something was badly wrong with me, I understood this, but until that moment at the party I had not been able to put my finger on it. It was not quite the teeth, not quite the job, not quite the dole, but something that went beyond all of these, something to do with who I was. I realised, when the uncle asked me what I did, that my self-esteem was shot: I did nothing, I *was* nothing, I never would be anything until I got a break, but I could not hope to get a break until I stopped feeling this crushing worthlessness, this inability to move and function in the world, and I would not stop feeling like that until I got the break, so I was essentially fucked. Even then – and this was what truly frightened me – I didn't know if I was capable any longer of feeling differently – of being light-hearted, of being someone who went to parties and laughed and danced and confidently announced what they did with a sense of pride. I secretly feared that already I might be beyond feeling anything: that the phone could ring tomorrow and it could be someone asking me to become Literary Editor of the *Guardian*, or telling me my entire family had been wiped out in an inferno, and either way the best I would be able to manage would be an effortful half-shrug.

This was how I felt, and still I did not recognise it as a condition that might be treatable. I knew by now that depression was an illness – people at college had been granted permission to defer exams because of it, and in my ignorance I secretly sneered at such weakness: no one *likes* exams, but we don't all turn into Woody Allen and beg a doctor's note to dodge them, I used to think. I even knew by then that it could be fatal; that summer I graduated, it had taken my friend Henry at the age of 23. I just didn't know that it was happening to me. I thought I was simply mired in self-pity, rejection, toothache and poverty, and it didn't occur to me for a moment to bother a doctor with it.

After some weeks, one of my pleading letters and apparently fruitless interviews paid a small dividend: I was offered one day's work a week at a major literary agency as a receptionist-cum-office factotum. It was not where my skills set was best suited, I felt, but it was a toe in the door, and for this opportunity they were going to pay me an incredible 40 pounds, instantly doubling my weekly income. Unlike my arrangement with the American historian for whom I did odd snippets of research in the university library, there would be no envelope of used fivers; this was an upstanding company and they had to put me through the payroll, which meant that I had to declare the 40 pounds to the benefits office. As a reward for achieving gainful employment, the Department of Health and Social Security took away my housing benefit, which significantly exceeded the monthly income I would now receive from my one day's work. It was at that point that I loudly lost patience with the Job Centre.

'You've crossed the threshold,' said the pie-faced boy flatly from behind the glass partition, presumably in place to stop me, and many like me, from killing him.

'How can I have crossed the threshold if I'm going to be getting less money in total?'

'Because you're earning. So we can't go on giving you housing benefit.'

'But I'm working *one day a week!*'

'It puts you over the threshold.'

I had a glimpse, in that moment, of how easy it is to demoralise people with the intransigence of the system, how quickly one can be made to feel impotent against the monolithic stupidity of government bureaucracy. Everyone thinks theirs is a special case, but to *Them,* no one is a special case. In the Job Centre, nearer to the threshold than the boy could have imagined, and roused to a pitch of emotional energy I had not experienced for months, I shouted, clearly and loudly enough to include the whole room. 'LAST WEEK!' I crashed my fist on the counter and the boy flinched in his glass case, '*Last week,* I stood in that queue and listened to two blokes having a conversation about fencing stolen tellies while they waited for their dole! There are people here just TAKING THE PISS! But I *want* to work! Do you think I want to be here, looking at your face? I've got a degree from Cambridge Fucking University! And now I've got some work, you want to punish me for it? You're actually telling me that I would be better off sitting on my arse taking handouts than getting a real job because the minute I do something useful you make it impossible for me to live? What kind of incentive is that?'

There was a resonant silence; even the screaming toddlers had been shocked mute. My fellow unemployed were staring, but not, apparently, in admiration. Too late, I suspected the Cambridge Fucking University bit might have lost me the sympathy vote. The boy contemplated me for a moment, more in curiosity than hostility, and after a thoughtful pause, said, 'Yeah, but you've crossed the threshold.'

So I found myself in the unusual position of telling the literary agency that I would be glad to take them up on their offer of a day's phone-answering, but I would much prefer it if they *didn't* pay me, which appeared to suit them quite well. In fact, if you counted the train fare, I was actually paying 15 pounds – more than one third of my dole – for the privilege of a job for which I was undertrained and overqualified and which – let's be honest – I was not even especially good at, forever losing calls in some eternal holding-pen in the ether. All this is standard practice for arts graduates, of course, but my sense of having finally taken a step forward was countered by the permanent sense of running up a down escalator. I was still waiting for my formal invitation to join the world.

I was unemployed for ten months, a mere blip, a parenthesis, and yet equalled only in torpor by the five months I spent on maternity leave, years later; something to do with the featurelessness of the days, perhaps, that stretches them out of all recognisable shape. My wisdom teeth, I had come to believe, were totemic; almost as soon as they had been wrenched out and the resulting elephantiasis had subsided, I got a call offering me a full-time job in London with a small literary agency, who had evidently heard about my unparalleled telephone skills from the larger agency. The teeth I kept in a Tic-Tac box, still bloodied, to remind me of how bad those months had been, because it was all going to be sunnier once I was in London, closer to the heart of things, closer to where I wanted to be (and where was that? What *did* I want to be? I had no clear idea, except the certainty I had known, growing up, that it was all happening somewhere else, and I was missing it). It was the spring of 1997 and we had a new government, too, brimming with progressive values for the first time in my life: things, I firmly believed, could only get better.

My inertia lifted slightly when I started work, but the underlying darkness did not. None of my friends were yet in London and I was chronically lonely, renting a tiny cell at an extremity of the District Line, in the house of a woman who made it very clear I was not welcome in any of the other rooms when she was at home – and she never went out. To avoid going home, I mooched around the city or sat in pubs hunched over the fat typescripts of novels I had to report on for my new job, eking out a pint until closing time. I was earning, true – the usual starting salary for an arts administration job (spotting an advertisement in the window of Pret a Manger, I was dismayed to find I could be earning considerably more pouring coffee) – but my cost of living had increased exponentially; in fact, the one more or less cancelled out the other.

A few weeks into my new job, I began to experience a resurgence of that strange, frenetic energy that had occurred in Spain;

sitting at my desk in my little office, I would find myself jigging frantically in my seat and clutching the edge of the desk, seized with that same urgent desire to burst out of the door and run and run through the city – where to, I had no idea, but I felt I needed to be unleashed. I became extremely agitated, unable to concentrate and alarmed by that sensation that I might be about to explode out of my own head, that my skull was too small and fragile to contain all this pent-up energy. That same claustrophobia, the fear of being stifled that had bound me in Cambridge returned now, but with this frenzied edge; there grew a frightening feeling of being trapped – at home, at work – and an urgent sense that something had to change imminently or the situation would become critical. The only thing I was able to do with all this sinister energy was write; I junked everything about the novel I had been working on since the end of university except the plot, pulled it to shreds and scrabbled through them to see what could be salvaged; sitting up every night on the end of my bed in front of my obsolete computer (thrown out by my father's college) with the keyboard balanced on my lap because the room was too small for a desk, I bled words in a torrent, haemorrhaged them on to the screen, losing myself in the unique thrill of being someone else – there was a high, a distinct shift in brain chemistry, an almost sexual anticipation about this kind of flurry, and often I didn't notice the night had passed until I heard the ragged dawn chorus. Soon I had a hundred pages, and this, I knew, would save me; with this novel I would be able to soar, and be calm and breathe again. I was elated; my hopes became extravagant, and entirely disproportionate.

It was the era of the big auction and the inflated advance; scant pages of first novels by youthful authors often fetched six figures and were slavered over by the press for five minutes, until they were published, when everyone piled in to give the book a good kicking. Regularly a handful of pedestrian chapters by some undergraduate would cross my desk for a reader's report; I would scathingly dismiss them, only to learn the next day that the writer had palmed 50 grand for his sub-Salinger musings. I can do better than that, I thought; this was a wave I could catch. My idea was completely brilliant (said the voice of unassailable hypomanic over-confidence), my characters compelling, I had been writing this quite exceptional and ground-breaking prose masterpiece for a couple of weeks with almost no sleep, I was so consumed by it that I could barely think of anything else and would smuggle chapters into work on a disk so that I could go on writing it when no one was looking, and now I was going to get my break, my six-figure advance, my launch to recognition and reward. I showed my new improved chapters to a literary agent I knew and trusted and waited with over-revving optimism for him to call back and tell me he had sold them in 17 territories over the weekend.

The men in white have a word for this Tiggerish state of mind: they call it 'grandiosity'. My mother had warned me about it in the past, though neither she nor I knew it as a feature of hypomania; she thought of it as another example of my not having a very firm grip on reality. Though I was often prone to feeling smothered by dark, negative thoughts, I was also capable of these stratospheric leaps in which, with the flimsiest encouragement, I became certain that the universe was bent double in its efforts to ensure me a fairy-tale ending. It was not that I thought I was great – I so often thought I was the polar opposite of great, that I was such a disastrous, worthless, ruined car-crash of a life that vanity had never been prominent among my flaws – just that, in certain moods, what in other people might have remained modest hope escalated in me to a pitch of near-delusion. Love was the worst: falling in love had this effect on me every time. It was a lot like being high, except that my mind could do this all on its own, and only a crashing disappointment could rein it back.

I didn't sleep for most of the weekend. The agent called back the following Monday, having read my pages, and asked me to drop by his office on my way home. There he explained, quite rightly and with faultless diplomacy, that what I had was an interesting idea that needed a great deal more thought and that, in any case, it was probably not suited to his list. He suggested another agent who might be appropriate. I nodded bravely, and distantly heard somebody with my voice thank him for his helpful comments, but the sensation I experienced was exactly equivalent to the moment when you miss a chair sitting down and smash your coccyx on a stone floor: a lightning bolt of pain and nausea in equal measure.

I made it home on the bus, detouring only to buy a bottle of undrinkable wine at the Costcutter. My flatmate was out. I wanted to call someone, but didn't know who – and to say what, anyway? Guess what – *I'm shit?* The one thing I had believed I could do – it seemed I had been mistaken. I had failed, definitively. There would be no six-figure advance, no Booker Prize, no illustrious career. I would measure out my life typing other people's letters. But as I prowled purposelessly around the flat with my bottle, entering first one room then another, ignoring the need to turn on the lights as the shadows lengthened and spread over the walls, what roiled in me was not despair but fury – not at the agent, but at myself. Where a rational person would have been grateful for constructive criticism and set about correcting what needed to be corrected, I saw only a steel shutter crashing down; this was, as far as I was concerned, the end of the world. Lit with this white rage

I paced the flat feverishly with that strange, surging light-headedness, and it seemed to me that I had to give vent to it or I would in some way combust. I was too far out now to be calmed or talked down, even if there had been anyone there to do the talking. Only a physical lashing-out would exorcise the furious energy surging behind my eyes, it seemed, but it would not have been enough to break some object, even many objects – it was myself that I wanted to hurt. My prowling took me to the bathroom and by now I was fully in the grip of something quite alien, not merely drunk but self-immolating; there was a momentary urge to put my fist through the mirror but then I caught the glitter of a pair of nail scissors on the shelf and before the thought properly had time to solidify I had snatched them up and slashed the length of my left arm.

For a moment I regarded my arm with mild surprise, as if someone else had done it. Beads of blood sprang along the line of the gash and in the instant I gripped the scissors in my fist and with a deep cry of rage I did it again, and again, and again, and then I did the other arm, and there was no sense of catharsis, no release in it, but what I felt overwhelmingly was a sense of justice. I *deserved* this. I *ought* to be hurt, because I had failed. It was right that I should punish myself, because I hated myself. By the time the fury was all spent, time had hiccupped forward and it was late; I moved with caution, slowly, as if I were breakable. The house was silent, lagged by the darkness. My flatmate, when she came in and switched the light on, gave a little scream to find me slumped on the living-room floor in the dark, staring at the wall, my arms ribboned with cuts. They were only surface wounds – I looked as if I had held down a particularly spiteful cat – but God knows what she must have thought in that instant. We didn't speak about it, though a few days later she announced that she was going to have the decorators in and would need my room back.

Self-harm was never a feature of my depression; the idea of hiding oneself in the bathroom and methodically carving patterns into one's flesh with a secret toolkit has always been foreign to me and still shocks me cold – the surgical precision of it, the relished secrecy, are not in my nature. That moment of inflicting violent damage on myself – repeated only a couple of times, years later, though the urge often returned – was something other: a sudden compulsion, a fever of self-hatred, a brief journey out to a place of glittering dark and potential oblivion. Once it had subsided into regular old hopelessness, I could not explain it to myself, and thought it best to pretend the whole thing never happened.

It was only later that I learned that 'bipolar' or 'manic depression' are misleading terms, suggesting as they do that one must be in either one or the other of two neatly defined, separated and opposed states of mind. Much of the time, people with bipolar disorders will be neither, but sometimes they can experience what are termed 'mixed state' episodes, or 'agitated depression', where the negative, despairing feelings of depression are accompanied not by lethargy and fatigue but by all the frenzied malevolent energy of a manic episode, and this is where the illness becomes really dangerous. Drug and alcohol abuse and suicidal thoughts are more prevalent during mixed state episodes; one of the earliest studies of manic depression (by Emil Kraeplin in 1921) concluded that mixed states occur most frequently during periods of transition, as someone is cycling into or out of an episode of depression or mania, and recent studies in the US have shown that bipolar II disorder and cyclothymia (rapid-cycling episodes), being characterised by frequent changes of mood and a greater tendency to mixed state depression, carry the highest risk of suicide among all the subtypes of major mood disorders. Evidence shows that the majority of people with bipolar disorder who commit suicide do so impulsively during a mixed state episode, which makes perfect sense to me; only in mixed states have I experienced what I can only describe as that urgent compulsion to self-destruction, the knowledge that in that temporary unreason I would be capable of doing myself great damage. Neither is there any sense, in the fury of it, that this will pass; the present moment, the will to harm, is all that exists.

The Coach and Horses in Ray Street, in 1998, was one of the last outposts of old Fleet Street, its décor and its regulars all borrowed from Michael Frayn's 1967 novel *Towards the End of the Morning*. Here hacks drank with solemn dedication, as if it were a religious observance; on my initiation visit, shortly after I started working for the *Observer*, the first landmark proudly and solemnly pointed out to me was the bloodstain on the wall behind the hat stand, souvenir of a disagreement about an obscure point of political philosophy between two eminent columnists. The Coach seemed to me, new to this world at 24 and still embarrassingly green, to be the unofficial engine room of the newspaper. This was where ideas were ignited, deep friendships forged, affairs begun and messily ended, politics, literature and art thrashed out, the world put to rights, lunchtime after lunchtime, night after night, the one often sliding into the other without anyone noticing. It was the talk that did it for me, the thrill of being part of a group of clever, sardonic people with experience to share, and all of it carried along on a current of cheap booze; I never wanted to leave, and for most of the next seven years, I didn't.

Everyone I knew drank to excess, so it was hard to tell when the line had been crossed. Much of the time it was hard to see where the line had gone in the first place. I moved among journalists, novelists, comedians and poets, none of these professions famous for temperance; it was in the air we breathed, and more often than not it was free at some publicity event or other. When I first moved to the *Observer* my position was unpaid and untitled, so I had no income at all and barely anything in the bank; I would go without food all day, then find a book launch (someone was always having a book launch, in those more profligate times) in the evening where I could fill up on canapés and cheap white wine. By this means I successfully avoided buying groceries for weeks. But even in that culture, I occasionally encountered individuals for whom the pursuit of excess was something more than convivial or part of a professional lifestyle, in whom it was a mission, a wolfish hunger to see what lay beyond the furthest reaches. If you had it, you were drawn to it in others. The world divided into two kinds of people: those whose inner adult could be relied upon, be it ever so late, to tap its watch, purse its lips and remind them that they had to work in the morning, and those who were missing that mechanism, the wild-eyed ones who were compelled to keep going, and keep going, and keep going, because to go home would be to break the spell, to return to the ordinary, with its tiresome bondage to the laws of cause and effect. Not that I chased an altered-consciousness experi-ence for any sort of visionary purpose; neither the drinking nor my rather desultory experiments with drugs were part of a spiritual quest, and I didn't buy all that Blakean cod-Romantic hokum about the road of excess leading to the palace of wisdom – more often it led to waking up in a bus garage at the end of the line or on the bathroom floor of someone whose name you didn't know and whose party you had invited yourself to without having the slightest idea what postcode you were in. On some level, though, that kind of drinking was about the need to introduce an element of the unknown, a little magic dust. I had scrubbed religion from my life and since I had no other lexicon for the supernatural it was impossible for me to replace it with a different form of spirituality, but I found the landscape flat and colourless without it. The rational, daylight world was not enough; I missed a sense of the numinous and when I was fired up, setting out for the night, what I loved most was the unpredictability, the endlessly multiplying possibilities. Not knowing who I would run into, what parties they might know of, what picaresque journeys we might make around the city or where I would find myself the following morning restored a sense of adventure, a sense of stepping beyond what was known, or safe.

The Diagnostic and Statistical Manual (Fourth Edition), the handbook of American psychiatry, lists the following among the diagnostic criteria for hypomania: decreased need for sleep; increased talkativity; inflated self-esteem; over-optimism; uninhibited sociability; hypersexuality; flights of ideas; increased productivity (often with unusual and self-imposed working hours) and excessive involvement in pleasurable activities with lack of concern for painful consequences. Since this described most of the people I ran with most of the time, my over-excited moods were well camouflaged; I had no concept that this behaviour might be considered cause for concern, except by tight-lipped beige people who disapproved of life in general. And yet, on occasion, the still-tuned part of my mind was alert to a needle point of conscience telling me that I had gone too far; I had alarmed people, or upset them, or made them lose patience. In these moods, which sometimes lasted a few days, I felt constantly an urgent need to plug into the pulse of the city, to keep moving on to the next place, and the next, dragging whomever I could persuade along with me in search of what, I didn't know – somewhere I would know I was alive. I would talk and talk at anyone who would listen, and often even when they did not; I was a flurry of ideas and anecdotes, some of which made no sense at all – at one party I spent what seemed like hours insisting to a respected political writer that my father was a leader of the Peruvian Maoist terrorist group the Shining Path with such conviction that in that moment I completely believed myself (though I'm fairly sure he didn't).

No consequences: this was how it always felt in these taut, vibrant moods; there existed only the present moment, glorious and illuminated, and it was impossible to think of the reckoning that would come – the credit card bills, the shattered trust, the words that couldn't be snatched back or unsaid. Sometimes this recklessness was harmless (except to my bank account), like the time I decided it would be an excellent idea to teach myself New Testament Greek so that I could translate the Bible accurately for the first time in history and thereby disprove Christianity by high-lighting its inherent contradictions, and crashed around a bookshop buying up every textbook I could find on the subject, including a ferociously expensive Greek Bible, only to take them to Oxfam a few weeks later. Sometimes it involved other people, and was not harmless. *Wasted* is the most apt word; *I* was wasted, a lot of the time, but so was so much else: time, money, the goodwill and patience of friends, the trust of lovers, the opportunities.

And afterwards, always so much tear-stained shame; shame for what was done, what might have been done, what was said and sometimes what was only thought (my smudged memory found it hard to distinguish between the two); the juddering, vengeful remorse familiar to every drinker that comes at you late in the afternoon of the next day, sending you scurrying to your email to fire off a blanket apology to everyone you have ever met for being such an abominable, hateful human being. And always, in that late afternoon half-light, the knowledge of what my family would think of me, how little I resembled the daughter they would have hoped for; though they didn't know the half of it, I lived with the prickling suspicion that they must, somehow. At Sunday School, we were taught that Jesus is always watching over us, like a holy closed-circuit television; he could even read our secret thoughts, so we must always be sure not to do anything that would sadden or disappoint him, even if we thought no one would find out. On some level I had substituted my mother for Jesus as the embodiment of my conscience; when the euphoria faded, I looked at myself through her eyes and was sorrowfully disgusted with what I saw. Then I would furiously determine to be good from now on – to be a kinder, nobler, braver person, to give my money to charity instead of to the Coach and Horses, to volunteer for hospital visits, to make my life worthwhile somehow. It was just that, sometimes, I didn't seem to be in control of it.

Mostly your friends forgave you, if only because, as long as you don't become aggressive or violent, there is always comedy value in having a member of the group who is prepared to abandon completely all pretence to dignity; like Jeffrey Bernard's columns, they provide some fine anecdotes and the occasional flash of insight from the brink, and you can always be grateful that you weren't the worst person in the room. Except that sometimes – not often – I could become aggressive, especially if thwarted or hindered; like a teenager, I could rage in rebellion if, while I was flying up there at 30,000 feet, any well-intentioned friend or boyfriend made the mistake of suggesting that for my own good I should come down, or stop, or go home. I was capable of a fury that could catch light in an instant; this was a reflex reaction that bypassed sense, humility or the dues of friendship. People don't know what to do with you then; you have crossed over from being lively, spirited, wild, all those words people use to suggest someone who is fun to be around at parties, to being frightening, inappropriate, disturbing. I went on hurtling through my life at this pace for a year or so, somehow effecting a plausible contribution to my job, though nights often ended with just enough time to make it home, shower and scramble into the office again; often I managed weeks on hardly any sleep, and then when I nosedived, as I always did, I would squirrel myself away in the dark of my room and become invisible, and so since I was only ever seen by others when I was out and flying, everyone thought that this was who I always was.

There came, eventually, a crescendo. A garden party; one of those anachronistically elegant affairs, a white marquee in a rose garden in central London, the luminaries of the literary world turned out in fresh linen to toast themselves in the clean evening light of early summer. I was giddily over-excited at the prospect of it, being in the midst of all that talk; I wheeled around the party talking hectically to people I didn't know but who I was sure must be dying to get to know me, while my boyfriend gingerly tried to steer me away from making too great a fool of myself near anyone important. Eventually the dignitaries left and those who stayed on repaired to the nearby pub. By this time I was soaring: in my element, riotously happy, flirting with everyone, buying drinks for people I'd never met with money I didn't have, surging upwards, and at closing time someone I barely knew said they were going on to a private club. I had that edgy mood on me that didn't want to be told, so when my boyfriend came to find me, saying he was tired and wanted to go home, I grew defiant.

I was going to the club with these people, I announced, pointing to show who I meant. He wanted to know why I wanted to go with them, and I tried to explain that it was because I didn't want to stop, that at the club we could go on with the drinking and flirting and singing and keep taut and strung at that pitch until the small hours, because I knew that at home, in his little flat, I would end up provoking a fight just to have an outlet for it, because I was afraid that if I let the momentum stop I would flail, mid-air, like Wile E. Coyote, and realise with a dropping horror that there was nothing holding me up, but I was in no shape to articulate any of this and I can't have done it usefully because he seemed to end up under the misapprehension that I was interested in a particular member of the club-going detail – which was not the case at all: it was the group's energy I craved, and a place to be among people. He accused me of preferring this other man's company to his, I yelled at him, he yelled back in that infuriating tone of knowing better by being older, so like a father, and I recollect only shards of what happened next.

He tried to take my arm and lead me towards the door; something exploded behind my eyes at being forcibly manhandled and I hit out at his arm to make him let go; someone stepped in to separate us and then time slips, misses a few beats, and I am being bundled into a taxi by a couple of kind friends, while the pub seemed to have erupted into a spaghetti western saloon bar brawl; I watched as if from a great distance through the taxi's rear window as my boyfriend chased us up the street shouting something I couldn't hear, growing smaller and smaller.

The next day, he came to meet me after work in a pub near my office. I was bracing myself for a telling-off and had prepared a comprehensive speech of apology, but I was not prepared for the sight of his face and it stopped me dead; there was a sizeable bruise under his eye and his lip was split and swollen at one side. The worst of it was that he wore an expression not of reproach but of wounded concern. I hated myself then, really hated myself, and could not comprehend how I had become someone who could have done this. He said, without anger:

'I think you might need professional help.'

A momentary, chilling vision of AA meetings flickered, and immediately I began protesting that I didn't have a drink problem. Of course, everyone who drinks too much categorically asserts that they don't have a drink problem, and often goes on asserting so even as they're being wheeled away to have their liver taken out, encased in concrete and buried at sea, but I was and remain certain that drinking was not my problem. At least, it was not the cause of my problems; I never experienced a physical need to drink, and the thought of drinking early in the day I found revolting. Neither did I find it difficult not to drink, and would often give it up for a while with no hardship – a few days, a week or two, sometimes as much as a month if I felt particularly shabby or threadbare and my body pleaded for respite. No, I had no trouble at all in not drinking; in fact, I much preferred to stick with water than to have one or two glasses of wine – there was no magic in one glass. All or nothing; that was how it had to be.

I told him that there was something else beneath the drinking; a compulsion I could not explain and which sometimes frightened me, which meant that I drank the way I had the night before not for its own sake but because the drink provided an external corroboration for my speeding mind – it made sense of it, by providing a visible reason for the way I felt. My boyfriend was wise enough, and experienced enough, in the ways of drink to see that there was truth in this, and he offered to pay for me to see a shrink.

'I'm not *mad*,' I said, indignant. In my view the problem was that I did not want to answer to anyone, and the more he tried to rein me in, the more I was provoked to behave like a furious teenager, to run riot and lash out. The solution, as I saw it, would have been for him to ease up with the rules. I did not seriously think there was anything wrong with me.

He merely looked at me from under a bruised eyelid, and I agreed that, by way of apology, to prove that I meant it, I would give therapy a go.

Alcohol and depression have a close and complex relationship and often it can be difficult to distinguish between cause and effect. Drinking is usually seen as a cheerful, convivial activity, integral to our social lives, and for many of us a low mood or a bad day is often countered by a few drinks to cheer ourselves up. People suffering from depression often self-medicate with alcohol or drugs in the hope of boosting their mood – recent research by the Mental Health Foundation found that one in ten people in Britain admits to drinking to mask feelings of depression and anxiety – but the oft-repeated truth is that prolonged excessive drinking further damages the chemical balance in the areas of the brain associated with depression, promoting depressive episodes and related symptoms such as disrupted sleep patterns and anxiety attacks. Those with psychiatric disorders are twice as likely to be alcoholic as the general population, and in the case of bipolar disorder the ratio is five times as likely (and seems to be a particular risk to women; a study produced in 2003 found that women with bipolar disorder are more than seven times more likely to have alcohol misuse problems than women in the general population). This prevalence may be because, since alcohol enhances and exaggerates mood, there is a tendency in manic or hypomanic episodes to drink in order to prolong the pleasurable 'up' feeling and sense of disinhibition. A further problem is that the similarities between the mood swings caused by bipolar disorder and those caused by drinking and withdrawal can make it difficult to diagnose bipolar accurately in people who drink to excess. For obvious reasons, moderating or cutting out alcohol is a cornerstone of all self-management programmes for unipolar and bipolar forms of depression. I sometimes wonder why it took me so long to work this out, now that it seems so obvious, but the answer is partly that, whenever I cut out alcohol, I did so – as with everything else I did – in such an abrupt and extreme way that it immediately made me feel worse; without the support of other sustained lifestyle changes, my bouts of abstinence were short-lived and I soon swung back to the drinking culture. For a long time, the idea of moderation seemed incompatible with the life I led, and held very little enticement, partly because I was secretly afraid that if I stopped drinking I would no longer belong. Moderation – being 'sensible' – was for the beige people. I wanted brighter colours, even if they sometimes shaded into black.

'Do you often hit people?' the shrink asked mildly, poised over her notebook.

'No!' I said, alarmed, which was the truth – I hadn't properly hit anyone since primary school. From my recumbent position on her sofa I could read the spines of the books on the stack of shelves opposite, floor-to-ceiling bookshelves like those in my father's study, like those I dreamed of building in the house I would one day own when I was a successful grown-up, instead of piling all my books under the bed in a cramped room in someone else's flat as I had for the four years since leaving university. The spines were antique and solemn, with pleasingly erudite titles: plenty of Freud, Jung, Lacan. This was more like it, I decided, thinking of the church's Ruth and her biblical platitudes; this unsmiling woman in the book-lined room was the real thing, she had many, many degrees from different continents, she had read books whose titles I couldn't even understand, so she was sure to be able to fix me.

Though I had resisted at first, I was secretly rather pleased with the idea of the shrink; I felt it lent a certain edgy glamour. Betty Blue, Sylvia Plath – being unpredictable and slightly crazy was part of what made them sexy; maybe having a shrink would make me sexy too. Therapy was so remote from my experience that my only concept of it was cinematic; I could not have detailed for anyone the difference between a psychologist, a psychiatrist, a psychother-apist and a psychoanalyst, nor did I even know which mine was, but she came highly recommended by a friend to whom she had been highly recommended in turn by an eminent media shrink, and I did know that she was a Jungian, which suited me because I had written a dissertation on Jungian archetypes in fiction at college, so I thought I'd be able to spot what she was up to.

Hesitating at the door of her gabled house in a leafy north London street, I felt a quick buzz of nervous optimism, as if on a first date. It had not taken a great deal of self-examination to understand that in the truest core of myself, the pith of my mind where I could not alter the facts or fool anyone, I still believed that the root of all my problems was walking away from God. Intellectually I may have ditched Him, but it was not so simple to cast off the beliefs that were watermarked through me since I was old enough to understand stories. Beneath all the posturing, I saw it as a negative move; intellectually I believed that I had belatedly woken up to the mythical or metaphorical nature of religious faith, not to mention its contradictions and inherent bigotries, but emotionally I felt not that God no longer existed, only that I had wilfully turned my back on Him and run off to indulge my taste for the dissolute life, like the prodigal son. In my unconscious He was still there, patient, monolithic, resolute as ever, impervious to my denials. There was still a part of me that strongly suspected I could solve most of what was wrong with me by admitting my sins and returning to the church, determined to live a good Christian life, and which also knew very well that consciously rejecting one's salvation when one had been given the blessing of its revelation ranked very high in the league table of sins, up there with being gay or having an abortion. There was also a part of me that perversely craved the simplicity of that process of confession and forgiveness, the effort of someone else's prayers, the ease of being washed clean and given a new start – though most days I suspected that my soul was going to need more than just a washing in the blood of the Lamb. Sandblasting might just do it.

As a result, I lived in a permanent miasma of guilt, pursued by the fear of a God I was fervently trying not to believe in and couldn't quite shake off. And yet it was not as bluntly Old Testament as a dread of punishment; what I feared most in the scratchy, wakeful hours before first light was the thought that I had occasioned pain – that my rejection had hurt God and that it was up to me to make it better. As a child in Sunday School I had been taught that my sins were the reason for Christ's suffering on the cross, and that every time I behaved in a way that did not honour Him, I renewed that suffering; I was horrified to learn that I had the power to inflict such damage on someone who loved me. By the time I left college, I had understood what it meant to offer someone all the love you can muster, only to find they didn't want it; for all my fine liberal atheist bluster, the guilt I hefted about with me everywhere was the guilt of having done the same to Jesus.

So I was desperate for someone to whisk a detached and clinical and, above all, secular eye over my troubled mind and to reassure me professionally that my moods were not the result of spiritual delinquency. To my disappointment, the shrink had not a black leather reclining couch but a floral two-seater sofa-bed. When I lay down, as I assumed was customary, she suggested I might be more comfortable sitting up. I assured her that I wasn't; sitting up facing her was uncomfortably reminiscent of a tutorial at college, an hour to fill and me with no preparation attempting to busk and charm my way through.

There followed a long silence, during which I took in the spines of the books and listened to the minutes ratcheting up like so many pound coins dropping into a deep well, while I waited for her to do something. Then I realised she was expecting me to speak. A gobstopper of panic plugged my throat. What was the protocol? Was I meant to talk about my mother? My traumatic birth (if indeed it had been – I had no idea)? The fact that when I was six I wanted to be a boy and would answer only to 'Darren'? Should I just plunge in by announcing that although I had been blessed with a secure and loving family, a good education and a job I enjoyed, I sometimes thought about killing myself over trivial matters and was occasionally given to slashing myself up with nail scissors and sometimes feared that I might explode out of my own head? I didn't want her to think I was crazy, for goodness' sake.

After what seemed like about 15 pounds' worth of mutually expectant silence, she asked why I had felt the need to see her, so I grudgingly explained, mumbling through my teeth like a teenager forced to apologise, about the garden party and its aftermath. We stuttered forward through a lot of expensive silences for the next 45 minutes, all inarticulacy and reluctance on my part and with-held knowledge and gnomic nods on hers, and I left my first session feeling that it had been like sex without climax – the prom-ise of some kind of resolution that never quite arrived. She did, however, offer one extraordinary insight with regard to the garden party incident that I grasped immediately and with gratitude: she suggested that I might have experienced an allergic reaction to the preservative chemicals used in cheap wines and that I should in future stick to better quality wines or champagne to see if such an incident recurred.

'Well?' my boyfriend asked when I saw him that evening, as if hoping to find me now docile and pliable, or at least in possession of some useful nugget of advice that would show he was getting his money's worth, and I didn't know how to tell him of the solidify-ing disappointment I already felt, the sense that this was not what I needed and that it would not, however many hours I spent lying back and staring at her leather-bound Complete Freud, change anything.

'She said I should only drink champagne in future.'

'Anything else?'

'She thinks I have a problem with guilt.'

'For 60 quid she's spotted that you have a problem with guilt and her solution is that you only drink champagne?'

'Yep.'

I wanted her to fix me: that was the problem. Though I had no experience of analysis, I had spent years being instructed in how to live within a defined framework; I had gone to the shrink expecting her to act as a kind of animated self-help book. I had imagined she would dispense sage, non-religious advice that I could go home and follow, a set of bullet points to make me calmer and more wholesome; I wanted her to tell me how to live. If she had done so – if she had told me on the spot to stop drinking or change my relationship or make any number of practical steps in a programme of practical steps, I do believe I would have gone forth and obeyed, because I knew how to live like that; she could have become a hieratic substitute, an alternative form of salvation. I had failed to understand that I was the one who was supposed to be doing the work in these sessions, embarking on the inner journey that would enable me to better assess for myself how to orchestrate the messy business of being in the world, but this was never explained to me. All I heard was my own voice, strained and lurching, echoing around the bookstacks on the subject of nothing relevant and the lasting silences occasionally punctuated by her small 'Mm' or '*Ahh*', to the tune of 60 quid an hour. I began to suspect that people went to shrinks because they didn't have any friends and they had to pay someone to listen to them. *I* had friends, though – for the price of a round I could sit in the Coach and cheerfully bang on about myself for well over an hour, boring the arse off any number of people and not even minding if they got up and went somewhere more interesting while I was halfway through, because someone else was always bound to take their seat – you were more likely to get advice back, too, though not necessarily any you would want to follow. By the second session I had started to wonder what the point was supposed to be, and by the third I worried that I might be boring her, and spent the journey there inventing Dali-esque dreamscapes ripe with symbolism just to fill the gaps.

I lasted a little under two months, with no discernible effects. One day I asked her how long she thought it would take, and she produced an indulgent laugh. Analysis could be the work of a lifetime, she explained. Certainly I could not expect to see much benefit in under six months. For a moment, six months' worth of weekly 60-pound cheques danced a little phantasmagorical jig before my eyes – since the obvious non-productivity of the first session I had felt it unfair to hold my boyfriend to his promise to pay for the therapy – and I thought of all the cheering things I could buy with that money, which I didn't have to spare in the first place; holidays and jackets and meals out with friends, all the nice things that would, I felt, do much better at warding off another bout of blackness than an hour of awkward silences in Hampstead.

I left her, like a coward, in a letter, so that she couldn't talk me into staying. She would not be the last shrink I ran away from. The effort involved in getting to the weekly sessions; the aversion to any sort of obligation of my time; the artificial intimacy; the boredom – very quickly achieved – with the sound of my own voice talking about myself; the expense, which some deeply ingrained sense of prudence could never view as anything other than a frivolous extravagance, quite apart from the shame of revealing what I am underneath the careful persona – all these reasons bank up every time I begin with a new therapist until I conclude, usually within a month, that it has been an interesting experiment but is not worth the bother. There is also the problem of my misplaced expectations. The old truism says that therapy is the modern religion, but I had gone to that first shrink making the same demands as I had of the old religion: I had wanted her to give me absolution and guidance.

I had wanted her to be both priest and doctor: she was supposed to make me better, though at the same time I had not seriously expected her to tell me that I was actually *ill*. At one point during our brief acquaintance, she asked if there was any history of depression or manic depression in my family; I answered truthfully that I had no idea. I was from working people who didn't talk about that kind of thing and wouldn't have known what to call it even if they had had the inclination. There was one close living relative, I knew, who had experienced a number of what my mother darkly termed 'nervous breakdowns', though I had never really understood what characterised these episodes. As a child I imagined this person lying in a curtained room, exaggeratedly nervous as you might be before, say, getting on a rollercoaster, struck dumb and shaking uncontrollably – a sort of cross between a stroke, a panic attack and Parkinson's – and long afterwards this was how I pictured a nervous breakdown, so that I didn't even recognise when I had one of my own.

Anyway, I explained to the shrink, it could not be anything like that because my little episodes, my odd moods, were always circumstantial; they were a reaction, even if an entirely disproportionate one, to a recognisable cause. I could not press my mother for any further details either, because that would have meant telling her that I was seeing a shrink, and this was not a good prospect; in the imagining, all hint of rock and roll glamour evaporated and I felt only the sting of shame, the way I thought it would look to them. And to explain to them why I needed to see a shrink would involve giving up more details than I strictly wanted them to have about the way I lived. They should be protected from such knowledge, because they were good and kind and had had such hopes for me; even the idea of the way I lived hurt them, I knew, but at least they had only a blurry outline so far, and there was no reason to sharpen the focus. They might be doubly hurt to learn that I preferred to pay a stranger to listen to problems I would not have thought to discuss with them, and that would only pile another stone of guilt on to the heap on my chest that already threatened to crush the breath out of me at night. I feared, too, that they would come up with the same conclusion that chafed at me: that I could save myself all this money and grief if I would only come back to the church. I was wrong to fear this, as it turned out, and perhaps life might have gone differently if I had trusted their understanding and sympathy, but that discovery only came years later, when I could no longer hide myself. In the meantime, out of their sight, I went on barrelling between extremes, addicted to my confected melodramas and my overreactions, convincing myself that it was better to burn out this way than die of boredom.

3

Love and Death

Amid the arguments that proliferate over the causes of depression, one thing is widely agreed upon: depression has evolved as part of our inbuilt response to loss, which is also part of our capacity to form attachments. 'Depression is the flaw in love,' writes Andrew Solomon at the beginning of *The Noonday Demon*. 'To be creatures who love, we must be creatures who can despair at what we lose, and depression is the mechanism of that despair.' It may be reducible to a series of chemical equations, but then so is love. Alongside the biological, psychological and social factors that can contribute to depression, it seems to me that there is also an existential dimension, integral to our capacity to ask the big philosophical questions about the point of human existence. Depression is our human response to loss – of someone we loved, or of something that was bound up with our sense of self and our own value. The loss of hope, sometimes years after the original loss.

I grew up with a religious faith that offered a sense of purpose, self-worth, comfort, community, pre-fabricated answers to most of the important questions and, on top of all these benefits, the promise of eternal life. When, during my first year at university,

I found I could no longer square the tenets of this faith with my reason, I chose reason, but at the time I had no sense of the cost involved. To walk away from the safety of that structure into a landscape that offers no comforting, illusory shelter has been in many ways a liberation but also a profound loss, whose significance has taken years to understand. Christianity taught me that since the beginning of time I was loved unconditionally by the Creator of the universe; I chose instead to inhabit a world where love is flawed and transient and very often painful, and perhaps that loss has marked me more than I recognised.

Love, hope and depression have always existed, for me, in an uneasy, unbreakable triangular tension. Though love and hope are depression's two opposites, they are not its guaranteed antidotes, though having both makes it easier not to be overwhelmed by depression. Depression blots out love and hope until it seems impossible that you ever experienced either or ever will again. Even so, loving and being loved are ballast against the threat of despair and the sense of emptiness that depression throws over a life. Depression is the remotest place on earth. You feel yourself to be isolated from everything and everyone you once cared about, and not even those who love you can follow you there. You become fundamentally unlovable to yourself and then you believe it to be true objectively, and the absence of love is fertile ground for despair. This is the heart of the matter.

In his short story 'The Revival', Julian Barnes writes, 'Did he reflect that first love fixes a life for ever? Either it impels you to repeat the same kind of love and fetishises its components; or else it is there as warning, trap, counter-example.'

The first time I fell in love, at the age of 19, created a template for everything that came after.

I saw Daniel on my first day at university, glimpsed him across a courtyard, and turned back for a second look. The following day I saw him again in the college bar at lunchtime, at a table with a group of the graduate students. He was obviously much older, obviously American, clean-cut and square-jawed, dressed from head to foot in LL Bean – neatly pressed khakis, a dark green Goretex jacket for the great outdoors, sneakers as blindingly white as his teeth. I watched him with interest and when he turned around and looked straight at me I experienced a jolt – not desire, exactly, but something more like recognition.

Almost a week later, I was crossing a courtyard late at night after our matriculation dinner with a loud, jostling knot of new students, all of us illuminated and amped up by several bottles and rounds of shots; we had heard there was a party on a staircase somewhere. Daniel rounded a corner with a couple of other grad students and, as if we were old friends, he fell into step beside me. 'There's a party,' I explained, before he spoke, and quite naturally he took my hand and we followed the others across the river. The party turned out to be a very small room spilling over with a large number of very drunk people dancing, some on the table or the bed. We stood on the threshold in a rhombus of light as a stream of people pushed past us in both directions, still holding hands. 'Daniel,' he offered, half-turning with a frank smile.

'I'm Steph.'

'I know,' he said.

He asked me to meet him the next day for tea in Grantchester. We walked out across the meadows on a path that flanked the river, under a wide sky speared at the horizon by lines of poplars and distant church towers, and I learned about Daniel. He was 36 and from New York; he was in England for a year studying for a Masters in philosophy because he wanted to write a book; he didn't have a girlfriend. He was funny and wry, but he became passionate on the subjects of poetry, art and music; he seemed to have read everything I had ever read and far more that I hadn't, and for a whole afternoon we talked with a kind of urgency that was wholly unknown to me. I had never been so ignited by the possibilities of conversation with someone; not with my one previous boyfriend, Paul, or the occasional flirtations I had had in Spain. Daniel so exactly matched every detail of what I had hoped to find in someone that there was only one logical conclusion: Daniel must be the person God had been keeping for me all along, and now He had finally guided us together, despite my imperfect Christian life. My faith may have wavered many times on an intellectual level, but on this point I was utterly trusting, childlike in my certainty that finding my soul mate had always been the major element of God's plan for my life. How could it not be? It was God who had decreed that it was not good for man to be alone (the fact that I no longer believed in the Creation story didn't deter me from clinging to this part of it) and therefore it must be his intention for all of us to find that all-encompassing connection. All through my teens in the church youth group, since we were first old enough to contemplate the opposite sex, it had been impressed upon us that, while the world would talk frivolously about 'finding Mr Right', we could have faith that God really did have Mr (or Miss!) Right already planned out for us; all we had to do was trust Him and He would perform like a divine dating agency. This was my understanding, anyway. And now, incredibly, finally, it was happening for me. I didn't mention this to Daniel at the time – I thought it might be premature – but I believed it almost instantly, with all the force of faith.

We met for coffee and dinner several more times in the two weeks that followed, and each time there was such dynamism in the way we talked, and in the fact that, since that night on the crowded staircase, there had been no explicit reference to the existence of a physical attraction; instead, it was acknowledged tacitly, in brief touches of hands or held looks, and although there was a beautiful tension in this limbo, I wondered how to affect this stasis. Daniel consumed every conscious moment in a way that was so exhaustive it reminded me of my earliest crush. I knew precisely when Daniel came into college for his lunch, so that I could coincide with him in the canteen; I knew which days his rowing crew and mine would be training on the river; I knew which afternoons I should reroute my journey to the supermarket to take me past the Philosophy Faculty (which was in fact on the other side of the town, so not technically a rerouting so much as incipient stalking), but I did not know how to nudge us towards an acknowledgement of that immediate understanding that had happened when he had taken my hand before he had even told me his name.

Then Daniel asked me if I would go to the MCR dinner with him, an extravagant black-tie event for the graduate students that took place once a term; this, being the first, was a crucial moment to consolidate early flirtations or establish them on a more formal footing by asking someone as your official date. I was only concerned about whether I, as an undergraduate, would be out of place. 'Please come,' Daniel said. 'When I go to these parties and you're not there, I feel as if I'm only half there myself.'

A few days later, I was apprehended on my way out of the

college bar at lunchtime by another graduate student, Michael, a doughy, pink-faced German with a permanent sneer.

'I heard you're going to the dinner with Daniel.'

'Yes, why?'

He glanced at his friend and sniggered. I took a step back, irked.

'Just thought we should let you know you're wasting your time. Daniel's not into women.'

'Oh, for f—'

'It's true, he told us – he doesn't go out with women.' Michael sneered widely. 'Why don't you go ahead and ask him? You can always come with me instead,' he called, as I walked away.

Later, Daniel took me out of college to a dark-beamed pub in the town, as if he didn't want to be seen. It was a wet afternoon; clouds banked up behind the towers of the colleges. I was silent and pent as I scurried to keep up with him along the wet cobbles, knotted with the fear that my euphoria of the past fortnight was about to be shattered and that I would have to bear not only rejection and the ruin of all my tender hope, but also the ridiculous shame of discovering that I had mistaken a *coup de foudre* for someone who had only wanted to be my gay best friend.

'You're upset,' Daniel said, scanning my face. 'There's something you want to ask me, right?'

'Michael said something…' I brushed the rain off my face and hid my words in my pint.

'Ah, Michael. I think Michael might be jealous.'

I looked at him.

'Well?'

'I'm so sorry.' He tried to find something suitably contrite to do with his hands, finally folding his fingers together in a prayerful triangle. 'Of course I should have mentioned it before but I was just enjoying being around you, I guess in a way I was getting a kick out of imagining my life was different, that I didn't have to tell you. It was unfair of me.' He spread his hands out flat on the table and smiled bashfully, like a child caught out in a deliberate fib. 'So here we are.'

'So it's true!' I half-rose, appalled, shaking my head against this revelation as if to dislodge it. 'Were you not even going to tell me you're gay?'

Daniel stared at me for a moment, thrown, and then he laughed so hard that he got beer up his nose. When he'd recovered enough to speak, he wiped his eyes and said, 'Michael said I'm *gay*?'

'He said you told him you don't go out with women.'

'Ah. Yes, I guess it would be that black and white for Michael. It's true that I don't date women, but I assure you I'm not gay.'

'I don't understand.'

'Uh…' Daniel scratched the back of his neck and looked over his shoulder. 'Actually I'm a Jesuit.'

The pause that followed was the silence of the nonplussed. The only image that came clearly to my mind was Monty Python's Spanish Inquisition, or granite-faced men in black robes beating small children. I tried a quick mental word-association game: Jesuits-Jesuitical-legalistic-reformation-counter-reformation-torture-damnation… None of this could be made to correspond with Daniel, handsome, clean-cut Daniel, sitting opposite me in a Cambridge pub with his LL Bean sports jacket, his pale chiselled jaw and his off-kilter smile. I said, very slowly, 'So you're a – *priest*?'

'Not yet. I'm not ordained. But I have taken vows.'

'*Vows*? Like a monk?'

'Yes. Poverty, obedience and – uh – you know.' More scratching of the neck. 'Chastity.'

'Are they serious?'

'I'm afraid so.'

'But you've got a laptop!' Barely anyone I knew had a laptop in 1993, certainly not students.

'It belongs to the Society. I don't actually own anything for myself.'

'What about your shoes?'

'Again, technically, not my property, although I shouldn't think they'll ask for those back.'

'So you get round the poverty one on a technicality. Does that work for the others?'

Daniel grinned. 'They're as serious as marriage vows. Maybe more so.'

'But you drink beer!' I protested again, pointing, as if the weight of all this evidence might force him to admit that, okay, he wasn't really serious after all. 'You go to parties – I've seen you!'

'I'm a Jesuit, not an Anchorite. We're supposed to be out in the world.' There was a brief pause. 'I had to tell my confessor about you in the first week,' he added.

'But we haven't–'

'It's a question of intent,' Daniel said significantly.

'And what did he say?'

'He said he thinks God has brought us together for a reason.'

'You know, clerical dress actually counts as black tie.' Daniel took my arm as we passed through the heavy wooden door of Old Hall and into the crush of the MCR dinner. 'I almost wore the dog collar – don't you think that would have been funny? That would have made them look – with you in that dress.'

'We'd have looked like a vicars and tarts party,' I muttered. I was still thrown by the Jesuit thing, but since Daniel seemed so relaxed about spending time with me I tried not to regard it as an entirely closed door. He seemed to have a remarkably Zen attitude for a Catholic. Now that he was 'out', we talked a lot about faith; my doubts, his doubts, the elements that our two very different versions of Christianity had in common, the frequent impasse between faith and reason. If there could have been anybody qualified to help me to a mature understanding of the nature of faith, it would have been Daniel. I might have risen to the challenge of someone who could show me how it was possible to embrace science and philosophy and reason, yet hold on to a belief in the supernatural. Daniel was an Ivy League graduate, had several degrees and talked about God in a conceptual way that would have been anathema to those in my church who took a more literal interpretation of the Bible. But Daniel didn't talk me back to faith, because love got clumsily in the way.

We drank at the MCR dinner; for me this was routine by now, but I had not seen Daniel drink so much before – usually he kept to his tidy two pints – and on our way from the Old Hall to the bar to join the others, he steered me to the right and then grabbed my hand and ran with me, laughing, through the courtyard and across the lawn by the river. There, under a velvet sky, Daniel took my face in both hands and kissed me for a long time, raked his hands down the front of my body and around my waist, and just as suddenly leaped back as if stuck with a cattle prod and hurled himself towards the river bank where he stood, hunched over and rocking, hands tangled in his hair. I stood nervously beside him, still hoping that this might just be an aside, a parenthetical twinge of conscience, while he repeated 'sorry' through his hands, but I was not sure if the apology was meant for me or the Almighty.

The following day, Daniel told me he felt we should not see one another while he took some time to seek God's guidance; he had crossed a line, he knew, and he needed to spend some time in prayer and fasting and talking to his spiritual advisors about what it all might mean. For two weeks, I believed I had lost him; the weather turned autumnal in supportive pathetic fallacy, and there were days of sitting bleakly, staring out of windows at the rain, while I waited for Daniel to get back in touch, though I presumed it would only be to tell me that the Society were having him removed to a monastery somewhere, or perhaps castrated, like Abelard (I was still not clear on the working methods of the Jesuits). This, I understood, was a broken heart, and I had not had one before; the fact that I was now, for the first time, surrounded by a large number of people I was entitled to call friends only threw into relief how acutely alone I felt without Daniel and how without him it seemed like less than half a life.

When he eventually came to see me, the verdict was inconclusive. This was a crucial time for him, he explained; the two years between taking vows and being ordained were a time of great testing, to judge whether he was truly called to the priesthood, and he had chosen to put himself in the most extreme situation by studying not at a Jesuit seminary but in a real university, thousands of miles from the people who knew him, where he was likely to meet girls. If his calling remained steadfast through that, then he was walking the right path, but he wanted to keep an open mind – maybe this year would show him that God had another path in mind for him, but either way it was clear to him that I was the instrument God had chosen to illuminate his calling. I sensed that

I was supposed to feel honoured by this, but I was beginning to resent God for dragging me into this experiment. I too had been given to understand that God had a plan for my life, and even when I doubted the entire foundation of my faith, the very existence of God, I couldn't shake the desire to believe in this part: that a path was already plotted for me and that all that was required on my part was the wisdom to recognise it. Of course, in my version of predestination, the path only included good things (it could never be God's will, for example, that I should get a serious illness), but the point was that I was the star of my own biopic, so it was something of a slight to find that this same God might have cast me as a mere supporting role in Daniel's more important drama.

Despite the fact that I had, in those first few weeks, fallen in love with Daniel, the relationship evolved into a curious kind of intimacy that was careful to avoid any contact that might be construed as sexual, like something from a Jane Austen novel. He had fortified his defences after that night, and although we seemed to onlookers like a couple in the way we talked and the time we spent together, I knew that he had taken a step back. Something had been lost.

To the rest of the college, for whom Daniel was already a novelty – a plain-clothes priest, and a good-looking one at that! – we provided a handy source of amusement and gossip. That the priest and the wild girl with the platform boots and the little dresses should be so close possessed a frisson all its own; it was a trope of English farce – we were a *Carry On* film and *The Thorn Birds* all at once – and because it entertained my friends to speculate about our bizarre relationship, I allowed them to go on imagining what they would without too much effort to correct their lewd guesswork. Stories appeared in the gossip column of the college magazine, abundant with heavy-handed puns, and Daniel appeared to enjoy this notoriety enormously; it amused him that everyone assumed the obvious when in fact the obvious was precisely what our friendship was not about. He even joked about Christ and Mary Magdalene, which I found ironic rather than insulting.

'Wouldn't they laugh if they knew we can spend a whole evening arguing about New Testament Greek translation?' Daniel said one day, throwing down the latest copy of the magazine.

'I'm sure they'd piss themselves,' I said, drily. Daniel always affected to miss the bitterness in my tone whenever the conversation skirted the elephant in the room, the desire we were attempting to sublimate. We might have gone on like this indefinitely – an expedition to Ely Cathedral, a day trip to London to have tea with my mother and brother, cosy pubs on winter afternoons, wind-scoured walks across the fields, my tentative but constant hope that he would realise I was his destiny – if we hadn't both been sideswiped by a sudden death.

Daniel's telegram came near the end of term, before Christmas; a friend, a fellow priest, had been murdered in Colombia. I found Daniel in the college dining room in the evening, pale and removed, holding himself with the dignified detachment that grief bestows, as if he alone had been granted a glimpse beneath the surface of life. It was a look I could identify, but not identify with; I didn't know at the time that I would learn it fully in a matter of weeks. Daniel explained that the Jesuits in the part of Colombia where he had previously worked as a missionary were also involved in social care and in aiding those caught up in drugs and gang violence. His friend had been engaged in such work, when one of the gangs he was helping had accused him of betraying them to their rivals. His body had been dumped in the night on the church steps. It was not so long since Daniel had been living there himself.

He told me this story quietly, but he was almost vibrating with contained distress. I placed my hand on his across the table but he gently withdrew it.

'Look at this,' he said suddenly, biting back anger and gesturing to the vaulted ceilings and oil paintings of the college's dining hall. He was angry with himself, I surmised, for being here, in the midst of all this medieval opulence, indulging in the life of a student, playing at having a girlfriend, far from the front line where his brothers were trying to make a difference to those who needed it and being shot for their trouble. I offered to walk with him, but he said he needed to go and see someone. I knew he had a mentor in the city – the Society's support network was watertight, especially for young would-be priests let loose in a co-ed university, and this mentor's role was, as far as I could see, a combination of life-coach and therapist. But I understood, at that moment, the limits of what I could be to Daniel; in the moment of his deepest grief, I could not reach him, and nothing I could offer was of any use. This was a Jesuit thing, and he needed to be among those who understood without words. I suppose I had known all along where Daniel's loyalties would finally fall, but I saw clearly that night that I could never give him the sustenance he drew from his faith and all that accompanied it, and that I would never be the fulcrum of his world in the way that he now was of mine. But what was I to do with all this love, now that it had been ignited?

*D*eath crashed into my life at around the same time, yanking me out of my new-found student hedonism and back to the prescribed world of the church. My mother wrote to me shortly before the end of my first term to let me know that Rory was getting worse and would very likely have to have another operation. Rory was the son of friends of my parents in the church, and though he was a year younger than me, I had spent a lot of time with him growing up because we had both been involved in the young people's drama group. Rory was a talented actor and an outstanding comic; he gave the impression of being wired up to a different current from everyone else, so fizzing with energy that he seemed to crackle. He had a wicked laugh and a wealth of funny voices, and everyone was agreed that Rory would end up on the telly one day. But he had also been born with a heart complication and had undergone operations as a child, though these had been so successful, and so long ago, that most people had forgotten that there was a shadow waiting to catch up with him.

Rory had been taken ill unexpectedly the summer I returned from Spain and went almost immediately to college; he had been fitted with a pacemaker and I had meant to visit him in hospital but in the frenzy of my first term, with Daniel and my new friends and parties every weekend and three separate essays every week, I still hadn't got around to it when my mother's letter arrived. I did feel a little guilty about this, but I reasoned that I could see him as soon as I came back for the vacation; after all, it wasn't as if I was his closest friend in the world, and he was bound to be out soon anyway, perhaps even by Christmas.

By Christmas, Rory had deteriorated so fast that it was decided his only hope was a full heart transplant as soon as a donor could be found. The church organised a flurry of all-night prayer vigils, fasts and days of intercession; the youth group echoed these or joined in, and the church leaders did shifts by Rory's bedside praying for healing. The youth group had planned a New Year's house party at a retreat in Sussex (when my friends at college had asked about my New Year plans, I had only mentioned the 'house party' bit, hinting at scenes of Home Counties country-pile debauchery. Nothing could have been further from the truth). Then we heard that a donor heart had been found and Rory's operation was scheduled for New Year's Eve. The party element was quickly superseded by an all-night prayer vigil in real time, which would carry Rory through his operation; with all of us there together, we could support and encourage one another if we felt afraid, and we could update our prayers with regular bulletins from the hospital.

The prevailing mood that evening was largely upbeat. Here we were, gathered to do something practical with our prayers and fully expecting a miracle; we all knew Rory to a greater or lesser extent, but for some of us – me, anyway – it was also a question of flexing our faith, throwing down a gauntlet to God. Come on then – You say You can heal the sick, let's see some direct action. The pastor of the church came to the retreat early to give us a pep talk. We were going to spend the night praying for healing, he reminded us, and though we held to our faith that God had the power to heal Rory and restore him to a full and active life, we must bear in mind the possibility that He might have other plans. This night would be a test not just of our faith, but also of our trust in God; if we lost Rory, we must be strong enough to understand that God was taking him for a reason.

The group shifted uncomfortably as we glanced at one another. We were young and most of us had never been this close to death; the faith we had been taught was not a faith of mortification, punishment and prohibition, but rather one that emphasised joy, fulfilment and the kind of self-esteem that comes from the certainty of being loved and understood. A favourite verse that could be adapted to any situation was Romans 8:28: 'for we know that all things work together for good to those who love God.' But it took quite a leap of imagination to believe that God's version of what was good for us might not be the same as our interpretation, and it hadn't really occurred to most of us that God might choose to withhold the gift of healing in Rory's case – why ever would He? What good could possibly come out of Rory's death? I knew very well all the theological sophistry required to counter the eternal paradox of a loving God who allows suffering and could parrot it as well as anyone – we were all prepared with such apologetics every time the youth group went out evangelising, since it was usually the first question you could expect from the more hostile man in the street. Now, as we prepared to see in 1994 by begging God through the night not to let our friend die, I found the theology, and my own faith, pitifully insufficient.

Rory remained critical through the night and into the days that followed, though by the time I returned to college, he had begun to stabilise. My wilting faith had been galvanised, largely by guilt, and I determined to live a better life this term, as if Rory's life hanging in the balance was directly dependent on my behaviour, as if by renouncing the drinking and the parties and my ungodly desire for Daniel I might somehow tip the scales in the celestial realms and persuade the Lord to give Rory another chance. I went back to church with renewed vigour; I prayed morning and night. Rory died from a secondary infection in the middle of January, the day before my twentieth birthday, without regaining consciousness.

I had been to the cinema; when I returned to college there was a message in my pigeon hole asking me to telephone my mother urgently. I knew immediately, but when I called her from the Porter's Lodge, I couldn't speak. The receiver swung, unattended, as I ran out into the rain-slick street in search of the only person who could understand and would be able to find the right words, sensitive and wise enough to take the sting away.

Daniel was riding his bike past the college at the moment I ran out into the street, in what might almost have been serendipity. I threw myself into his path and as he swerved on to the curb to avoid me, I blurted, 'Rory died!'

He dropped his bike, scooped me into his arms and said, 'Bummer.'

Not quite the clear-eyed theological wisdom I'd been hoping for, but carrying more real feeling than a thousand platitudes.

Daniel took me up to the roof of my building in college; four storeys up, you could look out across the tree line to the row of spires lit like Christmas trees and the turbulent sky beyond. I felt like a child abandoned in a dark room, whirling about not even knowing if there was a door.

'You want to yell, don't you?' Daniel shouted into the wind.

'What?'

'I said, you want to yell at God. You want to yell *WHY?*'

I nodded.

'Well, go on then. He can take it.'

So there, on the roof, I screamed into the rain and wind; I screamed at God and the 'why' encompassed everything: taking Rory, taking Daniel, making me like this, so trapped inside myself and full of darkness and chronically unsuited to being simply happy, and when I had screamed myself limp I began to cry and folded myself quietly into Daniel's chest.

'I do love you, you know,' Daniel said gently. I did know, actually. Just not in the way that I wanted.

Rory's funeral was beautiful. It was packed with friends from his school and college as well as the church and the youth group, and because he had known and accepted that he may not come through his operation, he had had the opportunity to choose the music, poems and readings he most wanted to celebrate his life by those who loved him. Rory was an exemplary lesson in dying well, in full acceptance and faith and gratitude for the time he had been given; he did go gently and with dignity into that good night, to judge by the funeral and the accounts of his family, no raging for him against the dying of the light. There are those atheists who argue that the comforts of religious belief are a poor compensation for the damage it does in the world; a valid point, and one I've argued myself in more strident moments, but so is the necessity of comfort. I know only that I envy Rory the grace and certainty with which he faced death. But at the funeral I was raging, partly on his behalf but mainly for myself. God, I was raging fiercely inside, and I desperately sought a sign that I was not alone.

Everyone was grieving, that was clear; no one could make it through a reading or a poem without folding several times and having to stop, reassemble themselves, breathe, begin again. But there was also a determination to be joyful, to counter the sadness by clinging to the repeated mantra that God must be planning to do a great work through Rory's death. This is where faith comes into its own, this is its apotheosis: this refusal to see death as an ending. It felt to me as if everyone else could see beyond the horizon and was determined to look at the bigger picture, and I was merely squinting into the distance, seeing nothing.

I had travelled down on the train with that sharp awareness of mortality, the peculiar sense of being peeled that comes with grief; as if you have lost a layer of skin, leaving all your nerve endings exposed, but to compensate you have gained a kind of metaphysical X-ray vision. In front of me a couple had been arguing about their holiday plans; I almost intervened to let them know that it really wasn't important, that an 18-year-old boy with everything to live for had just died, and that they were going to die too one day, perhaps sooner than they knew, and there really wasn't time to waste. I thought I had reached a new insight into the innate sorrow of life, the ineluctable fact of death and the randomness of catastrophe, and I couldn't make this fit with the notion that all things work together for good to those who love God.

How was *this* good? I wanted to shout at the funeral, where it seemed to me then that this vast unspoken *why* overshadowed all the beautiful words. Will no one stand up and say that this was a *tragedy*? Will no one admit that, just maybe, *this,* God's so-called will, is not the best thing that could have happened – that maybe the best thing would have been for Rory to get better and still be with us? That his death was simply fucking *awful* and *wrong* and a *waste* and why must we dress it up in all this optimism and blind trust and justification, as if we have to protect God from potential criticism? I imagine that those closest to Rory wrestled with these questions privately, but I ached to hear someone voice them so that I might learn a satisfactory answer.

Why was I raging so hard? Rory was not my brother or my boyfriend, I had not even made the effort to see him in hospital, but his death had become symbolic of something much bigger. I was angry that I had trusted God to heal Rory, and He had let me down – let us all down, except that to me, everyone else appeared to be tying themselves in philosophical knots to excuse the God we want to believe is loving and benevolent, and that made me angrier still. At that moment I felt, with brand-new clarity, that all this sophistry was a waste of effort. The much simpler conclusion was that God was not there, never had been; it was just a charming story, and while I envied those who could accept it, who leaned on it to take the sting out of life's cruelty, I knew that I was no longer among them.

The relief that came with this realisation was like dropping a heavy rucksack down the side of a mountain and facing the climb unburdened. The erosion of my childhood faith was completed at Rory's funeral. There was an irony in the way a voice in my head repeated, all through the journey back to Cambridge, a Bible verse I had often heard quoted: 'For you shall know the truth, and the truth shall set you free.' Never had I felt freer than in facing, clear-eyed and straight on, the truth that life is a series of collisions of random chances; that there is no plan or pattern or fate or any higher power guiding us; that we are alone in the universe, our lives shaped by biology, economics and physics, and that life is unjust, unpredictable and often cruel; that in this shadow of death we had to wring every last drop out of life while we had the chance. Suddenly I felt far lighter looking the universe in the face like this, in all its implacable heartlessness, than I ever had been trying to hold on to a comforting myth that smoothed away all the rough edges.

I told Daniel that I no longer found it possible to believe in God.

'Yes, you're bound to feel like that,' he said, being grave and mature. 'I can help you through it.'

I looked at him, and realised that he could not help me through it; I resented his smug condescending certainty, his all-consuming faith that had made him a surrogate confessor and counsellor to half the college but still allowed him to treat me like some

Arthurian test God had set for him and which he had passed with distinction, as if he were Sir Galahad.

'Fuck off, Daniel,' I said. 'You can't be everyone's saviour.'

G.K. Chesterton famously said that when a man stops believing in God, he doesn't believe in nothing – he believes in anything. Christians are fond of quoting this, but Chesterton was wrong. For years I believed in nothing. I wish I could say that, having concluded that one life is all you get, I had thrown myself into some kind of activism that proved humanist values could be just as passionate as spiritual ones; I wish I could say that I hurled myself heart and soul into student politics, or Amnesty, or Friends of the Earth or running the marathon for cancer research, but I didn't. Instead I hurled myself into self-gratification, by whatever means was affordable, but it was not a replacement faith, only a kind of nihilism. Losing faith did not make me a better person; it made me harder, more cynical, more selfish, less grounded – though perhaps, on the plus side, less of a hypocrite. Through all of it, though, I did go on believing in love.

People hold to a religious faith for many reasons, but Philip Larkin's poem 'Faith Healing' crystallises for me the particular attraction of the kind of church in which I grew up, which is in many ways the attraction of Christ himself as the gospels describe him, and the more charismatic of his followers through the ages; the unique pull of being made to feel that you are truly seen, and understood and – in spite of all your manifold flaws and failings – perfectly and completely loved. The poem describes women lining up for a blessing from a preacher; the last stanza reads:

> In everyone there sleeps
> A sense of life lived according to love.
> To some it means the difference they could make
> By loving others, but across most it sweeps
> As all they might have done had they been loved.
> That nothing cures. An immense slackening ache,
> As when, thawing, the rigid landscape weeps,
> Spreads slowly through them – that, and the voice above
> Saying Dear child, *and all time has disproved.*

I had grown up being told that I was cushioned on all sides by this kind of unswerving divine love. Now I understood that it was a fiction devised to cover an elemental human need and I rejected that fiction in favour of what I felt was a more honest acceptance of the world and our place in it, but that did not eliminate the fierce need for love; if anything, it intensified it. Christians are also fond of talking about 'the God-shaped hole', an image probably derived from Pascal's *Pensées*:

> 'What else does this craving, and this helplessness, proclaim but that there was once in man a true happiness, of which all that now remains is the empty print and trace? This he tries in vain to fill with everything around him, seeking in things that are not there the help he cannot find in those that are, though none can help, since this infinite abyss can be filled only with an infinite and immutable object; in other words by God himself.'
>
> 10.148

The God-shaped hole is only another name for the desire to be loved, if not perfectly, then at least comprehensively. The loss of faith is a profound change in any circumstance: it separates you from your background, from those with whom you once shared the same view of the world, and creates a tectonic shift in your sense of self, but particularly so when the faith you have known all your life and now jettisoned promised you purpose and unconditional love that stretched even beyond death. To abandon it is to choose to be metaphysically alone and to face death as an absolute; I felt, and still feel, that there is courage in this, or at least a kind of honesty, but I did not realise at the time how much I had lost by demolishing the structure that had sustained me for almost two decades. I had never completely bought it, mind you; I couldn't quite let go of the suspicion that if God loved me that much, it was probably out of pity, or a slight remorse that He had screwed things up so badly when making me, and it had struck me many times during my teens that, although God's love was supposed to be all-encompassing, it was a pretty poor abstract substitute for the love of an actual person. Even so, although I could no longer contort my intellect and my reason into the positions required to maintain a belief in the supernatural or the divine, the need for that kind of love did not disappear. It was merely transposed to the human sphere, which was probably too much to ask of anyone.

For years I believed that love would save me from the black weather that descended; once I found it, I would hold it up like a talisman to ward off despair. The only obvious remedy to being metaphysically alone, I concluded, was to avoid being literally alone; how could you despair, I thought, if you were truly loved? Though I no longer believed that there was a divine plan for my life, I could not let go of the conviction that there was someone meant for me, someone who would be everything Daniel had been and everything that he was not, and then I would be complete, but

I was always in some way looking for Daniel, long after he had gone back to the States, long after I had left college and myself inflicted many needless heartbreaks on others. My understanding of love was inherently off-kilter; I sought drama, angst, guilt, a sense of transgression; I went into every relationship with one eye on the door and if it failed to be sufficiently Ted-and-Sylvia I grew quickly bored and looked elsewhere. I was not kind; I disregarded the feelings of others often, but it was all collateral damage in my own quest for something that remained always just out of reach. I believed that when I found it – and I held with absolute certainty to the knowledge that I would – I could finally stop all the flailing and running and be at peace, at home, and I went on believing that I would recognise it instantly when I found it, just as Daniel and I had recognised one another before we had even spoken; the instinctive knowledge of likeness.

Another death bookended my time at university, the summer I graduated; like Rory's, its resonances went beyond the blunt fact of it. If Rory's death took from me the last possibility of faith, Henry's death erased the possibility of suicide as a dark maudlin fantasy to flirt with and roll around my imagination late at night, because I saw from the other side what happens to those who are left behind.

Henry was a fellow first-year English undergraduate but he was a year older than the rest of us because he had started at college once already, the previous year, and dropped out halfway through for reasons that neither he nor anyone else quite explained – he half-joked about 'finding himself' – but I came to understand that Henry was considered to be exceptional. He was, it was whispered, rather highly strung, but was so brilliant that he had a special dispensation from the college which allowed him to appear and disappear at will without the inconvenience of having to take exams or hand in work. There seemed no injustice in this; Henry, it was generally agreed, was not like the rest of us, who were only mortal, bound to the earth. Henry was not subject to normal rules, and nor should he be.

I was thrilled by him because I had never met a real live genius and he was just what I had hoped to find at Cambridge – eccentrically dressed, tall and handsome with a glittering, dangerous mind and a presence that made everyone around him seem lacklustre by comparison. You wanted to be wherever Henry was, even though whenever I talked to him I felt hopelessly cloth-tongued and oafish and worryingly ill-read, despite the fact that I had spent most of my life doing nothing but reading. I couldn't dazzle with words in the way that Henry could, and I was always a little in awe of him. He wrote songs and poetry, he was a gifted actor and photographer, he seemed to be at the eye of every artistic endeavour; like many people who live with extremes of light and dark, he hid his shadows well and did everything with a flourish.

He disappeared again halfway through that first year – people talked of Africa, and when he reappeared the following autumn he was transfigured. Gone were the green velvet smoking jacket and the John Lennon glasses; instead he was tanned and bearded, his hair long and bleached white-blond by the sun, like a stained-glass Jesus. He was starting the first-year course over again and we had moved on, so although we remained friends, I saw less of him that year, and by the time we were in our final year he had dropped out again. By this time, no one was really sure about Henry's status as far as the college was concerned. He still showed up frequently – his friends and girlfriend were there – but the idea that Henry would ever finish his degree seemed remote. I knew by then that his long absences were due to depressive illness, a sort of breakdown, but I was not sure that I really understood what was meant by *breakdown* and every time he returned he seemed to shine; I worried about what would happen to him in the future, when his friends had all moved on and he no longer had the university as a home from home. A friend remarked at the time that Henry would never graduate because he refused to write what the exam board wanted to read – he insisted on being too original, too iconoclastic to fit the strictures of the system – and I agreed, and wished he could just see the wisdom of playing the game for long enough to get a degree because, I said, parroting my father's advice to me, he could always go off and be all bohemian afterwards, but at least he would have that to fall back on, which just shows how little I understood about Henry, and about illnesses of the mind in general.

Once, in a lecture on Sylvia Plath, I heard Germaine Greer use a phrase that burned like neon: Plath, Greer said, 'carried suicide with her like a coin in her pocket she was waiting to spend.' This phrase came instantly to mind the overcast morning that I stood on the Silver Street bridge, scuffing bored patterns in the dust while I waited for tourists who might want a punting trip along the Backs, and Henry's friend Tim came cycling up, ashen, to tell me that Henry was dead. He did not say how, though ghoulishly it was the first thing I wanted to ask; he said only that Henry had been at home with his parents. Tim had spoken to him the night before, and Henry had planned to come to Cambridge that weekend; somehow, in the blank hours that followed, he had arrived at a place where he could no longer go on.

'He wanted to talk on the phone,' Tim explained quietly, scratching at the peeling paintwork on his handlebars. Stillness muffled the street. I felt a sickened punch in my solar plexus; the feeling that comes from stepping off a kerb without looking and only just avoiding an oncoming car. Oddly, the news was a shock, but not a surprise. 'I was impatient – I was going out. I told him we'd talk at the weekend.'

'You can't blame yourself,' I said, reflexively, knowing how pointless the words would sound. At the same time I was wondering what more I could have done. I had seen Henry rarely in the past months; we had drifted out of one another's orbit and I had not made much effort to keep up with him when he left Cambridge. Could *I* blame myself? What about his family, his girlfriend, his doctors? I have little doubt that they will have done; suicide leaves a ragged absence that can't be filled with well-meant words and clogs instead with *if only*s and thoughts of everything you might have done but didn't. Later, listening to people talk about Henry, I heard for the first time the words 'manic depression' used of someone other than Virginia Woolf or Byron, a real person I had laughed and smoked and played guitar with, and it frightened me because naively I had thought such things existed only in dead literary heroes; now, suddenly, this label was being applied to someone I had known and I realised that it could exist even in my safely bordered world. But it frightened me more because of how nearly it touched my life; I remembered the nights when I had lain awake feeling that I could not stand to go on for another day, and remembered how those nights had always passed, eventually. I imagined Henry in that moment – the moment when, so far, I had always managed to scrabble with my fingernails for a shred of hope, for the belief that there might be some shift, some change in the light around the next corner. Henry had come to the end of hope, and I was ashamed of my frivolous imaginings, for toying so lightly with the idea of self-destruction. It never occurred to me that what had affected him might also have touched me. Henry, in my eyes, was sufficiently iconic to have had a mind that defied normal constraints. He belonged up there with Plath, Woolf, Lowell and all the others whose minds were so far-reaching, so remarkable, that they couldn't fit in the world. I, by contrast, was just ordinary, given to foolish, shameful thoughts of suicide when things went wrong. I would no more have equated my experience with Henry's than I would have compared myself to Van Gogh, so that after Henry I became further convinced that 'depression' as a legitimate illness was something that happened to other people – brilliant, eminent people – and bore no relation to my own dark moods.

There are people who consider suicide to be an act of cowardice, but they must be people who have never known the ways in which depression paralyses reason and strips you of all belief in the change of seasons. They are right, of course, when they point out that others have endured prison camps and unthinkable torture, deprivation and grief and survived by clinging to life, and if you try to reduce suicide to rational cause and effect in this way then yes, it will often leave the victim looking pathetic and selfish. He lost his job? Her husband left? What, and they just *gave up*? But these are never the sole reasons, and those who look from the outside are able to take a longer view: things can only get better. From inside depression you can find no truth or comfort in this promise, and when the present and the future become unbearable, your mind turns to the possibility of non-existence. The virtue of resilience is a legacy of our western Christian heritage – chin up, onwards and upwards, shoulder to the wheel – we revere the ability to endure adversity and scorn those who appear to buckle under life's expected hardships, as if theirs is a moral weakness, a failure of character. But none of us should ever presume to judge someone else's despair.

Later, over the years that followed Henry's death, I gradually came to realise that I, too, carried this coin in my pocket. From time to time I have reached to feel its outline, testing its solidity, reassuring myself that it is still there in case of emergencies. On a couple of occasions I have taken it out, turned it over in my hands and given serious thought to spending it and in those moments I have thought not only of the people I would leave with the weight of guilt and regret, but also of Henry, of all the times I have wished I could have persuaded him to go on, to turn and exist, defiantly, in spite of the dark. Other friends have died since then, and relatives, but it is Henry that I see most often. I don't mean that I have visions or anything superstitious – only that sometimes, on a crowded street or Tube platform, I will catch sight, above the crowd, of a head of long blond hair and instinctively I will move to catch up with Henry as he was then, aged 23. Then the boy will turn and I will see with a jolt that it is not Henry, and I am always surprised by the sudden plunge of disappointment at that moment, as if I'd really imagined it could have been, as if I'd never truly believed the report of his death, as if I hoped he'd just been away on one of his long absences, finding himself, all this time.

Before Daniel left for New York at the end of my first year at university, he gave me a book by the Pulitzer-winning Catholic writer Annie Dillard. Since the murder of his friend, he had withdrawn from me significantly; we had remained friends, but his manner was deliberately avuncular and he markedly avoided any intimation of desire, even to the extent that he jokingly offered to set me up with his friends. I went on loving Daniel, but I also wanted to hurt him, as if by sleeping with people I didn't care about I might somehow, through jealousy, dislodge his calling or shock him into realising that he had made a mistake. With no one to answer to – not my parents, not the church, not even Daniel, because I owed him nothing, I thought angrily – I grew wilder and more reckless, and the more I tried to hurt Daniel with my behaviour, like a teenager seeking to provoke a parent, the more magnanimously forgiving and compassionate he became and the more I felt condescended to and enraged by his patience, until the night I crashed furiously drunk into a quiet dinner he was having with some graduate student friends, all of them hanging on his every word as if it was the Last Supper, and with blazing, unfocused eyes informed them all that Daniel was not Jesus-fucking-Christ before bursting into tears and trying to slap him.

He half-carried me back to my room, the good shepherd and the crazy lost prodigal daughter, while I thrashed and sobbed the whole way, howling 'it's your fault, I could have been good, I could have been good', as if he were responsible for the turbulence in my head, as if I might have become someone else, someone who was happier in her own skin and whom I was better able to like, if he had only loved me like a man instead of a spiritual mentor. And yet he did go on loving me, in his own way; he saw the extremes in me, the warring contradictions, and beyond them he saw some quality

138

that he thought was worthwhile. The essay he had marked for me in the Annie Dillard book was called 'Living Like Weasels'. The author, encountering a weasel in the woods, recalls a hunter who shot an eagle out of the sky and found hanging from the bird's throat by its teeth the dry and bleached skull of a weasel – as the eagle seized it, the weasel had twisted and in fierce blind instinct locked its jaws and refused to let go, even in death, as its flesh was pecked from its body. Dillard reflects on whether we could learn to live with such tenacity, such pure adherence to true instinct. Daniel had underlined for me these final paragraphs:

'We could, you know. We can live any way we want. People take vows of poverty, chastity and obedience – even of silence – by choice. The thing is to stalk your calling in a certain skilled and supple way, to locate the most tender and live spot and plug into that pulse…I think it would be well, and proper, and obedient, and pure, to grasp your one necessity and not let it go, to dangle from it limp wherever it takes you. Seize it and let it seize you up aloft, even till your eyes burn out and drop.'

In the margin he had written simply, 'YOU'. I didn't ask what he meant by this. Was it praise or exhortation? Did he mean that this was how he saw me, or was he willing me to live in this way after he had gone? I no longer knew what my calling was, nor how to find it. I had no cause, no faith, nothing greater than myself to fight for and give myself over to, a past I wanted to erase and no future that I could see; nothing except the present moment, which more often than not simply bored me.

A year after he left, Daniel wrote me a long letter. His father had died, he told me, and it had started him wondering again if he had made the right choice; watching his father in his last days, surrounded by his children and grandchildren, Daniel had pictured his own ending, alone, without family, and had once again been pricked with questions about whether his calling was worth the sacrifices. Faith and doubt were locked in a constant dialogue, he assured me, and you never reach the end of it. There is no resolution: this is part of what faith means. Don't give up, weasel. He wrote that he missed me. 'Bit bloody late,' I thought, and brought down the shutters hard against any memory of what I had felt for Daniel. I did not write back, because I knew that we could never be friends, and because I did not want to have to remember.

'You know we'll never be friends,' said B, the man who eventually superseded Daniel, ten years later, in the first letter he wrote to me. I was 30 by then, with a young son whose father I had not seen since before he was born; I had stopped expecting love to crash over me again, until I collided with B. Though he went on to become the most complete and intimate friend I have known, the person who has known and understood me best, I grasped his meaning: we could not, if this love failed, retain only the outline of it. We would gamble all we had and all we believed on this connection; it had to be all or nothing. He understood all or nothing well because this was how he also lived; his heart was fierce and uncompromising. It could not be less than honest. He understood what it meant to seek out extremes and to walk through the dark places, he was familiar with the demons, and perhaps it was this that we recognised in one another. With him I had the immediate sense, just as I had had on first meeting Daniel, of stripping away all the niceties of politeness and small talk and piercing to the marrow of what mattered. B called it 'the vanity of recognition', and so it was; we saw ourselves mirrored in the other and it was possible to believe, for a while, in the notion of complete connection. I admired him because I thought he was unswervingly true to himself, in a way that I had not witnessed in anyone before (except, perhaps, Daniel or Henry); he seemed genuinely not to care what anyone thought of him, and this showed not as a contrived attitude of being difficult, rather it struck me as true independence of mind. The less he cared about making himself liked, the more people were drawn to him. I knew he was unique, just as I knew that, after so much running and so many wrong turns, for the first time I was able to contemplate promising someone a lifetime.

Early on, waking jetlagged into a white dawn in a room high above an American city, I propped myself on one elbow to watch him sleeping and understood that love always contains the shadow of its own ending. In the euphoria of finding him, I already knew how it would feel to lose him, even if that loss came decades from now, as we had promised one another it would, even if it was death that took him away and not the failure of love, which seemed then impossible. In that moment I wondered how I would bear it, how I could stand to live without him, and whether the gift of having him would outweigh the pain of that loss when it came; as I lay beside him I wished briefly that I had not met him, and had not discovered how much was possible. I could have lived my life without this kind of love and perhaps I could have achieved an equilibrium of sorts, based on a low-level disappointment that nothing had ever measured up to my hopes. Now that B had pulled back the curtain to reveal breadths and depths and colours I had not been told were possible, I knew I could never again accept less than this, at the same time that I feared it could not be sustained at this pitch. Leaving him that time at the airport, I thought, prefigured every leaving, every departure that we would endure until the final, irreversible parting; already I felt the breath of it. Everything was magnified and sharper, more profound, more significant; the world possessed the clarity and structure of a movie. We had the sensation of having discovered some profound secret of the universe, of becoming suddenly wise and benevolent. It was both seismic and commonplace, but it was more than I had ever dared to hope for. With him the world made sense, and at last I made sense; it felt a bit like coming home.

Was it love, I wonder? We talked endlessly, often through the night, about what love meant, what we had thought of as love before we met and how we now realised we had been merely sleep-walking; we pursued our version of love all around the country and from coast to coast of the United States; we filled boxes with letters dense with metaphor about how we had derailed one another's lives and in doing so, found everything that we believed had been lacking. But this love existed mainly as an abstraction, a Platonic form we were trying to pull down into a world of solid shapes, and it didn't, or couldn't, survive the transition. It thrived in a state of hypomanic euphoria, in letters and airport lounges and talking until dawn; we could not make it fit into a world of children and bills and deadlines and supermarkets. We were always on the move, always out of time. It is telling, perhaps, that we were happiest – at least in my recollection – in Los Angeles, the ultimate Unreal City, where we sloped around like giggling vampires, two pale, chain-smoking misfits taking pride in the shock we occasioned among the taut, varnished Angelinos with our bruised hangovers, our irreverence and our disdain for their ideas of what mattered. There is a photograph of us, taken by a waiter in a Santa Monica café; we are gripping one another's wrists across the table as if one of us were in danger of falling down a sheer cliff, and our eyes are laughing. We radiate an unassailable confidence in the entity we make together; we know, in that instant, what it means to walk that bit taller because you are loved, to have your self-belief bolstered by someone else's belief in you. Other people fell in love with us because of it – we both found ourselves pursued by others – 'everyone sees *it*, and wants a part of it,' B wrote to me (and why couldn't evolution do something about the injustice of *that?* When you're lit up with love, everyone is attracted to your happiness, and when you're shrivelled with loneliness and most in need of someone, that need becomes inherently repellent – that can't be the most efficient way to run a species). When I look at this photograph I think, perhaps this is as good as it gets. It was, at least, the only time I remember when part of me was not straining to be elsewhere.

The end of it was as dramatic and unexpected as the way it had ignited. 'We would never have made each other happy,' B said, but it took me a long time to recognise the truth of this. I knew only that in the time we spent together I had come to believe that the demons had gone for good. At 31, I was still convinced that the dark moods which fell on me from time to time were all circumstantial, just the result of my usual incapacity to respond to set-backs with any posture of grace or maturity, my particular vulnerability to being tripped on my face by any small ruck in the carpet of life, because no one had ever really suggested that it might be otherwise. Even the severe depression I had experienced after my son was born I explained away with reference to the circumstances. Occasionally, a suspicion had inched its way over the threshold – what if this thing is part of me? What if I achieve whatever it is I think I need to achieve in order to be happy, and it comes back anyway? What then? No: when everything was finally going well, I assured myself – as if this much had been promised to me long ago and was beyond doubt – there would be no further grounds for such bouts of despair, no more reflex thoughts of self-destruction. When I first met B, I was amazed and a little baffled by the high regard he seemed to have for me, and rather than being flattered, it made me anxious; I feared that I had unwittingly duped him, and that when he realised I was not nearly as great as he seemed to imagine, it was going to come as a huge disappointment. Instead, the opposite happened; he continued to believe that I could reach greater heights than I had thought to aim for, and because I respected his judgement in all other things, I began tentatively to wonder if he might also be right on this point, and if I was the one with a skewed view of myself. He made me want to be better, to make myself worthy of the faith he had in me. With him walking beside me, I believed I would be protected; there would be no more demons, no more blackness, no more frenzy or fury or scissors in the night, no more bottles of pills, no more medication. If he loved me, I must therefore be lovable, and I would be safe.

He was right in one regard: we could not be friends. It was as fruitless as taking a thousand-piece jigsaw puzzle, throwing out all the pieces but five and still trying to make a recognisable picture. After one abortive attempt to have dinner after the rupture, I saw that we were in danger of becoming angry and defensive, inflicting needless damage with words, and words were the core, the reactor, of everything we had been and done and felt; I wanted to save us from the potential hurt of them, and so we simply cut all contact. And just like that, the person who had shaped every minute of my days and illuminated the future was gone.

We calibrate grief in our western, Anglo–Saxon culture; implicitly we grade the propriety of its indulgence according to an established scale of loss. There are griefs that are sanctioned by society, and those that are not. In her beautiful memoir *Giving Up The Ghost*, Hilary Mantel writes about her deep grief for the children she knew she would never have, and how difficult it was to articulate this pain in front of anyone. The death of an 80-year-old father is perceived to be less tragic than if he had died at 40. A mother who loses a young child is entitled to the highest degree of sympathy; her loss is considered greater than that of a woman who loses an unborn child, and even then, to miscarry at six months is seen as 'worse' than at six weeks. Either way, that grief is still more valid in the world than that of someone who mourns only the idea of a child, the death of a hope. But loss is always loss to the person knocked sideways by it; you grieve not only for the one who is lost, but for the hoped-for future that has been snatched away, for all that will now not happen. I did not see or speak to B again. He did not die, but he vanished as succinctly and comprehensively from my life as if he had, and predictably I plummeted.

The fall happened in slow motion this time; it was almost graceful. For a while I didn't feel anything at all and simply moved remotely through the world, wholly detached, as if I stood at my own shoulder watching the frame by frame shattering of the girl who gave up sleeping and eating and sometimes stepped out on to the fire escape late at night to smoke only to realise later that she had been sitting there for hours staring at the trees and had forgotten why she ever went outside in the first place. If B had been my husband or fiancé and been killed in an accident, the world would have granted me permission for distress – a whole future annihilated – and I would have been given time off work and treated with great gentleness. Strangers would have been queuing up to make me cups of tea. But although I felt that the effect on my life was the same, to the rest of the world I had merely split up with my boyfriend, and for Christ's sake I was a modern woman, I should be seen to laugh disdainfully, buy shoes and move on. It would not have done to let anyone see what damage had been wrought, so I strapped on the well-practised smile and went into the office and once again pretended to be fine so as not to inflict my pain on everyone else. A friend called inviting B and me to dinner; I had to tell her it would just be me from now on. 'But I thought you were–' she said, baffled. 'You know. For good. You seemed so…*right*. What happened?' I had no answer to that.

I tried to move on; in fact, I delayed the worst of the fall by almost six months by quickly finding an understudy, someone who could replace B straight away in my affections in the hope that the part of my mind that dealt in love, famously blind, might not even notice the substitution, like a well-meaning parent trying to replace a dead pet before their child gets home from school. Naturally, it makes things worse; the child instinctively knows, just as the heart always knows. But the heart – the bruised, stupid, faithful heart – is so stubborn; it insists on clinging fiercely, long after you have wished it would let go, long after such tenacity has ceased to be useful, like a dead weasel gripping an eagle's throat.

4

Deeper Dark

By the time my son was born, at the beginning of 2002, the relationship that began him had already splintered apart in resentment and accusation. It had been a disastrous collision of lives from every angle. I had hurtled into him during a particularly lost and furious phase and though it was mutually antagonistic from the start, there was now this baby whose impending existence, though initially a shock, had continued as a deliberate choice.

I felt quite open to the whole business, at first; this had happened, it was not what I would have planned or what anyone had intended, but here it was, this life that had been unexpectedly handed to us, as if in a prize draw we didn't know we had entered, and it was a good thing, we thought, a positive thing, to roll with this new plot twist, see what lay down this alternative path that had opened up. I thought this mainly because I had absolutely no notion of what having a baby entailed. He was approximately halfway to completion when his father concluded it was not such a good thing after all and made the decision to return to his previous life, and I remained, like the stooge of a bad practical joke, with this convex body I no longer recognised, feeling as if I had been persuaded into buying something very expensive that I was not sure I had wanted in the first place and now learned was non-refundable.

I was 27, and keenly aware that my friends all thought from the beginning that the choice I made was by some distance my greatest act of wilful stupidity to date. No one actually stated it as baldly as this; they didn't say, 'you must be insane', but the judgement was there every time they said, 'are you *really* sure?' and 'you're very *brave*, but have you thought it through?', where *brave* was a synonym for pig-headed, and *have you thought it through* meant try thinking it through again, you moron, before it's too late. I had thought it through, obviously; since I made the discovery I had done nothing else, but I had thought it through according to my own stubborn, blinkered and not especially well-informed arguments, so there was not much rationalising involved. Therefore, because everyone expected that, at a certain point, I would find that I could not cope and would come whimpering back admitting that they had all been right and that, yes, this time I had screwed up my life royally and irreparably, it was very important that no one should be able to detect when that moment came, particularly because I was beginning to agree with them. In fact, it became imperative that, at every stage of what I was only just coming to realise would be a long, long road, I must be seen by the rest of the world – friends, colleagues, parents, the ex, if he showed up – to be coping, and not only coping but blooming, thriving on the challenge, spinning all my plates with panache and a showman's smile. Christ, I thought: this is going to take some acting.

They thought I was stupid because, looking in from the outside, I had what appeared to be a very desirable life. I was living in the heart of London, in a tiny studio in which it was possible to open the fridge while lying in bed, and in which the bed was also the dining table, desk and ironing board, but this was no bother to me because I could walk into the West End in ten minutes and anyway I was hardly ever at home. I was writing about books, comedy and music and every night there was something to keep me out in town – a gig, a show, a party or several – and I spent my days on the *Observer* books' desk and my nights zipping around town from one event to the next on my new motorbike, bought with the advance for my first novel, which had been finally hammered into an acceptable shape and sold to a publisher.

But at six months pregnant and feeling less inclined to linger in Soho bars until the dead hours of the morning, I was beginning to find the flat less accommodating now that I had to live in it. It was on the fourth floor, had no lift and no washing machine – the nearest launderette was half a mile away. In a parking bay a little way down the street the red motorbike stood abandoned; I passed it every morning on my way to work and gave it a quick once-over since I was intending to sell it, but had left it too late to ride it to the dealer; as with most aspects of my life at the time, I was just sort of hoping the problem would resolve itself, perhaps in the form of elves who would sell it for me in the night and leave an envelope stuffed with money under the mat. One day I came down to find that it had been knocked on its side in the night; it lay there reproachfully with one of its wing mirrors snapped off and I was winded by an awful pang of remorse and misplaced compassion. I had neglected it and now some uncaring person had come along and hurt it when I wasn't looking; and how, the unspoken subtext continued, did I imagine I could take care of a small human being when I couldn't even be bothered to look after a bike that had cost me most of my precious book advance?

People solicitously asked what I intended to do about the flat; how I was going to *manage*. They asked this so often that I realised they wanted to be reassured that I was not seriously imagining bringing a newborn baby home to a one-room flat with no washing machine four floors above a falafel shop. It'll be fine, I would blithely reply, because I hadn't allowed myself to think about it. I was still, in most important ways, standing back in disbelief from my situation, feeling – in the brief interstices when I admitted feeling of any kind – that this could not possibly be happening, that it was all a terrible misunderstanding, some failure of bureaucracy at a remote level and not what was intended for my life at all, and waiting faithfully for the *deus ex machina* to arrive and restore order. A resentment towards the launderette had been brewing for some time, but that was as much for the atmosphere as the inconvenience, that particular warm damp fug of melancholy and poverty; as autumn drew on, with my mound of baby and my bulging bag of washing, on the bench in the launderette I felt like an extra from *EastEnders*, and it occurred to me that I would like it even less if I had to make the trek every day in the depths of winter with a baby – I had been given to understand that babies created laundry on an industrial scale. I supposed that I ought to think about moving somewhere more family-friendly, but where? This was London: if I wanted a bigger flat, even a one-bedroom, I was looking at a minimum 50 per cent increase in rent, and then there was the matter of childcare. I had been to look at a couple of day-care nurseries in central London and learned that a full-time place would cost as much as the bigger flat I couldn't afford, so that it was as if I had one day capriciously chosen to rent two flats, but with no change in my income. The only way it could be done was to move into an outlying borough so remote that it would take me an hour on the Tube to get into town, and if I was going to move that far out I may as well move out of London altogether and into the commuter belt, and it was then that I was struck by a terrible sense of inevitability.

Once the obvious solution of moving home had suggested itself, I rebelled against it so completely that I might well have been stupid enough to attempt to stay in the studio with the plywood walls so thin I could hear my neighbours sneeze in the night, had I not tried to get up from my desk one day at work and discovered that I could no longer walk.

Almost seven months pregnant, I took two steps towards the printer as I might on any other day and with no warning experienced an onslaught of pain that felt – there is no good way to explain this – like being vaginally penetrated by a three-foot sword. A howl ripped from my throat and I grabbed on to a filing cabinet as my legs buckled, clinging with my fingertips like a doomed mountaineer as it became apparent that I could not support my own now considerable weight. Help, I called, weakly, and someone kindly wheeled a chair underneath me just in time. I shunted in slow increments back to my desk, shaken. Must have stood awkwardly, I thought, so I tried again, just to check. Again, the shrieking bolt of pain, the same impossibility of movement. I remained at my desk in a state of some consternation. This could be a problem come six o'clock, I thought. How was I supposed to get home? Although home was a five-minute walk from the office, it might just as well involve a double marathon if I couldn't stand up. Perhaps they would have to find a wheelchair or call an ambulance to move me less than quarter of a mile, and that would really blow my cover.

So far the performance had been going very well, as far as I could tell: my friends and colleagues were adequately convinced that I was completely blasé about the whole baby thing and had barely even noticed. Around the office I was – most of the time – cheery and wisecracking, and probably more than usually efficient at my job, now that the days of long lunches and murky, industrial hangovers were in the past. At lunchtime I would join my friends in the Coach, pretending to be quite happy with my mineral water and only occasionally having to excuse myself to pass out from low blood pressure or run to the loo to throw up from the effects of other people's cigarettes. I spent the summer at the Edinburgh festival, zigzagging across the city from one fringe show to another, sometimes seven or eight in a day, and doing a reasonable impression, given the enforced sobriety, of someone having a good time, someone whose company was still tolerable. I carried on reviewing gigs and comedy shows, often cramming my awkward bulk into heaving, sweaty basement bars with no seating in the middle of the night to hear obscure bands, when all the pregnancy magazines informed me in a breezy tone that what I should be doing, for my baby's sake, was putting my feet up with a light chicken pasta snack cooked by my husband, who should then indulge me with an aromatherapy foot massage. Often I dragged myself across London on the bus to see friends even for half an hour, when the aggregate journey time was three times that, because company had become such a precious commodity, and because all these things were a necessary distraction if the façade were to hold intact; I could not risk my friends finding me a drag, though I feared it was inevitable. Whenever I was finally at home with no one to see, I lay on my bed with the lights off and cried into a pillow, sometimes for hours at a time, often from sheer relief at being able to relax the efforts of playing this role, and in the morning I would put on the happy face again before striding out into the street. The acting was more exhausting than the pregnancy.

I had even managed to pretend to myself to some extent that I was not really pregnant; I walked a lot, went to the gym, swam and took up yoga and was certainly fitter, if not slimmer, than I had been in years, though in recent weeks I had been aware of a growing murmur of light pain in the general region of my pelvis after long walks, a kind of slow ache that faded after a short rest but came to life again in a series of twinges on stairs, or whenever I tried to get in or out of the shower or bed. Having identified this pain, I then ignored it with brio, in case pandering to it hampered my ability to pretend in public and in some way drew attention to my vulnerability or, worst of all, meant that I needed to ask someone for help. This went on successfully until the day I lost the ability to walk. My friend Euan half-carried me, limping and with an arm hooked heavily around his shoulders, to my door, as he had many times when I was drunk, while I repeatedly insisted, with as much conviction as any drunk, that I was absolutely fine, bloody *fine*, for goodness' sake; it was essential that he should leave before I was overwhelmed by the need to put my face in the pillow and collapse.

Reluctantly, a doctor was consulted; she sent me to a physiotherapist, who pronounced that I had a reasonably serious case of symphysis pubis dysfunction. I recoiled, appalled; it sounded like a venereal condition. It was quite rare, the physiotherapist confided, one woman in 300, as if I should be in some way impressed, or proud of my achievement. Apparently, the ligament that held the two halves of my pelvis together, softened by pregnancy hormones, had stretched too far and was now tearing. If I rested – by which she meant on a sofa, permanently, like an invalid, for the next two months – I might prevent lasting damage. I must learn to keep my legs together at all times, she admonished, and I waited for her to add, with a Carry-On nudge and a wink, 'though you should have thought of that seven months ago!', and when she didn't, I said it for her. She didn't feel the need to laugh. Some women, she informed me, with a headmistress's eye, had the condition so severely that the pelvis separated entirely and it could take a series of operations over *years* before they could walk normally again. Above all, she said, I should take extreme care when giving birth, as if I were going to have some choice in the matter. On no account must I let them put me in stirrups, she said darkly, implying that such a thing could happen without my consent, before I'd even realised what they were up to. I was not to swim any more, nor attempt any yoga positions that involved moving my legs in different directions, and I was instructed to use special techniques for climbing stairs and getting in and out of beds, cars and baths. I must be very careful about sexual intercourse, she said. I barked out a short laugh, which sounded harsher and more bitter than I had intended, and explained that although this was not an immediate issue, it was certainly advice I would be heeding in the future, though at the time I could not begin to picture any future in which I might even contemplate having sex, or anyone would want to contemplate having sex with me. I was then handed a special belt to hold my pelvis together, similar to those thick elasticated black ones Bananarama used to wear in the eighties, but more surgical and truss-like, and a pair of crutches.

Eventually I called my mother and admitted defeat. I was thinking it might make sense, I explained, if I moved out of London for the first few months at least; it would make things easier to have them nearby. This was fraught diplomatic terrain; I knew that they wanted to help me with the baby, but I had hoped not to have to depend on them. Even now I was not asking to move back in with them; I had been so determined not to impose the mess of my life on them too closely, and to show, for the sake of my self-esteem and their sanity, that I could remain independent to a degree. I also believed that we would not survive my adult self suddenly being present in their house any more than we would have when I left university, despite the changed circumstances; my mother must have known too that any invitation to move home would have pushed me in the opposite direction, though her instinct was to gather me in and take care of me. Nevertheless, she had been keeping an eye on the property pages of the local paper, waiting for the day when I would realise the need for compromise, and just before I made that call, she had found a neat little two-bedroom house, fully furnished, only ten minutes down the road and available to let immediately, for considerably less than I was paying for my one room above the falafel shop – this was very far from the heart of London, after all. It was very far from the heart of anywhere. My parents would have called this divine providence; I conceded a certain serendipity in the timing, but it was hard to avoid a sense of fatalism as well. I gave in, not graciously but with limp resignation, in recognition of the fact that I had squandered every other choice. I was no longer in control of my future, it seemed.

Research into the brain responses of animals who are placed under stresses beyond their control has found that they became extremely passive and exhibited symptoms of depression, which did not occur when the animals were able to control the stress levels themselves. Paul Gilbert, Professor of Clinical Psychology at the University of Derby, who has worked extensively on the evolutionary causes and functions of depression, writes in his book

Overcoming Depression that feeling trapped and unable to control one's environment is one of the most common triggers for depression as well as one of the most commonly reported feelings of those who are depressed. This may be because the sense of being trapped activates the body's natural fight-or-flight response, raising levels of the stress hormone cortisol, which adversely affects the balance of the brain's mood chemicals, especially serotonin. Evolution designed this response to deliver a short-term solution to a temporary threat. But if you are trapped in a situation – a job, a relationship, a place – that keeps you permanently feeling an urgent desire to escape with no possibility of running away, these stress levels will remain permanently elevated, in turn affecting the brain's ability to regulate mood. The connection between stress and depression is well researched and documented and, as Professor Gilbert goes on to explain, part of the purpose of cognitive therapy is to equip people better to cope with stress so that, like the animals in the experiment, they feel increasingly able to control it and less vulnerable to the sense of being powerless.

At the beginning of November, my father and brother came to move my belongings out of London, to bear me out of my life and, like a character in a nineteenth-century novel, away into this strange, removed world of confinement that would be both new and grimly familiar, as old as my earliest unhappiness. I stood in the middle of the room on my crutches, redundant with this enormous, useless body, pointing mutely as they hefted countless boxes of books, my only real possessions, down four flights of stairs. If I tried to lift anything they would reprimand me in unison, peeping simultaneously over the load they were carrying like an old-fashioned double act. As we drove through the streets of south London, I watched in wordless grief the passing of the big colonnaded Georgian houses, the squat little terraces, the faceless, square-edged blocks and the colourful rows of shops, cafés and pubs as if I were seeing them for the last time, as if they were precious things that belonged to me, that I had worked hard and saved up for and which were now being ripped away against my will. Over Clapham Common the sky wore a pearly, optimistic sheen, the grass still thickly scattered with brown leaves; in the late-afternoon light people who still had London, who had not fatally wounded their chances of remaining in the midst of its glorious turbulence, casually jogged, pushed buggies or walked their dogs, while through the rear window I watched it all slipping away and felt a great upsurge of loss and homesickness, and a sense of waste, of my own culpability, like a newly sentenced prisoner being driven away and realising for the first time the true cost of her crime.

The village had grown in the ten years since I had lived there, spreading slowly outwards at its edges like an unattended spillage, but I perceived it as smaller. This might have been a consequence of the house my mother had found, which appeared to have been vacated in a hurry by the owners, a separating couple, who had left it stuffed with their own, somehow oppressive, floral furnishings. Though it had more rooms than my studio in Clerkenwell, these did not amount to much more square footage, and the ceilings seemed unusually low compared to those I had been used to, which added to the feeling of a lid having closed over my head. At first I avoided the worst of the claustrophobia because, despite the physiotherapist's advice, it was impossible financially for me to stop working yet, so I gathered my crutches and commuted to London for two hours a day for the rest of November and December. My parents, concerned at this display of misplaced determination, offered to lend me whatever money I would lose by starting my leave early, but I would not hear of it; partly because I had already determined that I could and would not take their money, but mainly because it was not really about the money at all, but about my sense of who I was. For as long as I abjured ante-natal groups and baby boutiques and instead continued to go into my office and engage in discussions with my colleagues about books and films and current affairs I would be able to keep an attenuated connection to my life, to the person I used to be and still thought of as myself and still, foolishly, imagined I would return to at some point, once this was all over, as if she were still progressing, oblivious, along her own, happier trajectory and would do so until our paths could converge, so that I could assume her identity once more. It meant that my existence was not confined to the house with the pink soft furnishings and the closed-in ceilings, and that was worth any amount of pain, I felt. I had become increasingly unable to be alone, now that I was not technically alone at all – not because I was afraid of anything external, but because I already sensed the danger to my state of mind and was holding it at a distance for as long as I could.

While post-natal depression is now commonly discussed in magazines and as part of post-natal care, depression in pregnancy is often overlooked and seems more difficult to talk about. Recent research in the US has shown that as many as ten per cent of pregnant women experience depression but few receive adequate treatment, sometimes because the common symptoms – changes in appetite, sleep patterns and loss of energy – are confused with symptoms of pregnancy, but often because women feel they can't admit to depressive feelings at a time when they are expected to be happy and excited, and often feel desperately guilty if they can't manufacture the delight they are supposed to feel. Until quite recently, it was widely believed by healthcare professionals that the elevated levels of oestrogen and progesterone present during pregnancy protected women against depression, and that the condition therefore could not exist. Pregnant women who experience depression may come to believe that their depression is a sign that they don't love their baby enough, that they will be a bad mother, and this guilt may be compounded if they read, as I did while I was pregnant, articles on the supposed links between high levels of stress hormones during pregnancy and the risk of miscarriage or foetal defects such as premature birth, low birth weight, high blood pressure, heart problems and predisposition to anxiety and depression and even autism.

Even for those women who do seek help, treatment is more complicated because of potential side effects from medication. In 2006, in response to new studies on the link between commonly used SSRI antidepressants such as Prozac and Zoloft and health conditions in newborn babies such as respiratory complications and drug withdrawal symptoms, the American College of Obstetricians and Gynaecologists recommended that the use of SSRI antidepressants during pregnancy should be assessed on an individual basis, weighing up the risks of untreated depression against potential harm from drugs. Non-drug treatments such as talking therapies can be helpful, but much of the available literature blithely recommends the most useful defence against depression during pregnancy is ensuring you are surrounded by plenty of practical and emotional support and doing all you can to reduce stress – rather failing to acknowledge that for many women it is precisely the absence of such practical and emotional support and the inability to resolve stresses that will have precipitated the depression in the first place. For those women who are also working and/or caring for other children and are used to managing and coping well with busy lives, it can be extremely difficult to admit to needing more help and support from friends and family, especially if there is a sense of guilt attached to being depressed or feeling incapable. Greater recognition of depression during pregnancy and information from health-care services might do much to alleviate a problem that leaves many women feeling isolated and trapped, and would also be a positive step towards reducing the high risk of post-natal depression in those same women.

The trains grew increasingly hot and crowded with Christmas shoppers and their loot, especially when I returned in the evenings, looking with my egregious hump and my crutches as if I were making damn sure people would offer me their seat, like someone who has contrived an excuse too intricate to be strictly plausible. Though the crutches and the truss-like belt helped to an extent, the pain of getting myself to and from London each day, moving through the world, simply negotiating my physical place in it, was almost unbearable; I couldn't douse it in painkillers because of the baby, so I attempted to cultivate a mind-over-matter absence from my physical body, which gave me a permanently clenched and slightly terrified expression. 'You shouldn't be here!' cried everyone I encountered in the workplace, from the security guard on the door to the editor, but I couldn't explain to them that the pain of not being there would be immeasurably worse. I was stranded between two worlds: I had neither the companionship and solidity of a family life, the sense of embarking on the next step of a shared journey, nor the unencumbered focus of a single professional. My mind still existed in the latter, while my body did not. I had never felt such a profound alienation from my own life, and I could only locate a consistent sense of identity in the context of my work. I understood why so many people became depressed, even suicidal, after losing their jobs or being forced to retire; in the absence of a secure, loving relationship, significance is conferred largely by achievement, by the measure of your usefulness. I would have been quite happy to remain at my desk until the moment I went into labour and hop back again straight afterwards, like the women from more holistic cultures who were always held up as role models in my natural birth yoga classes, and who apparently barely broke stride as their babies slipped out serenely and organically and were gathered in some sort of woven sling as the women continued about their work in the fields. Clearly, no one could comprehend my desire to keep coming into the office on crutches from 50 miles away when I should have been at home resting. Someone offered to find out whether I could claim sick leave and maternity leave simultaneously, not understanding in their concern that it was not really about the money; I was so desperate not to be left alone in that house that I would have worked voluntarily if I'd had to.

I went out for what I believed would be the last time in my life just before Christmas, two weeks before the baby was due. A colleague was giving a party at her house and I had arranged to stay with a friend in London. My parents fretted that something might happen while I was out of their reach; they seemed to be entertaining dark fantasies of my delivering the baby on a Soho pavement or on the Tube. I explained that I had a phone and anyway, they had hospitals in London; I was probably still a patient at one of them, since I had not been organised enough to tell anyone I was moving. They felt very strongly that I shouldn't go; I had been a month premature myself, my mother reminded me, as if in this I had unwittingly set my own child a bad example. In fact I had no real desire to go to the party; I was exhausted and wanted only now to lie down until someone came to take this burden away, but I felt a kind of frantic need to absorb this one evening, which I knew would be the last chance to play at my old life for a long time, perhaps ever, to shore up the memory of company and friends and laughter as a buffer against the cold empty days I could already see ahead. Anyway, I was still in the business of pretending I could do everything; I would not be persuaded to stay at home.

After the party, a group of us went on to a Soho members' club, where we stayed until the early hours of the morning. Unusually, I was with a crowd that were not big drinkers, but although I was awash with mineral water, as the hours crept by I found myself startled by the same fear that had sometimes stalked my drinking nights; the fear that if I were to admit my exhaustion and go home, the magic would be broken and I would be flung out into the black and white world. I was so tired, so aware of my symphony of aches and twinges and the great thudding lunges of the baby, that I could barely focus, never mind hold a conversation, but I could not be the one to suggest we went home, knowing that this would be the last of these nights and that tomorrow, in daylight, I would return to the village to wait in solitary confinement. So I was still at the corner table when Bono, who knew my friend Sean, came over to join us.

'When the time comes,' Bono pronounced, 'take all the drugs you can get. You don't want to be even considering natural birth.

That's like *choosing* to have the flu.' I thanked him for his wisdom, though I was secretly disappointed; my yoga teacher had made it sound as though natural birth were infallible.

'Do you have a name for him?' Bono asked.

This question, like many other necessary preparations for the baby's arrival, I had left unresolved, because to decide on a name would mean accepting the solid contours of the situation; so far, I had allowed the baby to remain a sort of abstraction, a project I was supposed to be organising but was continually putting off because I suspected I lacked the required skills. In so far as I had considered it at all, I was favouring Kingsley, in homage to one of my favourite writers. I now found Kingsley would not survive an airing in front of all these people.

'Patrick,' I said. I didn't know where it had come from – perhaps a subliminal response to the Irishness in the air – but as I said it, I did a quick mental calculation and was pleased to find that I had never met a Patrick I didn't get on with, but could count at least three that I liked very much. Some time after two, the friend with whom I was staying noticed that I was falling asleep in my chair. The sight of the crutches seemed to excite Bono's charitable instincts.

'How are you getting home?' he asked us anxiously.

'We'll look for a taxi,' I said, waving imprecisely towards the street, although now that I was on my feet, I was faced with the possibility that there might not be too many empty taxis breezing about Soho at this time of night, so close to Christmas.

'You will not!' Bono cried. 'You'll take my car! It's just outside.' He pointed.

'Well, thank you, but – how will we get it back to you?' I said.

He gave me an odd look.

'He can come back for me when he's dropped you,' he said, and I realised that of course Bono was not about to hand me his keys, of course his car came with a little man to drive it. Gallantly he took my arm – the gesture was cosmetic, since all my combined weight was actually leaning on the crutches – and walked my friend and me to where his driver was waiting. As we passed through the bar, I heard a thin girl at a table near the door whisper to her friend, 'Is that Bono's wife?' and for a moment I wished my ex could have been there to see, just so that I could say, *see*? Fuck you, I'm doing fine, I'm hanging out with Bono. Or she might have said, 'Is *that* Bono's *wife?*', incredulous that he would even let me out of the house looking as wrecked and monstrous as I did – I was too tired to assess the inflections.

The following day, back in the village for good, I looked out through the net curtains to the identical houses across the stretch of tarmac at the end of our cul-de-sac as clouds squeezed the last thin light from the sky by mid-afternoon and sealed in evening, and thought, 'Bono lent me his car last night.' Then I thought, '*So?*' What did that mean, in the wider picture? It meant nothing, except that my life was ridiculous. I had squandered everything I had worked for, and the thing I had feared most had finally happened: the village had reeled me back in the end. I was back where I started. I did, at least, have a name for the baby: I was more or less contractually obliged to call him Patrick, otherwise it would mean that I had lied to Bono, which was probably a mortal sin.

'I don't know if I'm unhappy because I'm not free, or if I'm not free because I'm unhappy,' muses Jean Seberg in Godard's *Au Bout de Souffle*. I was quite clear on that point: this time I was unequivocally unhappy because I was not free, but since I was the architect of my own confinement it seemed inappropriate, not to say futile, to protest aloud. I had chosen this sentence myself, reclassifying it as an adventure, before it was far enough advanced for me to know better; there was, it turned out, nothing adventurous about being imprisoned in your own body in a tiny terraced house in a non-descript village just beyond the fringes of suburbia. Friends in London kept saying 'what a lovely place for a child to grow up!' as if to reassure me that there was a point to my exile, that it was not just a punishment for not having better judgement, though I noticed that none of them had elected to live there, not even the ones who had children. When I was feeling generous, though, I acknowledged that they were right; though our village was some-what off the beaten track and offered little to lure visitors, most of its indigenous shops now replaced by estate agents and its historic pubs all owned by chains, the next town along, only five miles away, was exactly the kind of place that attracted affluent young families looking to move from London for the schools and green spaces while remaining a tolerable distance from the capital. There was National Trust downland on every side, and wide parks and play areas. Since I had been away, it had even acquired a Costa Coffee, two gastropubs and a Pizza Express; objectively, it was hardly the Gulag, by anyone's standards. All its horror lay in its associations, in everything it represented in my memory. I had worked so hard to get away from here. All that hard-won freedom, those glimpses of a kind of life I had not thought could belong to me and now, it seemed, I had voluntarily reduced myself to a posi-tion where, in a very short time, I would once again have to ask my mother's permission to go out.

Time passed almost imperceptibly in the little house once I stopped going up to London; I lived in a state of suspended anima-tion, trapped behind my net curtains like one of those bloated aquarium fish behind glass. I began to believe that the slow revolution of days and nights were nothing but a hallucination, and that I was condemned permanently to this limbo, in which my body would remain colonised and unrecognisable. All the attempts to ignore the condition of my pelvic ligament over the previous few weeks had worsened it considerably, so that I could not even risk short walks; instead I spent the day rapt in front of my computer as if at a shrine, obsessively connected to my office email, a far more assiduous and attentive correspondent in my absence than I ever had been in person. I spent so much time emailing suggestions and comments to my colleagues on the desk that they had to remind me, kindly but sternly, that what happened on the pages was no longer any of my business. 'Relax!' they said. 'You really don't need to worry about it any more, you know, we can manage perfectly well.' This stark assertion of my expendability made me cry, though they meant it nicely, as if they thought my concern were really for the paper rather than for myself, as if I weren't worrying about the pages as a desperate last-ditch bid to pretend I had nothing more pressing to worry about; it almost crushed me to hear that I could easily be done without. I offered to come in over Christmas if they were short-staffed, and they said that wouldn't be necessary.

I had been told, by one of my few friends who had already had a baby, that there would come a day of unexpurgated weeping, a kind of extreme emotional purge in which I would be assailed by such a force of feeling that I would fear it would rip me apart, and that this day of sorrows would be the surest sign of the baby's imminent arrival. I found a reference to this emotional Niagara in one of the books I had long since stopped reading because their radiant families bore no resemblance to my strangely mutated life;

it was, the book confidently exclaimed, the body's equivalent of nesting, a way of clearing out all the unnecessary preoccupations and feelings to leave you a cleansed vessel, pristine and ready to receive all the new (and, it was implied, superior) emotions that would come with motherhood. This struck me as somewhat whimsical, not to say condescending. I had not really experienced the fabled nesting instinct either; there was a desultory effort to stick some Winnie the Pooh stickers around the baby's room, but when I stepped back to look at them they seemed so forlorn, such a poor compensation for all the disadvantages he would be coming into, namely having me as his mother, that I gave up. My mother, on the other hand, had done nothing but wash and iron little baby-gros and vests for weeks, laying them out on the spare bed in the baby's room so that I could choose what to pack for the hospital. They seemed disembodied, lying there, like the sloughed-off skins of tiny ghosts. It seemed absurd to be choosing clothes for some-one who did not yet exist in the world.

On a blank morning in mid-January, a week before my twenty-eighth birthday, I began to cry over my breakfast and continued for the next 12 hours. I did not call anyone; there was no comfort to be had, no practical assistance – I could not even have explained why I was crying. I felt I would be rent, broken entirely, by a grief that was vast as a cathedral, metaphysical in its dimensions, a grief that encompassed all of humankind and that seemed fiercer and more terrifying than any black episode I had previously known. I cried for myself, for my lost life and my loneliness and my stupid, stubborn fear of looking weak, my repeated fault of pushing away the people who loved me; I cried for all the times I had hurt and all the times I had wanted my life to be over, all the people I had lost or been disappointed by, or disappointed in my turn; I cried for my child, for his lack of a proper family, for the utter inadequacy of myself, for the world he was coming into, in which people could now fly planes into buildings in the name of their god, and other people responded by bombing women and children in the name of theirs. I remembered a recent conversation with my ultra-leftist friend Nick, when I had been fretting about the baby being disadvantaged by the lack of a father; Nick had shrugged and said, 'He's white, male, middle-class and he'll have a British passport. He's already won life's lottery several times over.' Then my sorrow expanded and crossed borders: I cried for all the children who had not won life's lottery; for all the victims of war and terrorism and famine and natural disaster and everyone who suffered; I wanted to help them all, to gather them up, but they were too many and I couldn't even help myself. I cried for the warm certainty of faith, lost to me as surely as the happy ignorance of childhood; I cried for my parents and the sudden recognition of their mortality and how much I had let them down; I cried for the impossibility of love, and after several hours I cried simply because I did not know how to stop. I lay on my side on the bed and watched the light fade to be replaced by the dirty orange gloom of streetlamps through the window, feeling that I could not physically contain this intensity of grief; in that moment, I felt overwhelmingly that I could not carry on. I did not want to be sentient, to be conscious, to keep on waking up to this day after day. The baby tussled and fought in his confines; the surprising strength of his movements seemed wholly unconnected to me and my desire to fall asleep and never wake up, to never have to feel again. It seemed curious and inappropriate that he should have so much life-force when I could feel no impetus to go on living. I cried long into the evening as shadows overtook the empty house, moving only intermittently to use the bathroom. I did not have the motivation even to switch on a light. At some point I must have fallen asleep in my clothes, because despite my wishes I did wake, into a colourless dawn that seemed marginally less terrible than the one before; though I no longer wanted to die, the pain that ricocheted the length of my body suggested that I might be about to, and I realised that this must be it.

I was quite adamant that I did not have post-natal depression. At first the only audience for these defiant denials was myself, until one day, some weeks after the baby was born, the health visitor arrived with a brisk questionnaire apparently designed to rate my state of mind. I was considered at special risk, she said significantly, because of being on my own. In fact, I had barely been on my own for a moment during the first few weeks: my mother had stayed with us for a fortnight, during which we slept in shifts and she kept an experienced eye on us as I accustomed myself to the reality that the baby was staying and appeared to be no respecter of my needs. My father, who was still working, came straight round every evening, and my brother travelled up from Oxford as often as he could, strikingly impressed with his new nephew; my girlfriends made the trip down from London at weekends with designer clothes for the baby and luxury bath oils for me, fascinated in an almost pornographic way with the spectacle of my having crossed the border into motherhood ahead of them, and just as clearly overwhelmed with relief that they had not. On their first visit, they had crashed through the sedate maternity ward in their heels like a scene from *Sex and the City*, brandishing silver balloons and bottles of champagne, and seemed rather taken aback to find me unable to drink because of the painkillers. They took special delight in hearing about the physical details of childbirth and begged for stories of gynaecological trauma, glancing wide-eyed at one another and nodding earnestly, as if I had returned from a holiday destination they had been considering to warn them of muggings and tropical diseases airbrushed from the brochure. Whatever else I may have achieved, I certainly de-romanticised childbirth for my friends, and probably became their most effective prophylactic for the next few years. I always thought I was glad to see them, I looked forward to their visits as ardently as any prisoner, but after they had left I realised that I felt as if something had been stolen from me, or as if I had missed an important flight. They brought with them gusts of the outside world that I couldn't have; I resented their laughter, their skinny jeans, their taut stomachs and unencumbered lives, their bulletins from a life with which I no longer had any commerce, and although I would have been distraught if they had stopped visiting, I sometimes felt it would make the process of my obliteration easier and quicker. Sometimes my parents' friends came round to visit, bringing gifts, and this made me anxious; people from the church I hadn't seen in years, and in their presence I became guilty and confused, as if they must all be thinking 'See? None of this would have happened if you'd just lived the way we taught you.' I was surrounded on all sides by kindness and practical support; what I lacked was intimacy, an equal partner in this enterprise. I was being looked after by my parents just as I was attempting to look after my own child; I was being fussed over and cared for by many different grown-ups, to the extent that I no longer felt like an adult myself, but I wasn't sure I wanted to explain the distinction to the health visitor, who reminded me of a Beatrix Potter mouse, all neat, contained efficiency and quick, scurrying movements.

The questionnaire turned out to be surprisingly easy to fake. It consisted of ten statements with four possible variants on Always, Often, Rarely, Never.

I have been able to laugh and see the funny side of things, it began.

I considered. *Was* there a funny side to this? My life had been razed to rubble, I was two stone overweight, I still couldn't walk properly without pain so I could not exercise the pounds away, I hadn't slept in months and the baby cried incessantly from colic. Surrounded by care and assistance, I felt more alone than I had ever felt. Was there some nugget of comedy I was failing to dig out?

'As much as I ever did!' I circled triumphantly, looking up for approval. The health visitor nodded encouragement.

Things have been getting on top of me.

Now this *was* funny, I thought, this tone of wry understatement. Had any new mother in the history of the species ever seriously ticked the option *No, I have been coping as well as ever*? Who could honestly say that? Nigella? Miriam Stoppard? I did, anyway; dishonestly, but with a confident stroke.

I have been so unhappy that I have been crying. Yes, most of the time; Yes, quite often; Only occasionally; No, never.

I glanced at the health visitor. Would she be able to tell?

'No, never!' I circled it with a flourish that I thought would be a dead give-away, dashed off the other answers in a similar fashion and handed back the paper, hoping that she would accuse me of lying. I wanted her to see through me, because then, I reasoned, I would get help without the embarrassment of having to ask for it, without having to come out and admit that I couldn't cope.

Instead, the health visitor glanced over my answers and smiled broadly.

'Well, we don't need to worry about *you*, then, do we?' she said.

I contrived a smile in return, frantically willing her to read between the lines, but she tidied her things into her bag and left, apparently convinced by my fraudulent buoyancy.

After she had gone, I leaned against the wall with a fleeting sense of having got away with something. Well, I thought, I fooled *her*, didn't I? Clever me. Later, pushing the baby through the grey, vacant streets, I realised it was not so clever after all, and that I had lied to the one person who was sufficiently unconnected to me not to require this performance of competence, the one person who could have listened objectively and offered impartial advice. Now that I thought about it, I couldn't see what exactly had been achieved by persuading the health visitor that everything was going swimmingly, except to prove to myself that my acting skills were still holding fast.

If I had answered the questionnaire truthfully I would have come out with top marks, but I didn't need the Edinburgh Post-Natal Depression Scale to tell me that something was wrong. I understood this at the most basic level, because there had been a conspicuous absence of joy so far in this experience, and surely you were supposed to feel happy when you had a new baby, surely that was the natural way of things? No one looking on could have accused me of being a bad mother; I was not neglectful or short-tempered or unkind: to any impartial observer, I was doing a fine job. I was obsessively anxious about his well-being and attentive to his every need; I fretted over the correct number of blankets, the temperature of the house, whether I was bathing him too little or too often. I sat up all night in the armchair watching Open University programmes about integers and Wagner so that he could sleep face down on my front when that was the only position that soothed his colic; I submitted to the indignity and discomfort of breastfeeding, which I loathed both while I was doing it and when I was not, because I was told it was in his best interests; I never failed to leap immediately to his summons, regardless of exhaustion; I sang songs and told stories and anyone watching might have said that, if anything, I needed to relax and remember to take some time for myself, that I fussed too much over the baby. Only I knew the dark motivations behind my earnest care; only I knew that I was overcompensating out of guilt, because in my heart I knew that I *was* a bad mother. I must be a bad mother because I didn't feel what I was supposed to feel. In truth, I didn't feel anything at all. I was simply empty, scoured, a flimsy wicker framework built around a void. At my core, where a well of fierce maternal love was supposed to be, there was only absence, and to disguise this absence I put on a fervent show of motherhood.

I had been uncomfortably aware of this absence during my pregnancy but had buried my anxiety, choosing to believe that the maternal bond I was not yet feeling would somehow be conferred on me at the moment of birth; I assumed it was a biological imperative, that the appearance of the baby would effect some elemental shift in my psyche and the instincts would magically come flooding in. Now we were several weeks in, and still this did not seem to have happened. In the delivery room, when he took his first breath and his first jagged cry, my mother, who was with me, cried too with emotion, and this seemed to me the natural response; I was glad someone did. I was too stunned to do anything except clumsily receive his slippery little body and stare, as if I could not for the life of me work out how this had happened. Even now, when I watched him feeding or sleeping, I struggled to make the connection between him and myself; like the complicated mathematics I sometimes watched in the dead hours of the night, I could not work out how the two parts of the equation related to one another. I tried saying, '*my* baby' or '*my* son' aloud, over and over, but the words seemed disengaged from any meaning that I might apprehend. I had no sense that he was part of me; I understood that it was my job to feed and clean him and keep him warm, and my body went about performing these tasks with a greater or lesser degree of competence, depending on my tiredness, but the vital part of me was absent. It was not that I didn't love the baby; I knew that I loved him, but I knew it only at a conceptual level, in the same way that I knew an atom is composed of neutrons and electrons, or that Jupiter has 63 moons. I seemed incapable of experiencing this love in any empirical sense; I was shut off from my ability to feel, and this induced a greater anxiety: that my professions of love for the baby were therefore not valid. If a friend had confided that she *really* loved her boyfriend but most of the time she wished he would just go away and stop making demands on her, I would have felt compelled to suggest that perhaps she didn't actually love him as much as she imagined; perhaps what she loved was the *idea* of a boyfriend rather than the real everyday fact of that particular individual, yet this was how I felt about the baby. Could I honestly claim to love him when a thousand times a day I wished someone would come and take him away – not permanently, just for, you know, six and a half days of the week or so? Yet this love did exist; I felt intimations of it sometimes that were almost feral. It broke my heart to see him with a cold or suffering with his teeth; then I would have done anything to take the pain on his behalf, and if anyone ever tried to harm him, I knew I could kill them violently, without reflection.

It occurred to me that for the first time in my life, I was in a relationship in which the other person's needs and desires were more important than my own, and this realisation revealed to me once again the inadequacy of my capacity to love. One evening a few years earlier, at a play in London, I had run into an old friend from college whom I had not seen in a while and who after university had set out on a promising career in the theatre. I asked what he was doing now and he explained that a year earlier his partner had become seriously ill and so they had moved away, to Scotland, and that he, my friend, was no longer directing but had taken on several temping jobs to support them so that his partner could have the treatment he needed. I came away from the encounter shocked and full of admiration, but also a little shamed, and it was the shame of knowing that I did not have it in me to do the same. I could not, at that time, imagine loving anyone so much that I would have abandoned my career and my ambitions to care for them, and the knowledge made me sad; perhaps it was true that, in Larkin's words, 'I was too selfish, withdrawn and easily bored to love.' Now it had happened, without my planning it; now I had been obliged to give up everything that mattered to me to care for another person, and I did not feel that I had risen particularly well to the challenge.

Still, I did not believe that I had anything like post-natal depression, because I had misunderstood the condition to be a causeless and inexplicable thing that landed out of the blue on new mothers, and that it could be identified precisely by its lack of correspondence to circumstance. My own emptiness, by contrast, had a very clear and obvious set of causes, and there was nothing any doctor or health visitor could do about those. But it was precisely what I thought of as the logical nature of my unhappiness that allowed me to cling on to a tiny shred of hope. Though almost unbearable from day to day, my present situation was at least finite; there was an agreed date, four months away, on which I would return to work and in my mind this had become transfigured into my release date, on which I would be approvingly told that I had served my sentence and learned my lesson and I would be allowed to return to my old life. This belief, that I simply had to wait it out, steeled me to endure the featureless wind-stricken days of February and March, wheeling the baby around the village in thin rain, counting the hours, always counting the hours down to a reunion with life. The only question I had answered truthfully on the Edinburgh Scale questionnaire had been the final one: *The thought of harming myself has occurred to me.*

I checked 'Never', and unusually it was true. Unlike my previous experiences of despair, since having the baby I had not entertained thoughts of ending my life, partly because I would not have had the energy to organise it, but mainly because I felt in some way I had already ceased to exist. I had been diverted into a siding; life was passing elsewhere, I imagined, but mine was temporarily stalled and it seemed to me that it would be less painful to my mind if I didn't struggle but quietly accepted it and waited for the days to pass.

Gradually, there came an incremental change in the light; spring spread over the village, and as I became better able to walk again I ventured further afield with the baby, to parks and woodland where I introduced him to flowers and ducks. His colic and crying abated and, like a painting being restored, beneath its murk was revealed a bright, cheerful nature; he slept through the night now and so did I, and we appeared to have reached a kind of accord. In preparation for returning to work I stopped breastfeeding, with such profound relief that it incurred an instant fine of guilt; for the first time in more than a year my body was being given a reprieve from someone else's demands, and although it was nowhere near its former shape, it was at least back within my jurisdiction. In the same month I returned to work and my first novel was published to mostly generous reviews; there was a little party, for which my parents had the baby overnight and I managed to fit into my old jeans. My publisher gave a speech, my friends all raised their glasses and cheered, I drank too much, danced until the early morning and felt that finally I was able to inhabit a version of my old self, even if temporarily. All those lonely winter days traipsing the abandoned streets of the village with the pram seemed then like a parenthesis, a necessary test of endurance that had been passed and left behind. People asked if I felt guilty about leaving the baby in a nursery at such a young age and the question surprised me: why would I feel guilty about placing him in the care of people who had professional qualifications in looking after babies, people who had been trained and had chosen to do this for a living, and who I trusted were infinitely more clued-up than I about how to entertain him? My only concern regarding the nursery was how I was going to continue to pay for it.

As I eased back into my life at work I grew progressively lighter, in body and mind, and for a while I began to believe that we had survived the worst of the storm and that it might even be possible to build out of it a functioning version of life in which I balanced my needs and his to everyone's satisfaction. Now that I was back in the current of the world, nourished by the energy of the city and able to resume something like a life of the mind, I returned to the baby galvanised, with the sense that there was more of me now to offer him. I could not understand mothers who felt guilty about working; rather, I knew these weekday absences to be necessary to my sanity and therefore to my ability to care for him. He was usually asleep by the time I got home, so that I saw him only for an hour in the mornings and at weekends; I missed him and valued my time with him more for having been away. Sometimes my parents would look after him overnight and then I would go to a party in London and become almost aggressive in my pursuit of transformation, slipping back into my old life for one night with a daring sense of transgression, like someone having an affair. Once again I found I had two lives; my existence had been polarised into extremes. Either I was alone in the silence of my pink floral sitting room, watching the last of the daylight slide slowly down the walls and fade as the baby slept upstairs, or I was miles away, being somebody else, somebody who stayed out all night in thickly smogged bars or clubs, trying to devour a week's worth of drink, cigarettes and dancing before dawn came and I had to return to my sterilised other world. My childless friends, who mainly saw me on the nights I stayed in London, seemed delighted by my swift return to what they saw as normality; I was pronounced to be 'fun' once more. The division of myself was complete.

I did not like myself much after these nights out; the hangovers seemed physical projections of a sense of filth that adhered to me after these rendezvous with my uninhibited, irresponsible alter ego. I would wake painfully in a friend's spare room or sofa bed, usually in my clothes, mouth tasting as if I had licked a pub carpet, and think, *I am somebody's mother.* I did not want to be this person any longer, this person who never knew when it was time to go home, but neither did I want to be the person who sat alone night after night in a remote village miles from all her friends, wishing her life were different, and there didn't seem to be anything in between. I began to suspect that this polarisation was retarding my transition to adulthood – a transition which had apparently not, to my disappointment, been effected automatically by motherhood. Maturity, I guessed, would be reached by a synthesis of these two opposites, but I could not see how it could be done. If I had a partner, I thought, if I lived in London, I could invite people round in the evenings and I would not have to choose between my friends and my child, between company and responsibility; I could learn a different way of living, one that perhaps involved moderation. Another possible answer might have been to find different friends, ones who might better understand my altered circumstances, but where would I find such people? I had shied away from mother-and-baby groups partly because I had always been daunted by organised gatherings of strangers and did not see that my social confidence would be enhanced by the mere fact that we were all in charge of small people, but mostly because I was cowed by these competent Home Counties mothers, the ones I passed with a shy greeting outside the nursery, with their celebrity-endorsed buggies, their detached houses and four-wheel-drives, their husbands who commuted to banks in the City and wore pastel Ralph Lauren polo shirts and khaki shorts with deck shoes at the weekends. Their lives seemed more unrecognisable to me than those of my childless friends and, besides, it was a fact of social selection that couples socialised with other couples; single, you are not immediately categorisable and couples feel uneasy around you – you remain an unknown quantity, a loose cannon. There are groups for single parents, you know, the health visitor told me enthusiastically, and I determined instantly never to go near one; I had a fierce aversion to being herded into a group on the basis of supposed common interests at the best of times – how much worse would it be if that common theme was our collective problem, a difficulty that, while not necessarily of our own making, we nevertheless carried with a slight sense of shame and diffidence, knowing that it was usually perceived from outside as failure? The split life seemed a better prospect than this.

I thought I had withstood the worst of the darkness that shadowed this new path I had taken. Towards the end of 2002, as my son neared his first Christmas, came the first hint that it might not be quite over, that there might be a deeper dark, a force gathered far beneath the surface, like a supervolcano, whose terrible power, once roused, could wreak devastation on a scale not yet imagined. It began with a letter from the Child Support Agency. Money was a problem; I had been back at work for less than six months and already it was quite clear that things could not continue as they were for much longer. My salary was not sufficient to cover all my outgoings and the ferocious costs of the nursery as well; I was surviving temporarily on the last of the money from my first book, but that would soon be gone and I was relying on the Child Support Agency to collect the money I had been promised when my son's father and I split up. This letter, which had taken the best part of a year to process, made it clear that no such money would be forthcoming and explained why. If I wanted to challenge their decision, it said, I must submit an appeal to a tribunal. The appeals process, it went on, usually took upwards of six months.

At the same time, my boss at the paper was to take a six-month sabbatical to finish a book, and I was asked to take over as Literary Editor while he was away. Instantly I knew that I should not agree; I was finding it hard enough to manage the commute, the writing, the attempt to maintain a functioning home with clean clothes and food in the cupboards, added to the fact that the baby still woke in the night, sometimes several times, and I was carrying a year's worth of sleep deprivation. I had not known it was possible to be so tired, and the new job would mean far longer hours and full responsibility for an entire desk of a national broadsheet, together with its budget, at a time when I did not feel competent to take responsibility for a trip to the supermarket. In any other circumstances I would have been thrilled to have been given this opportunity, and I was proud; I could not stand the thought that if I declined the offer, they might appoint someone with whom I did not get on, or – worse – that I would have to be subordinate to someone I did not think was as good as I would have been. I was also afraid that if I admitted that I was not sure I could manage, it would become an indelible mark against me, and that if any chance for a promotion should arise in the future, I would be thought of as the person who couldn't handle it because I was a single parent. I was determined not to let this idea cross anyone's mind for a second. Periodically, colleagues and acquaintances would coincide with me in corridors or lifts and warmly offer praise and admiration. They didn't know how I did it, looking after a baby on my own and doing the day job and writing the books! You put me to shame, said one woman, smiling, I haven't even got a baby and I still can't get around to writing my novel. I wanted desperately to maintain this illusion; the more they told me I was wonderful, the more afraid I became of letting them all down by revealing the disarray beneath the pretence. I experienced a fleeting kind of nausea when I agreed to the new job; the kind of anxiety I usually felt before boarding a plane, the stirrings of a panic attack, but I let it pass. Everything would be fine. Besides, I was in no position to turn down the chance of extra money.

The crisis came with a slow, inexorable build-up followed by a rapid plummet, like those log-flume water rides at funfairs, where your little log-shaped boat is drawn with painful slowness up a conveyor belt at 45 degrees before rounding a corner and hurtling at speed over a precipice, drowning you in its own wake. Once the ascent has started there is nothing you could do to avoid the crash, even if you wanted to. I began to research my child-support appeal on the Internet late into the night, and very soon it had grown into a frantic obsession which took priority over sleep or eating; I convinced myself that it was more necessary than either, since until I could compile a compelling case I could not persuade the CSA to open an appeal, and soon I was going to have to start borrowing money from the bank.

The first intimation of what was brewing came towards the end of the year, when I was asked to give a speech at my old comprehensive to those pupils who had taken their exams in the summer and were returning to collect their certificates. It seemed that I had been chosen because I was considered to represent an unusual level of achievement for a former pupil, and my task was to appear as a role model, to inspire these insouciant, multiply-pierced teens that if they applied themselves then they too might one day get to appear occasionally on Radio 4. The very idea was horrifying – more so because I couldn't have felt less able to inspire or more miscast as a role model – but because I am bad at saying no, I agreed. As the night of the presentation drew closer, I found that I was not only reluctant, but actively terrified. I had spoken publicly many times, to larger and more demanding audiences than this, and yet the thought of standing up on stage, particularly at my old school, prompted waves of panic, jagged breathing, shaking and crying. I did not know why I was having this reaction – it frightened me as much as the speech itself – and I determined that I was going to call the headmaster and cancel, explain that I was not well enough, but I put off this call for so long that I could not reasonably abandon them at the last minute. I remember little about the content of the speech, though I vividly recall vomiting from anxiety beforehand and feeling that I would have done anything for a reprieve, staring wildly across the sea of young faces beside their gratified parents, some expectant, some cynical, and the gently indulgent expressions of my former teachers above their folded arms. All I wanted to say to these kids was, don't end up like this, back here in this town, losing everything. Get out as early as you can, and don't have any kids yourself. In the event I didn't say this, and whatever I did say seemed to pass off all right, but this adrenalised terror didn't abate; instead it followed me and insinuated itself invisibly into other areas of my life.

After Christmas I took over as literary editor, and for the first few weeks I believed myself to be on top of the job: I attended meetings, produced pages that people seemed generally to be pleased with, and wrote a weekly column that betrayed no hint of my unravelling mind, despite the fact that I had not slept more than two or three hours a night for nearly a month. I felt that if they just left me alone to get on with it, if nothing unexpected happens and no one makes any additional demands of me, I might just keep this operation together until my boss returns. Of course, it doesn't work like that on newspapers. Events upset your best-laid plans, and your business is to respond to them immediately, even in the rarefied world of book reviewing. In the third week of my tenure, it happened that halfway through our production schedule the editor wanted to change my page layouts, introducing new elements which would require extra pieces to be commissioned, new pictures to be found, the whole design to be torn up and begun from scratch. This happened with relative frequency and I knew what needed to be done, had done it many times before; it was just that suddenly the work involved seemed monstrous and impossible, as if I had just been asked to land a stricken aircraft. Instead of making the calls and speaking to the designers and sub-editors who needed to be alerted, I locked myself in the loo, where I cried and hyperventilated until I almost passed out. Later in the day, a young assistant from the picture desk approached to ask me how they should illustrate the new piece, which I had not yet commissioned, and I burst into tears and screamed at her, 'Stop asking me fucking *questions!*' Then I ran out of the building and pounded the streets in tears for an hour before coming back to my desk, but the break had achieved nothing; the tasks that faced me seemed even more daunting than before I ran away. The picture assistant kept her distance, even after I apologised. Apparently no one paid this outburst much attention; it can be a stressful profession and we were all used to sudden panics and tempers flaring. I was known to be volatile, but was generally thought to know what I was doing.

Somehow, the work seemed to get done, but I could not be said to be on top of it. Instead I began to flail wildly, like someone who has just realised their parachute will not open. Fear of the world, a horror of the simplest decisions, became the defining feature of my landscape. First I stopped returning non-urgent calls, then I stopped returning all calls, then I stopped listening to my messages altogether. I could not cope with confronting my financial situation, so I stopped opening bills and bank statements. Very soon I stopped opening any mail at all, and the light-headed, heart-racing, dry-mouthed panic attack would begin when I heard the crash of letters through the door in the morning; I would hide them in a cupboard without looking, so that I wouldn't have to worry about who was demanding what. After my first month in my boss's job, I had a meeting with the managing editor about my budget. He showed me the figures and observed that I had gone over by a small amount; it was neither a reproach nor a criticism, merely a remark, but I immediately burst into tears. 'It doesn't matter,' the managing editor said hastily, alarmed, 'it will be easy to rectify, you can make up the balance next month,' but all I heard was someone else telling me I was in more debt; my mind could not make the distinction between the collapse of my personal finances and the budget for which I was responsible at work. All the deficits blurred into one and I became convinced that the managing editor was going to demand the sum I had overspent there and then out of my own pocket, which in turn made me think of all the red bills ticking away unopened in the cupboard at home and wonder what would happen when they eventually detonated. He asked if I was all right and I explained that I had had a bit of a cold and was probably a little run down. I did not tell him about my true state of mind, that every minor decision paralysed me with fear and that I barely felt I had the skills to make a cup of tea, never mind manage a department, because I was afraid I would lose the job, and because I still would not be seen to look weak or incompetent. He sympathised and, smiling, said not to worry, at least my boss would be back in another five months and then I could have a nice well-earned holiday.

'Five months' dropped like two stones through the murky waters of my consciousness and sank slowly out of sight. I saw those months laid out before me without parole, days and days like this one, days that were impossible hurdles to be overcome only to find they were followed by more days, more demands, more hours to be endured. I recognised that more or less since the middle of my pregnancy, since I understood that I was to be a single parent, I had been sustaining myself with the false hope of a series of deadlines; landmarks which, I deluded myself, would herald a return to myself, the restoration of life to its former contours and texture: once the baby's born; once he sleeps through the night; once I stop breastfeeding; once I get back to work; once I have a boyfriend; once I get the money sorted. I now realised, with appalling clarity, that there would be no such return. This would simply go on and on, these demands, for years and years, with no prospect of respite, with no hope, I thought, of ever feeling differently, of ever engaging fully with my child, with my life. I would get up in the dark and come home in the dark, spend the day in an office pretending to cope with a job I should have loved but could not face before coming home to work on a legal case that I did not hope to win, and the bills would mount up and how would I ever again find time to write, how could I manage normality if I was terrified of the telephone and the postman? Before my son was born I had confected pastel-coloured romantic fantasies of our life together, in which I was someone more relaxed and creative, the kind of mother who invented long, captivating magical stories or acted out epic adventures and, later, in which we were more like best friends than mother and son, and would go on cycling holidays and road trips and I would introduce him to film, theatre, books and music, and as an adult he would tell friends with fond recollection of his bohemian, fun-filled childhood. These fantasies had not survived; more often than not now I would find myself simply staring at him with dumb incomprehension. How could I ever play games or make up stories when I could barely find the resolve to get up in the mornings, when I had to force myself to sing 'If you're happy and you know it, clap your hands' with tears sluicing down my face? It was like asking someone with a shattered spine to help you move house.

This was not the kind of depression I had experienced when he was first born: the flatlining of emotion, the sense of anomie and absence from myself. This was something altogether more primitive and more threatening, borne along by its own violent energy: I felt that the foundations of my mind had been assaulted. I was very much present in my own consciousness and aware of a lurid anguish, a psychic pain that nothing would relieve – not sleep nor, I was now certain, even the most dramatic change of fortunes, such as winning the lottery – and I began to feel that if this pain would not go away, and could not be endured, the only thing left for me was somehow to escape it. I had come to the end of my resources; I had run dry. There was nothing left in me to summon to the struggle of staying afloat and I wanted to be free of the obligation to try. What if I stopped thrashing altogether and allowed the waters to close over my head, if I could just sink into darkness?

I had always assumed that having a breakdown meant that you shut down altogether, and that you would know you were having one if you lost your grip on reason. Once, after university, I had wondered aloud to my mother if I might be depressed. 'You're not depressed,' she said, firmly. 'If you were depressed, you'd be like Linda.' Linda was a friend of hers who had suffered severe post-natal depression and had not got out of bed for two years. I learned later that mental pain is no different from physical pain in that people have different thresholds of endurance; some can mask it more effectively than others. Outwardly, I continued to function for a few more weeks. I forced myself to perform certain tasks: getting out of bed, showering and dressing myself and my son, feeding him, taking him to nursery, getting on the train, carrying out the series of duties that enabled four pages of book reviews and comment to appear each week. I affixed myself to this routine; only the predictability of it enabled me to go on putting one foot in front of the other. Inside, I was dismantled: the world had lost its outlines and I was unmoored, disorientated, raw and defenceless against contingencies. I cried if someone pushed past me at the bus stop; I cried if the lift or the bank machine were out of order; I shook and hyperventilated if the phone rang; I went into a full-throttle panic attack if plans were changed at the last minute. I was afraid that I would start to scream if anyone made any further demands on me, however trivial. I could no longer return friends' calls or emails; the thought of going out socially was horrifying, but I didn't want them to see me like this nor to have to explain why I had not been in touch for so long, so I simply withdrew. Weekends were the worst times; at least during the working week there was a pattern to which I could adhere, like scaffolding, to keep me upright. At the weekends, the nursery was closed. My only desire – the only thing of which I felt capable – was to hide under the duvet with no one's expectations to meet, but my son would wake some time before six, and once we had completed the routine of breakfast there was an entire day like a mountain trek at high altitude to be traversed. I was usually weeping by seven; the inane jingles of the jaunty children's programmes I put on to distract him scraped like someone taking my skin off with a potato peeler. Sometimes I would take him to the soft play area at the leisure centre, where he could plunge into a pool of brightly coloured balls, shrieking with delight; he always wanted me to join in, and sometimes the husk that I had become did venture into the colour-ful padded maze, but on those occasions my conscious self had rolled up and retreated inward; I felt I was bringing contagion into that bright, noisy inflatable temple of fun, and I would stop and look at myself, knee-deep in plastic balls, and experience the strong sensation that I was not there, that this was somebody else's life I had stumbled into by mistake. More often, I took the baby to my parents' house and went to bed for the afternoon while they entertained him as babies should be entertained. The nursery sent home a questionnaire for parents; one of the questions was 'How can we improve our service?' 'Open at weekends,' I wrote. It was not meant to be flippant; I would gladly have worked longer hours to afford whatever extra they charged. I had no impetus to engage with a lively, inquisitive child; I felt I was no use to him as a mother and, worse, I feared that my mood may be infecting him – how could it not? How could we go on like this, weekend after weekend, for all the remaining years of his childhood – how could I inflict that on him? Surely he would be better off without me, I began to think.

My friends thought I was very busy with work and the baby. To my colleagues I was present, though they might have agreed I seemed highly stressed, but perhaps they assumed that was the result of added responsibilities and that all new working mothers are prone to be a little snappy with the lack of sleep. My parents thought I was overworked, and suggested repeatedly that I should bite the bullet and step down at the paper, go back to my old, less demanding job, but I not only disregarded their advice and concern, I refuted it, assuring them I was just fine; I needed to cling on to the job with my fingernails, even as they splintered, because if I gave up on that, if I admitted defeat, there would be nothing to stop me falling. They noted that I had lost a lot of weight – I was now more than a stone below my usual weight before I was pregnant – and I assured them that this was normal, that my body was still adjusting, but the fact was that I could not eat. This had no relation to vanity or an awareness of my body; it was simply that I felt as if my throat had closed and I was permanently nauseous.

Presently I lost the ability to read – something of a handicap when your job is reviewing books. Though I was still awake most of the night, I could no longer concentrate on any text; instead I would spend hours staring blankly at the wall in the dark, or sometimes sitting on the floor, rocking and biting my fist, repeating the word 'No…no…no' over and over, or pacing in small circles in one spot, turning round and around, or punching my fist against the wall repeatedly, all of which actions, even while I was almost unconsciously engaged in them, I recognised in a detached part of my mind as the motions and gestures of a mad person, a movie asylum inmate. Since this existence was verging on insanity and could no longer really be classified as living, and since there would be no end to it, I began to ask myself why and for whose benefit I was insisting on prolonging this sorry charade?

Emotional weather is as hard to recall, once it has passed, as the external kind. Try to summon, in the glare of a blazing July day, the sensation of being frozen to the marrow, shivering in a cold wind that penetrates even your winter coat. You know you have known what it is to be cold; you can probably picture yourself on an iron-grey day wearing that coat, and you know that you will experience cold again, but in the fierce heat of summer it is very hard to conjure how it feels to be frozen. Being well, it is just as impossible to recreate what happens to your mind when you become suicidal. I feel now as if what I am describing happened to somebody else, a character in a novel I might have written. That it should be my own mind I am describing seems puzzling and improbable, as if someone had shown me a photograph of myself in front of a foreign landmark I had no memory of visiting; are you *sure* it's me? I want to say. When I try to recall what it was like to be that person during those months, it feels shameful and foolish, now that I am well, that I could have allowed myself to reach such depths. Perhaps it is this sense of shame about the inherent unreason of depression, together with the sense of personal responsibility for policing our own state of mind that keeps so many sufferers silent, until it is too late. Those of us who survive want to shunt it into the past, to pretend, embarrassed, that it never happened, and so those who come after us feel, wrongly, that they are the first to have felt this way and that they must carry it alone.

Recurring or obsessive thoughts of death, self-harm and suicide are on the basic checklist for any diagnosis of depression and I had experienced all of these before at some level, but the incremental descent of my mind towards despair this time had passed the theoretical level; there was a strong current of will bearing these thoughts along. I became convinced of the world's indifference, its cruel emphasis on success and strength. As a child I had been taught that I was special – not because of any native talents, but because of my place in God's plan. In my teens, at a youth group camp, one of the leaders had given me a Bible verse which they believed God had told them to pass on to me; it was Jeremiah 29:11: 'For I know the plans I have for you,' declares the Lord, 'plans to prosper you and not to harm you, plans to give you hope and a future.' I wrote the verse on a postcard and kept it inside my Bible, clinging to the message. There was a plan for my life, predetermined in the mists of eternity, and I could be confident that the dark moments, when they came, were testing times, intended not to harm but to strengthen me. I had been promised hope and a future. Now I glanced about at the ruin of myself and understood that there was no plan. No one would come looking for me. Christ had taught compassion for those who stumble but the real world was Darwinian. If I lost my job, I would be replaced by someone better, stronger, someone who did not fall apart, and if I could not make a living I would have to move back in with my parents and live like an invalid. My parents would take care of me, I didn't doubt that, but it would mean leaving them to care for my child as well, and there would come a day when they might need care themselves. I would lose my friends – they could not be expected to maintain contact with me out of charity – and besides, we would have nothing left in common: they would only remind me of what I had once thought possible and all that I had lost. If I could not shake this – and I did not believe I ever would – I would lose all sense of identity and of my place in the world. I would be forgotten, replaced, cast aside, unwanted; if I could not achieve I was no one, I was not worth the space I took up in the world. This was my perception, distorted certainly, but as Solomon writes in *The Noonday Demon*, there comes a point at which depression fulfils its own prophecies. 'There is a terrible cycle: the symptoms of depression cause depression. Loneliness causes depression, but depression also causes loneliness. If you cannot function, your life becomes as much of a mess as you had supposed it was…and that is authentically depressing.' And once it has you, there is no longer any hope or motivation to commit to the future.

Though this may sound like pedantry, feeling suicidal is not necessarily the same as wanting to be dead. Since none of us can actually imagine being dead, we picture it as a state of non-being, an almost comforting reprieve from the pain of consciousness. The guidance notes for counsellors at the Cambridge University Counselling Service put it like this: 'Most people who attempt suicide are ambivalent about killing themselves – frequently what they seek is to put a stop to unbearable feelings or a situation that seems intolerable. Someone who is suicidal may well be feeling frightened, trapped, hopeless, helpless, confused and distressed – and desperate to escape from his or her suffering rather than actually wanting to die.' Yet when you are in the grip of a suicidal impulse, you are unable to see your problems as temporary; they are simply unbearable and you look for an alternative to bearing them, even if your scrambled reason contemplates the act of self-destruction as if it were not irreversible. I began to nudge myself closer to the edge, in preparation. I hoarded non-prescription painkillers, Nurofen, paracetamol, aspirin; at night, I would tip my little stash on to the kitchen table and stare at them, as if they might suddenly do something unexpected. I would push them into constellations with my fingertips and wonder if I had collected enough to do the job, if I washed them down with a bottle of vodka. I had read somewhere that an overdose of paracetamol, if not gauged correctly, could be insufficient to kill but still cause massive organ failure and brain damage; this would be a problem, since the last thing I wanted was to find that I had survived in that state. I climbed a small step-ladder to grip the banister with both hands and pull myself up, to test whether, in the event, it would take my weight (I suspected not; the house was cheaply made), but although hanging was the means that most obviously presented itself, something about the act frightened me. I was not afraid of dying, but I was still a coward about pain – I didn't feel the need to actively court it. Because I had never had any interest in cooking, the most lethal implement in my kitchen drawer was a blunt fruit knife, and my plastic safety razors would not have done the job; in any case, wrist-slashing was too brutal and messy for my liking. My preferred method would have been a gentle carbon monoxide poisoning at the wheel of my car, but I didn't have a garage and the car was parked on a tarmac apron in full view of three neighbours' front windows; there was no chance that I could attach a hose to the exhaust and leave the engine running for long enough without someone seeing and intervening. It would have to be the pills, I decided, but every time I tipped them out on to the table in the agonising dead hours of the night I would become conscious of the sounds of my son upstairs, stirring in his sleep; the soft snuffles of his breathing, and I would grudgingly put away the toys of my despair.

I would like to say that it was the ties of love that held me back on those nights, but this would be untrue, or true only in the most oblique sense. It was not the existence of such ties nor the acknowledgement of the love and support that I knew surrounded me that made me eventually chase the pills back into their various bottles, but the practical pull of duty and obligation. My son would wake in the morning and need to be fed and changed; the idea of his being left to cry unattended, hungry and dirty, perhaps for the best part of a day until my parents arrived in the evening, was unthinkable. And this was another obstacle: the thought that it would almost certainly be my parents who found me. It was one thing to take my leave of them all but it seemed an unnecessary cruelty to leave them with that indelible image. I did not want, in relieving my own pain, to inflict further pain on those who did not deserve any. It did not seem to me, at the time, that my death would in itself do irreparable damage; I thought myself quite clear-eyed in my assessment of the circumstances. My son was too small to have formed any lasting memory of me; this way, he would be free to grow up with normal people who could provide a proper family – my parents, should they be so inclined, or more likely they could have him adopted by a nice, childless couple with plenty of money who would dote on him, instead of being hindered always by this solipsistic wraith he had been unlucky enough to have been dealt as a mother. My moods were the sole generator of the emotional climate in our home, and since I found it impossible to imagine a time when I would not feel as shredded by despair as I did during those days, I could not bear the thought that I would be condemning him to live in such darkness throughout his childhood. When I tried to look into the future I saw only the scene from Nick Hornby's *About A Boy*, when the 12-year-old hero returns from school to find his depressed single mother slumped over the table after a suicide attempt. This, I felt certain, was our unavoidable fate somewhere in the years ahead – though I knew I would never last until he was 12 – and I became determined that by pre-empting it now I could give him a better chance at happiness. My parents, too, I thought, would be secretly relieved; they would be spared all the emotional demands and disappointment I had exacted over the years, and they would still have my cheerful, pragmatic, high-achieving brother, who would more than compensate. I was a drain on everyone who cared about me, I concluded, and always had been; though I believed that they would be sad and might at first miss me, I was certain that there would be a deep unvoiced ripple of relief.

To spare my family the distress of anything so brutally factual as a corpse, I realised that I would have to go away to do this thing, and once it became clear that I would have to grit my teeth, sit on my hands and endure the overwhelming urge that came in the silent hours in favour of a modus operandi that involved planning and travel, the idea lost some of its sheen. For a while thoughts of suicide alternated with a fantasy of simply disappearing, a gentler form of self-eradication: I would withdraw what little money remained in my bank account, take the train to some remote part of the Scottish highlands, check into a hotel under a false name and there drink myself to death, or perhaps just lie down to freeze quietly at the edge of a loch. A couple of times I got as far as queuing for tickets at King's Cross, but again the practicalities always interrupted the impulse; it would occur to me, as I neared the moment when I was to approach the window and request a single to anywhere north of Aberdeen that I would need to telephone my parents to ask them to pick up the baby; they would ask why, and I would have to invent some work-related excuse, and then they would expect me back and I was left again with the miserable image of them waiting up for me, growing increasingly frantic with every passing hour and eventually calling the police – unless I told them not to expect me back, that I was slipping away for good, but what would I say – don't wait up, I may be some time? They would of course try to find me, which would make it impossible to disappear anonymously. On both occasions, after all this reasoning, I slunk out of the ticket queue and returned to my office with no one any the wiser, and the pain went on accumulating over the days and weeks like layers of sediment that had begun to compact and petrify.

Then, finally, the evening I was returning home on the train later than usual and found myself alone in a compartment with a door you could open from the inside. Perhaps it was only the overwhelming despair of that daily journey, away from London and all its invigorating life, into the early dusk, back to the silence and the hours of dread that waited for me in the little house with the low ceilings; suddenly I felt I could not last another day. Standing there, minutes from falling, I had an image of my mother and my son,

and myself as the line of continuity between them; I was struck, as
if for the first time, by the understanding that I had once been a
baby, that I had once been to my mother what my son now was to
me. All those hours of patient, thankless care, the frustration and
anxiety and tears, all that time and love invested: I had done it for
a total of 13 months and already it had changed the texture and
meaning of my life beyond measure, but she had done it for nearly
30 years – *30 years!* - and for what? So that I could dash myself to
pieces under the wheels of a Network South East commuter train?
Would I make that the culmination of her work as a mother? And
my son – would I leave him the legacy of believing that he was not
reason enough for his mother to go on living?

I stayed, not because I salvaged any hope that my life would
improve or that I would ever feel better, but out of a deep-lodged
sense of duty to the people who loved me. And yet many, many
people love their children, their partners, their parents, their friends
and still take their own life; the one does not negate the other. But
the sheer desperation of suicidal depression can override love and
duty – it even trumps the survival instinct, the fiercest and most
fundamental passion we own. In his memoir, *Experience*, Martin
Amis writes of his eldest daughter's mother, who committed suicide:
'If what she was suffering had been endurable, then she would have
endured.' This is the only compassionate judgement: you cannot
know how it was if you have never stood where they stood.

This was the nearest I had come to ending my life, and though
I stepped back at the last minute, I was profoundly frightened by
the experience. It was not a mad romantic impulse, like the
moment when Celia Johnson rushes on to the platform at the end
of *Brief Encounter*, with the idea of throwing herself under the
express. Putting myself so close to self-destruction had not been

cathartic; if anything, it had shown me that I might really be capable of the act. I did not feel a renewed connection with life, nor had the despair that had urged the gesture abated, yet the reasons for enduring would remain equally compelling and I was afraid that I would be caught permanently in this tension between the desire for oblivion and the need to carry on, as in Anne Stevenson's poem 'Vertigo':

Mind led body
to the edge of the precipice.
They stared in desire
at the naked abyss.
If you love me, said mind,
take that step into silence.
If you love me, said body,
turn and exist.

That same week, I went to the doctor to admit that I needed help. It was a conscious decision to turn and exist, to find some way to overcome this, and yet it felt like defeat. I had just turned 29 and it was the first time in my life that I had even contemplated consulting a medical doctor about my state of mind, which I still imagined to be wholly independent of somatic complaints and which therefore ought to have come under the jurisdiction of my will and was not the proper province of a general practitioner. But I had passed a certain point: after that moment on the train I was quite certain that if someone did not help me, or at least give me some hope, I would not last very much longer. There were two possibilities, both containing their own terror: either she would tell me that there was something seriously wrong with me, that I was on the verge of a kind of madness that would entail psychiatric hospitals and medication that would blunt me into bovine acquiescence and which would result in losing my job and my child being taken into care; or – and this was just as daunting – she would assert that there was nothing wrong with me, that plenty of people dealt with far worse circumstances than mine with pluck and fortitude and all that was required was a bit of good old British grit. Even then, in my desperation, I was miserably aware, as I knocked on her door, of a deep shame and stigma attached to what I was about to do. I was going to admit to an inability to bear a fairly minor set of hardships, and this felt like an admission of poor stamina at a much more fundamental level; a deplorable weakness of character.

Since 1952, the National Health Service in the United Kingdom has conducted a triennial Confidential Enquiry into Maternal Death to establish, with the aim of preventing, the most significant risks to the health of pregnant women and new mothers. While enormous improvements have been made in treating the most frequent killers – conditions such as infection, haemorrhaging, thromboembolism – the last two Confidential Enquiries show that the leading killer of new mothers in the UK is now suicide as a result of post-natal psychiatric illness. These figures are difficult to ascertain accurately, because until recently a woman's suicide was only considered to be officially linked to post-natal illness, and included in the enquiry, if it occurred within six weeks of the birth, whereas research now shows that for many women post-natal depression is prolonged or delayed and can increase in severity over many months. A suicide that occurs over a year after the birth of a child can still be directly related to post-natal depression, and collating these figures to see them included in the enquiry is painstaking work, but essential if health-care professionals are to build an accurate picture of how many families are affected by post-natal depression that goes untreated.

The majority of new mothers who commit suicide are suffering from the most severe form of post-natal depression, called puerperal psychosis (sometimes postpartum psychosis), an illness believed to be a form of bipolar disorder and which can be characterised by symptoms of mania, delusions (mothers frequently believe their child to have special powers or to be sent from God) or extreme suicidal tendencies and paranoia. Usually puerperal psychosis is characterised by rapid onset at around ten days after delivery, but some research suggests that symptoms can develop as much as six months after birth. While post-natal depression in greater or lesser degrees of severity can affect one women in ten, puerperal psychosis is much rarer, affecting one in 500 – except among women with a previous history of bipolar disorder, where the risk is between one in three and one in two. According to Dr Ian Jones of the Mood Disorders Research Unit at Cardiff University, one of the leading specialists in the associations between childbirth and bipolar disorder, the health services are failing women at high risk of severe post-natal illness because not enough is being done to monitor or advise them. 'Probably about half the cases where a woman has a really severe postpartum psychosis there will have been no prior indication,' he explains, 'but for a large number of women there will have been certain factors in their history that means their high risk could have been predicted. What the confidential enquiries have shown is that we're not doing that very well – the women themselves and the professionals looking after them have not been able to recognise that risk and no particular arrangements were made to help them, and it's causing women to kill themselves.' But he does see reason for cautious optimism. 'I think that is changing now,' he says, 'because there is a focus as a result of these enquiries to ask women about their mood history and make sure that those with symptoms of bipolar illness are referred to specialist psychiatrists to try to keep them well through pregnancy and after birth.'

What about those of us who may have no idea that a history of mood swings might be indicative of bipolar disorder before we come to have children? It seems that a far greater emphasis on assessing a woman's mental health and psychiatric history before birth as well as after might allow specialists to identify those women who may not even know they are in the high-risk category for severe post-natal illness. I don't know if what I experienced counts as puerperal psychosis – although some of the symptoms sound similar, the fact that my post-natal illness was at its most severe a year after my son's birth suggests that it was not, but even here there is ambiguity over the diagnostic criteria. Dr Jones explains that it is not possible to distinguish absolutely between puerperal psychosis and severe post-natal depression or to identify them as separate conditions; as with so many mood disorders, they seem to exist on a continuum. 'It's difficult because they can merge and part of the problem is trying to get away from some of these rigid category distinctions because often post-natal depression can merge into psychosis and there isn't really a cut-off point, they're just labels,' he says. 'But it is increasingly recognised that childbirth is an important trigger and it seems to be that, rather than psychiatric illness in general or even mood disorders in general, it's women with bipolar vulnerability who are particularly at risk at this time.'

For women who have had a previous episode of severe post-natal illness, the risk of recurrence is over 50 per cent. With better information, and more care taken to identify those who are especially vulnerable and then refer them to specialist care, many of those maternal deaths from suicide might be prevented. Of course, specialist perinatal psychiatric care is not on everyone's doorstep, especially in the UK where, like so much else in health care, it depends on where you live. Would knowing have made a difference to me, I wonder? It would not have changed the circumstances that piled stress on top of post-natal depression, but it might have allowed me to be more aware of what was happening to me, and those around me – friends, family, doctors and health visitors – to keep a closer watch on how I was coping. Yet I was identified as a potential risk immediately after my son's birth because I was a single parent, and how easily I dodged the questionnaire and persuaded everyone that I was doing just fine.

'Certainly more people are aware of the concept of post-natal depression,' says Dr Jones, 'but the problem is that it's such a wide concept and covers such a variety of illnesses that it can sometimes lose its impact. Some women have much more severe types of illness that don't fit within the model of diagnosis and the Edinburgh Scale and there are concerns that it's very easy to avoid it being recognised. What is needed in those instances is help from specialist perinatal psychiatric teams. The ideal would be that all women would have access to that kind of care.'

Perhaps there is cause for optimism; think of the progress made over the past 50 years in reducing the number of maternal deaths from physical causes. The evidence can't be ignored: depression is now a greater threat to the lives of new mothers than septicaemia, and care must be improved accordingly.

'I think I might be depressed,' I blurted at the doctor, before she had even offered me a seat. When she gently pushed for more details, I could only mumble, 'I can't carry on.' I may have said it several times. I didn't tell her about the train; I didn't need to. She said, sympathetically, 'I'm surprised it's taken you this long,' referring, I assumed, to the weight of being a single parent. So everyone had expected me to crack up long before now, I thought. I'd believed I had them all fooled, but all along they were just patiently waiting for the implosion. This was the extent of our consultation. There were no enquiries about previous episodes, nor about family history. She dashed off a prescription, gave a quick summary of potential side effects and warned me not to change the dose without prior authorisation, and then I was on my own again in the damp February wind, clutching my piece of paper like a certificate of failure.

Lots of people take these, I told myself, as I walked away from the pharmacy counter, clutching my last chance in 40-milligram doses. They were a common brand of selective serotonin reuptake inhibitors, the 'new generation' antidepressants known as SSRIs, of which Prozac is the most famous and Seroxat the most infamous; they work, as the name suggests, by restricting the amount of the neurotransmitter serotonin reabsorbed by the brain, keeping higher levels of serotonin in circulation and thereby restoring the depleted stores associated with depression to more normal functioning levels. Everybody's on them, I reassured myself. In America, they give it to their pets. This did nothing to lessen the deep shame I felt as I watched the pharmacist read the prescription.

The side effects, I soon learned, were legion. Almost immediately, I felt measurably worse, which was mildly interesting from a scientific angle, since I had not believed it was possible to feel any worse. For the first three weeks of the medication, I felt very much as I had in the early weeks of pregnancy: the same bone-deep exhaustion, the waterlogged limbs, the same constant nausea. My concentration became clouded; my vision blurred and I experienced frequent moments of vertigo, the sensation that fixed objects around me had started to slide and that I was in danger of falling. In public places, on public transport, this sensation became terrifying. My memory was shot; I could find fractured images of things I had done but I couldn't distinguish whether I had done them that morning or the week or year before, and this gave rise to a permanent paranoia, that I had forgotten or failed to do something critical. Sometimes I would find myself on the train to London unable to remember whether or not I had taken my son to the nursery, and I would be seized by a sudden panic that I might have left him at home unattended by mistake. Often I was overcome by a sense of unreality or detachment, of watching myself performing a series of actions as if through smeared glass, from a distance. I continued to show up for work but it was clear to other people that something was wrong, and I took a few days off, claiming flu. At least now, I thought, I had some tangible physical symptoms that I could use as an excuse for sick days, though it seemed peculiarly inverted that the acceptable, visible symptoms of illness should have been caused by the drugs that were supposed to cure the invisible symptoms of the illness I could not admit to. There was more to come, too: the enclosed leaflet promised a dazzling array of potential adverse reactions that included dry mouth, sweating, loss of libido, increased agitation, intense dreaming, seizures, suicidal tendencies and even coma, which seemed a high price to pay for something that was supposed to cheer you up. In my ignorance about antidepressants I had imagined they would impart, like a tab of Ecstasy, instant fuzzy joy, but the doctor had made clear that they could take several weeks to work and that I should not be deterred by any of the above side effects; the bene- fits would be seen in due course, as a reward for persistence. One could not stop and start this medicine at will, she had instructed, as I was effectively engaged in a process of altering my brain chem- istry, and interfering with that process could be fatal. I felt that a coma would act as its own deterrent, so I dutifully persisted.

Almost four weeks to the day, I woke up one morning and knew that the weight had lifted. I felt the way I had felt as a child, waking on the first day of the summer holidays; the nameless dread that accompanied me every morning had been replaced by a sense of clarity and optimism. Instead of feeling crushed by the enormity of everything that was expected of me, I thought briskly, 'Right, today I have to do this, this and this,' and got up and got on with it. This is how I used to feel! I thought, and the novelty of it was so strange and lovely that for a moment I thought I might cry. I could hear my son calling from his cot; he giggled when I went to pick him up and I giggled too, which shocked him temporarily into silence, and I realised it must have been the first time he had seen me laugh in months. The physical symptoms continued, the fatigue, nausea, dry mouth and loss of appetite, but they were countered by the extraordinary relief in my head. Once, when I was about ten, I was ducked in a swimming pool by some older boys horsing around; they meant no harm, but they held me under the water longer than they should have and I recall vividly struggling against the weight of them above me, my strained lungs burning, and the sensation of lightness when they finally let go, of being freed to burst up through the surface and snatch great gulps of air, the knowledge, even as a child, that I could have drowned. Coming out of depression felt something like this, and at first I laughed at my own stupidity – that I should have been so afraid of the pills and all their connotations seemed a ridiculous and misplaced point of pride. If only I had known it was this easy to cure, I would have gone long ago!

The relief lasted until the nightmares began. They appeared at first while I slept, as you might expect with nightmares, and always in them someone was about to die violently. Sometimes it was I who was being chased through streets and alleys and familiar buildings, by a man – always a man – who was no one I recognised, whose face I never clearly saw, but who I knew instinctively was intent on killing me and would not stop hunting me until he had succeeded. In these dreams I was in flight for my life, in blind terror; they were always what is known as 'lucid dreaming', where the dreamer has a measure of control over the narrative, like a virtual reality game. I could choose to some degree in which direction I ran but I could not make it end, and he was never far behind me, never far enough to hide or catch my breath. I would be screaming for help, for mercy, but inside the dream the screams were mute, though sometimes in the real world they were loud enough for me to wake myself up for a temporary respite, producing the odd reversal of roles that now it was I who woke my son up in the night, screaming. When this happened I would have to switch all the lights on and get up for a while; if I tried to turn over and go back to sleep, the dream would simply resume from where it had broken off, like a DVD. More frightening, though, were the dreams in which I was the murderer; in these I was every bit as brutal and relentless as the anonymous figure who pursued me through the labyrinthine streets of the unconscious, and when I caught up with my victim, as I often did, the fury I unleashed was monstrous. Sometimes the person I wanted to kill was a stranger, a character from my imagination, but sometimes it was someone I knew, and from these scenes I awoke shrieking as if unhinged. Always stabbing or bludgeoning, always that elemental contact with flesh, never a detached, cold-blooded shooting from a distance; this was Greek vengeance, carried out with a frenzy and rage I had not suspected myself to possess, even in imagination, an incredible lust to inflict destruction, and it shook me profoundly. On waking I carried the imprint of these dreams with me, the terror they engendered, and I began purposefully to stay awake longer and longer into the night to avoid closing my eyes. Sleep became a hostile, dangerous country where my reason could be taken hostage. Where had these images come from? The dreams I was having now were not a fear of cinematic images reproduced on the screen of my mind in sleep, images I knew to be fictional. The fear I experienced in these present nightmares was far deeper and more visceral; it was nothing less than the very real, physical terror of imminent death – mine or someone else's.

After a while these dreams, or the essence of them, began to leak out slowly, as if from a poorly-sealed room, into my daylight hours. Though I was no longer dangerously depressed, I was not restored to a full and happy life; I managed to work and take care of my son, but this was all. I did not go out socially as I still felt too fragile to act a part in company, nor did I engage in anything that might have been described as a leisure pursuit, but merely coping was good enough for now and I was resigned to taking small steps for the moment. But I became aware as the weeks passed of a malevolent force building in me, as yet deeply buried but gathering intensity; the same combination of terror and aggression that coloured my dreams, and it was already partly familiar. I was permanently agitated and found it hard to sit still, but in the past, when I had experienced these surges of energy, their innate element of violence had been contained, battened down, barring the few occasions when it had found outward expression in being directed at myself. Now I began to fear the capacity for violence suggested by the dreams. I had not known I had this in me, I had always thought of myself as a peaceful person, but it was growing more insistent. If someone pushed me in the bus queue or the cash machine was out of order, instead of the onset of tears I felt an instant, reflex response of aggression, a desire to lash out and break something. I kept it reined in, but now I carried myself through London gingerly, like an explosive device primed and ready, afraid that an unexpected jolt might set me off in a way that would cause damage I could not undo.

Was it the pills? Or was it part of me? These questions strike at the heart of psychiatric medication and all its implications, and open up the most complex question of all – what is 'the real me'? Is there any such thing? When I had experienced moods of elation, when I became reckless and uninhibited and over-confident and annoyed the hell out of everyone, was that the real me? Or the person I became when I was depressed, when I hated myself and found myself worthless and a failure and wanted to die – was that my true self? Or the competent, efficient, well-organised, funny and quite likeable person I knew I could be at moments in-between? Were these drugs breeding monsters out of thin air, or were they revealing a side of my mind that had previously lain dormant and undiscovered? I began to hate the drugs, but I was afraid that coming off them would be worse, and my relationship with them took on the shape of an abusive marriage. I wanted to be free of them, but I needed them; I knew without doubt that they had saved my life, and I was too scared of what I might become again without them. I hated the stigma of them, too; the fact that I was constantly having to make excuses for not drinking, the fact that I saw it change the way friends looked at me. Common these pills may be, but not so much so in Britain – or at least not publicly – that you don't notice the raised eyebrow. It was strange, I thought, that I was not ashamed of anyone knowing that I wore glasses for reading because my eyes do not function perfectly without intervention, but telling people that you can't control your moods without medical help carries different connotations. Is it because we are conditioned to see the mind as the locus of the self? Is it again these antiquated notions of fortitude and character, or is it that there exists a slight resentment of those who take medication to improve their mood, as if they are cheating their way to happiness?

I don't know these answers. I knew only that from the day the dreams began I became desperate to know when I could stop taking the pills and return to normal, though I suspected that the concept of 'normal' had lost its currency. My template of normality corresponded to my childless self and was therefore for ever out of reach. The doctor had warned me that as soon as the pills kicked in I would presume I was better and want to come off the drugs, but this was a false dawn, she assured me; whatever improvement I noticed was an effect of the drugs and therefore artificial, and that to see lasting changes in my mood I would need to stay on the medication for several months at the very least. I wondered, given that all my moods were now generated by high doses of serotonin being pumped around my system, how I would ever know if I was better. All my emotions had become chemical holograms. If I felt unhappy, was I really unhappy, or did it simply mean that the drugs were not working as efficiently as before? If I felt optimistic, was this merely the drugs obscuring the truth, or might I actually be improving?

After some time, the agitation and the dreams abated slightly to a level that was bearable, though, like the nausea and exhaustion, they never disappeared entirely. After almost a year, I felt an incremental ascent and I became convinced that I was well again, that my mind no longer needed its crutches. Circumstances conspired to make me believe life was not entirely without hope; my tenure as literary editor came to an end without my having bankrupted the paper; the child-support case was resolved more or less in my favour; my first novel won a small prize and I sold the new novel I had been working on. I told the doctor I was ready to live without the medication; to my surprise she agreed, and by minuscule degrees I reduced the dose and eventually quit without any of the alarming withdrawal symptoms detailed in the leaflet. The dreams disappeared; I was no longer frightened of my own mind. I felt I was returning to the world with a hard-won knowledge of how precariously we are balanced on its surface. Often I thought of how narrowly I had escaped, what might have happened if I had not gone to the doctor, and the possibilities made me shudder and hold my little boy closer. This was not the life I had imagined for myself, but it was life, and it had acquired deeper colours for all the shadows. I believed that I was better now, and that I could leave that entire episode in the past. Not long after coming off the drugs I met B, and it felt as if I had a future again, as if this were my reward for having endured the worst of the dark.

5

Turn and Exist

January, 2006. The plane touched down at JFK into a fog so opaque that no lights from the ground had been visible, so that when the wheels first struck the runway I cried out, thinking we were still several thousand feet up in a bank of cloud and that we must have hit a building. Suddenly, there were rooftops at eye-level; the light through the windows was thick and jaundiced. As we taxied towards the terminal, I understood that this whole journey was a mistake; my experiment, before it had even begun, was showing me a truth I already knew and from which I was running with my hands over my ears, all the way to New York, as if there I might be transformed. I was going to need the drugs again. There was no use pretending otherwise; I recognised very well this time the place I had reached, and I knew what would come next if I didn't go to the doctor and ask for them, but I had interposed this trip to New York between the unwilling acknowledgement of my state and the moment of doing something about it.

Compacted drifts of snow lined the gutters, stained and shapeless. The fog loosened once the yellow cab crossed the bridge into Manhattan, but the air between the buildings seemed to cling to objects, wrapping them in dingy shadows. Crawling through the Lower East Side, we passed a line of hipsters in tight denim queuing outside the Bowery Ballroom; I couldn't see who was playing, but all I could think of was that I was not one of them, and never would be. I felt both invisible and exposed: my arrival in this city that was supposed to save me had gone entirely unremarked by all its inhabitants. There had been no one there to meet me at the airport; there was no one waiting for me in SoHo, where I had the keys to a friend's apartment while she was in London; there was, in fact, no one at all to give a damn what happened to me while I was here. Ostensibly I was in the city as a journalist – I had contrived a piece of work that required me to interview a number of young New York writers as a legitimate pretext for the trip, and I had a meeting scheduled about a film I had been asked to write – but really it was a last-ditch attempt to deflect the storm that was approaching, or at least to ask some-one else to be my shelter from it. There was someone I had come to see, someone I had talked myself into believing would replace B, whom I had lost six months earlier.

Unfortunately, this person didn't know that it was his job to save me, because I hadn't told him; he thought he was just my friend, and just before I flew out he told me that he had family obligations over the weekend and was not free to meet until Monday. Since he quite reasonably thought I was in New York for work, he was not to have anticipated the utter desolation this news occasioned, and I hid it marvellously. Nine o'clock on a Friday evening; the streets of SoHo lay abandoned in the snow and I arrived feeling more alone and lost than I had at home, which had not been in the plan. I bought a coffee at Dean and Deluca across the street from my friend's apartment and sat by myself in the window, watching the snowdrifts slowly eroded by traffic. I used to enjoy wandering alone through New York; I thought it romantic and melancholic. Now it made me feel shipwrecked.

The week before had been my son's fourth birthday. For the first time in his life, I gave a party that included people beyond the family; in previous years the modest scope of our celebrations had been partly due to my lack of animus and partly to the fact that I didn't know any other children. None of my friends had any and the idea of inviting any of the parents of my son's colleagues from the nursery into the tiny house with the low ceilings inspired shudders of shame. But some months before his fourth birthday we had moved to a new town – bigger and more substantial, closer to London – one where I felt at least plugged back into some current of life. I thought that perhaps having a party would be the way to introduce ourselves into the neighbourhood, like characters in a Jane Austen novel giving a ball; besides, I was carrying three years' worth of cumulative guilt. Other children had birthday parties and he was now old enough to have noticed this; I could not postpone it indefinitely because I was afraid I might not endure the pain of having to be jolly for two hours. So I made a booking and sent out invitations; 20 children would fling themselves against padded walls for two hours in the leisure centre before being fed a combination of additives designed to ensure they went on bouncing and screaming for most of the night. My son was terribly excited and his joy infected me temporarily, as I realised with remorse what a simple and essential pleasure this was for him, remembering with a smile my own childhood delight at the opportunity to be a celebrity for an afternoon.

By the time the day came, I did not feel much like a Jane Austen character. I was ill again, and I knew it very well – had known it for at least two months, but I pretended to myself that it was tiredness,

overwork, stress – not *that*, not the other thing, the thing that was
supposed to have been vanquished by the pills two years earlier. If
I didn't acknowledge it by name, I thought, perhaps it would take
the hint and quietly slip away; perhaps tomorrow I would wake
and find it lifted off my chest. In clear-eyed moments I knew this
would not happen; I recognised every step along the path like an
escaped prisoner who has been tracked down and escorted back to
the cells. The difference was that this time I knew how to change
course. If I went to the doctor now, its progress could be halted
before I reached the point where I was contemplating jumping off
trains. But the pills would breed their monsters, and the imprint of
those dreams and their waking counterparts, the plain physical
terror in sleep and the corresponding conscious fear of what lay
submerged in my own mind, remained fresh two years on. It was
common, I knew, to respond adversely to medication; I knew of
someone who had been prescribed endless cocktails of antidepressants, each with its own uniquely distressing side effects, in the
seemingly imprecise hope of striking a winning combination, like
a burglar trying ineptly to crack a safe with guessed-at numbers.
Could I live like that? If I went to the doctor and the drugs did not
work, how many new drugs would I be willing to try in order to
relieve the present mood? What if there were drugs with worse side
effects? Might it not be simpler just to endure the original depression, or would it progress faster this time?

Books have always been my defence against the things I fear; I
arm myself with knowledge and crouch behind it, as if this might
make the source of the fear vanish, in the way that as a child I used
to read the *Star Wars* books before going to the film and then keep
my hands over my eyes in the cinema, in the same way that I know
more than any lay person ever needs to know about emergency

procedures on aeroplanes. Building a fortress of information helps with the illusion of control. Yet, unusually, I had deliberately avoided reading about depression or seeking out medical facts because to do so would be to accept that I was not *better*, that what happened in the two years following my son's birth was not an anomaly but merely part of a condition that would always hold out the promise of its return. Squashing my pride sufficiently to take medication for a one-off episode – easily rationalised away in the light of stress and post-natal difficulties – was one thing; concluding that it was something *in* me, that even if I produced an international bestseller, won the Nobel Prize, made more money than I could spend and found a fairy-tale romance it might *still* come back – this possibility threatened the very root of who I believed I was and everything I dared to hope for the future.

And it should not have come back now; I was so *angry* with it. It had no right to intrude – things were going well and I should have been happy. I wanted to be happy. My second book had been published and I had been commissioned by a production company in New York to turn it into a film. I had prevailed on the generosity of my employers to change the hours I worked, allowing me to work more often from home and so reducing my dependence on my parents, a crucial aid to ratcheting up my self-esteem. Then, in November of 2005, I made the radical decision to give up drinking for good, prompted by the experience of having embarrassed myself once too often in front of the man I was now feverishly trying to impress, who was not a drinker. I, too, would embrace that New York culture of rampant puritanism and perhaps this would win him; in the meantime, spurred on by my new-found spirit of self-denial, as the teetotal days progressed I challenged myself by giving up more pollutants: smoking, caffeine, dairy products, wheat, red meat, sugar. I didn't notice myself slipping into a troubling state of mind, so proud was I of all my self-discipline. By December I was living on water, fish and vegetables, and although I was unarguably physically healthier than I had been in months, friends began to question how much good all this abstinence was doing me on other levels; they detected a note of obsession in it. Might it not be more sensible, they suggested, to give things up incrementally, or at least wait, like normal people, until the new year? The Christmas party season had begun and I found that I had no desire to be in company: if I refused to eat, drink or smoke, and the only person I cared to flirt with was across the Atlantic, I wasn't sure what else you were supposed to do at a party. Already I was beginning to lose the capacity for jolly conversation with colleagues and casual acquaintances; increasingly, I stayed at home and developed an unhealthy addiction to the one activity that afforded me any pleasure: writing long letters by email to the man in New York. It struck me that these were exactly the kind of letters I used to write to B, collages of pastiche, confession, flirtation, poetry and sketches – I was simply putting a different name at the top, as if love could be transferred wholesale to preserve the continuity; this, I appreciated, was a temporary, surface solution, and it struck me too that addiction was not a metaphorical term, for this email correspondence had direct physical consequences, amplified by the problem of time zones. If the connection failed or I was obliged to be away from my computer, I began to have anxiety attacks; if I logged in first thing in the morning and he had not responded overnight, I would be hit by an instant despair, like a cartoon character concertinaed by a falling anvil. Sometimes I sat up all night until five or six in the morning, calculating that with a five hour time lag he would just about be returning home from a night out and potentially checking his messages; I grew increasingly agitated and unable to sleep, and developed a daytime terror of leaving the house in case I missed a message, though the tiny muffled voice of sense asked repeatedly what I imagined he might have to communicate that was so important I could not risk going to the supermarket. I could have solved this last problem by getting a BlackBerry but then, I felt, I would be wholly consumed by this weirdness; I knew this level of obsession was not normal – it was not even as if he was my lover or my partner: he was just a friend with whom I was enjoying a light-hearted long-distance flirtation. It was as if I were hard-wired to extremes; I had to binge on something, and having purged my life of all genuine, quantifiable intoxicants, my mind had turned of its own accord and grabbed on to something abstract and ridiculous.

I left the house long enough to attend the traditional pre-Christmas dinner organised by my group of girlfriends from university. In the restaurant I felt brittle and vulnerable; the music and riot of conversation frightened me and I found making conversation as effortful as breathing through plastic. My friends were thrown into consternation by my abstinence and treated me with anxious concern, as if I had just announced a terminal illness. One of them ventured to remark that, although my skin was glowing, I didn't seem to be very happy, and perhaps I might relax a bit if I had just one glass of wine? I shook my head; one glass would violate the standard I had set. It was an arbitrary standard, admittedly, but still I did not want to fall short. Later, staying overnight in someone's flat, I went to bed early and listened to the rest of them gathered around the kitchen table, lighting cigarettes and opening more bottles, airily discussing when and whether they thought of having children. I almost got up to contribute my cynical expertise to the symposium, but I did not have the energy. They would have to learn for themselves. When I was at home, alone, not sleeping, I wished frantically that I was in London among my friends. Now that I was in London among my friends, not sleeping, I found that it was not what I wanted at all. Where, then, did I want to be? The answer was that I did not know; I was homesick for a home I did not have, and I suspected that there was nowhere that could settle this restlessness, this permanent sense of not having found anywhere to belong. Still, New York seemed to be the only place that held out any possibility of reinvention. Since the end of my relationship with B the previous summer I had felt as if my life was in abeyance, suspended in a place that did not in any real sense exist, like the Wood Between the Worlds in C. S. Lewis's story *The Magician's Nephew*. If I could only get to New York, I thought, I could resume living in a meaningful way, as if there were a future to consider. My son drew a picture for my mother: a stick figure with a shock of static long hair and a rain of dashes down its face. She asked him who it was supposed to be; he replied, 'That's my sad mummy crying.'

I experienced his fourth birthday party numbed of all sensation. All I could think was that this should be a joyful moment, to be shored up in memory for old age; this was supposed to be fun. I watched his flushed little face, alternately ecstatic and tearful with excitement, and tried to urge myself to engage with what was happening. *Engage*, for Christ's sake, come on, what's the *matter* with you? Have some *fun*, dammit! Fortunately, professionally high-octane children's entertainers were part of the package so I was not charged with rallying them to organised games, since even smiling seemed as arduous as trying to disguise the pain of walking on a broken ankle. My father zigzagged about with the camera, clicking like a paparazzo, composing the official portrait of them all sitting importantly along two flanks of a long table, solemn as the Last Supper over their hunks of birthday cake. When all the children had been returned sticky and intact to their correct owners, we walked through the sheeting rain to the car.

'I had a lovely birthday, didn't I?' my son said, looking up anxiously, as if hoping for confirmation.

'Yes, sweetheart, you did.'

'How do you feel?' my father asked me. I think he was expecting me to say, laughingly, 'Exhausted!' or perhaps even 'proud'. What I felt was that I would like to go a long way away and lie down and not wake up.

'I feel like weeping,' I replied, truthfully.

Six days later I was walking up Broadway through shards of icy rain and I still felt like weeping. If someone had offered me this package a few months ago I would have thought I had won an unexpected prize: subsidised flight, beautiful loft apartment to myself, free of charge, long weekend in New York to mooch around galleries and bookshops, drink coffee and read the paper in the Village, complimentary tickets to a Broadway play, an interesting assignment, a meeting with the film people and the chance to see the only person in New York who really mattered. I was so lucky, I reminded myself, counting off each of my blessings like rosary beads. I should be *happy*. Why could I not be happy? To feel so bleak when I had so much: this was failure on a grand scale. On New Year's Eve, in a grand moment of darkness, I had blurted to my mother that I hated my life. 'But you have a lovely life,' she said, surprised. She was right, of course; I did have a lovely life by anyone's standards; why could nothing rouse me to feel it?

Uptown, at the Museum of Modern Art, I trudged dutifully through vast white rooms of De Koonings, Hockneys and Pollocks as if colour might penetrate my sense of desolation but they left me feeling ungrateful and unworthy, exposing the flaws in my belief that art, not religion, holds the answers to the fundamental questions about why we live. Apparently art, like faith, had its limits. So there were paintings in the world. *And?* They made no dent in my lack of affect.

On my way down through the gallery, on one of the floors below, I came across an exhibition of Walker Evans portraits of Depression-era New Yorkers on the subway. They stared straight ahead, a monochrome line-up of faces: stern, weary, defiant, mischievous, beautiful, complex. Meeting their eyes – these strangers in their old-style hats and coats – I experienced a sudden updraft of emotion. Look at them here, so vivid and emphatic in the faces they present to the camera; so knowing in their life's worth of pain and despair and joy and regret and hope, all of them dead now, as my parents would one day be dead, and as I would and – unthinkably – my son, everyone I had ever cared about. All these faces on the wall, ordinary people, poor, working people whose names were not recorded, and only this image remained. For a long while I couldn't move, and I realised I was crying at the immense futility of it, of all of us, and at this buckling sense of loss that had no specific object, and people were beginning to steer a curve around me until a man asked me if I was all right and I nodded dumbly but it was as if I had surged upward on a sudden current of connection. I stumbled out of the building and walked the streets for a long time feeling somehow visionary, illuminated by tragedy as if I had been granted an exclusive preview of the emptiness of life and that this had conferred on me an exemption from the usual rules. The sky above New York seemed to have been raised to a greater height, the air magnetised; it was a little like the sensation of insight that comes with bereavement and a little like being high. By the time I met my friend Gaby for coffee after the play I found I could not do much except cry. With great sensitivity, she suggested I go back to the SoHo loft, collect my bags and stay at her house in Brooklyn that night so that I wouldn't have to be alone.

Sitting on the platform at Broadway-Lafayette, waiting for the B train that would take me to Brooklyn, I held on to this sense of elevation, of something universal having been revealed, a great understanding of mortality, but it was already overwhelming me. In a different frame of mind I might have wanted to harness it, to channel it into some kind of writing, but instead I remained on the almost-deserted platform and felt held down, weighted to the little wooden bench by a generalised hopelessness. From time to time people traversed the platform and a D train would come hammering into the station in a dull gleam of steel, scoop them into its maw and exit noisily, while I watched as if I were the eye of the camera.

After about 40 minutes I understood that the B train was not going to come and by the time this had dawned I was sure I could not move. I did not have the necessary endurance, the sense of purpose, to cross the platform to the wall-mounted map and work out another route; I had memorised the B train – direct to Seventh Avenue, Park Slope – and to begin again, to summon the degree of decisive action involved in replanning, in changing trains, was now beyond me. The thought of returning to the surface and finding a cab was not even possible within the laws of the natural world. I had become entirely passive, anchored.

The bleakness of a mid-winter Sunday evening in an empty station, waiting alone for a train that never comes: who wouldn't find themselves existentially burdened? Now would be the time to go, I found myself thinking, again. No one knows me. No one knows I'm here. Each time the D train came surfing in on breakers of sparks, I felt the familiar tug towards annihilation, the lure of the step into silence. Rousing myself enough to drift to the edge of the platform, I thought how simple and obvious it would be just to let my body fall forwards, to be swallowed under the cars into the rush of hot air, the hiss and rattle of wheels, as if I might at the moment of impact evaporate into sooty, metallic steam and disperse, indistinguishable, incorporeal. Or, said the pragmatic part of myself that always struggled hastily to its feet at these moments, as if it had been caught napping, I could just get on the D train rather than jumping under it and ride it to its final stop, probably Coney Island if I could be bothered to look, and there I could disappear in a less violent way. I could become a missing person, anonymous, without fixed abode, a fantasy I still entertained as if sloughing off the identity I had accumulated would equate to freeing my mind from its present pain of existence. I had run away to New York as if I might outrun my own despair; now I was going to run even further, to Coney Island? Why not across the whole continent? Had I not yet learned that no matter which station I alighted on, no matter what name I called myself or how many chains of responsibility I wriggled out from like a sideshow escapologist, I carried the storm clouds with me, would always carry them, unless I fixed my mind or destroyed it.

I don't know how long I stayed in the station; time slowed

thickly and seemed to conspire with my inertia. If I lacked the impetus to work out the subway map, I also lacked the will to throw myself under a train, so I merely stood by the edge of the platform watching forlornly each sweep of lights around the bend that heralded the arrival of another train with a big mocking D affixed to its face, as if just one time, by sheer force of faith, I could transform it into a B, a tiny miracle to prove the universe wasn't wholly set against me. Eventually, I got on one of them, more for the illusion of having done something proactive than with any sense of direction. There was no relief in movement, only more fear. My earlier gladness at the prospect of not being alone for the evening was pushed aside by my aversion to being a burden to my friends, to being pitied, and the knowledge that avoiding this would mean drawing up all my strength to make conversation, to conceal the wreckage of my psyche so as not to spoil their dinner party. William Styron observes that those suffering from physical illness are usually granted a removal from the demands of ordinary life. 'However,' he goes on, 'the sufferer from depression has no such option and therefore finds himself, like a walking casualty of war, thrust into the most intolerable social and family situations. There he must, despite the anguish devouring his brain, present a face approximating the one that is associated with ordinary events and companionship.'

I had spent so much time approximating this face over the years; if it did not become any easier, it grew at least more familiar, its contours more worn-in. I adjusted it one more time and, guessing at a station, ascended into the sharp night air of Brooklyn.

The hope of transformation through a change of place had slid down a gutter with the last of the brown New York snow; if anything, I returned home feeling lonelier and more rootless. There would be no running away, no magical intervention; I was back now, and not better, probably worse, and since I knew that help was available and that I owed it to everyone around me to get it, I had no choice but to go to the doctor.

A different doctor since the last time, but he consulted the record on the screen and saw that I had form; he spoke gently and asked me two or three questions from the diagnostic check-list (feelings of hopelessness? Loss of energy? Thoughts of suicide? Welcome back!), then wrote me a prescription for the same SSRI antidepressants I had taken two years earlier. Nervous about contradicting authority, I explained politely that I didn't want to take drugs and he looked equally politely baffled.

'I wondered if there was something else,' I said. 'Something that wasn't drugs? Alternative treatments?'

He looked as if I had asked him for a Reiki massage. Without enthusiasm he produced a leaflet that would enable me to apply for a course of therapy.

'The waiting list is around 16 to 20 weeks,' he added. 'Although it might be slightly less for group therapy. In any case, I strongly recommend you take something in the meantime if you're feeling very bad.'

Group therapy conjured an image of white-tiled school changing rooms: all your flaws and blemishes exposed to potential mockery under a pitiless strip-light. Or a dim church basement full of shabby people mumbling in a circle on orange plastic chairs, clutching Styrofoam cups of thin coffee; how was such a concentration of other people's misery supposed to jolt us out of our own? Or was it the aggregate itself that was meant to be comforting? I declined the offer of group therapy.

'There is also a counselling service,' the doctor began, 'though that would not be with a qualified psychologist.'

'What about if I wanted to see a psychiatrist?'

This time he looked at me as if I had requested an audience with the Pope.

'Why would you want to see a psychiatrist?'

'Well, because it keeps coming back, I thought it might be something more serious.'

He explained briskly that NHS psychiatrists were in very short supply and were occupied in specialist units seeing patients with serious mental health problems, people who were a real danger to themselves and others. If I wanted to consult a psychiatrist, he said, I would have to do it privately. Perhaps he thought I was impugning his diagnostic skills. Perhaps it was simply that, with only a ten-minute appointment slot, the only options available to him in the current guidelines were to offer me medication as an interim measure while I joined the long slow queue for therapy, where demand still far outstrips supply and a five-month waiting list was one of the best you could hope to find in the country. He was not brusque, but he made clear that if I wanted alternative treatments I would have to experiment with those in my own time; he was offering proven pharmaceutical intervention which, yes, may have one or two uncomfortable side effects, but would at least alleviate my symptoms, and he seemed quite nonplussed by my reluctance to accept them.

I shrank back in my chair, feeling just as I had been afraid of feeling for so long before I found the courage to go ask for medical help the first time: that he might think I was frivolous, that I was aggrandising quite average problems, that I was imagining a label of serious illness where only ordinary problems existed. *I'm* a real danger to myself, I wanted to tell him, but I was afraid he wouldn't believe me and would tell me to stop being silly. Because I look normal, because I scrabble to keep a lid on it, because I only take off the necessary face when I'm alone, why would anyone believe that I need help? Maybe if I stopped trying to survive it and just allowed myself to collapse, maybe then he would take me seriously. But I couldn't do this, because I had to keep my job in order to care for my son, and to do that I had to hide the depression, and so the pattern continued.

Defeated, I walked home with nothing but a leaflet. Sixteen to 20 weeks was four or five months; it was like the prospect of pulling on to a motorway after a night of no sleep in the knowledge that there was no rest stop for the next several hundred miles. And there was no guarantee that the wait would be worthwhile; I had read that cognitive therapy was highly effective but I had no way of knowing whether it would work for me. My experience of talking cures did not lead to high expectations; to endure another five months of feeling as I now felt, only to wait for one more failed attempt to communicate it, to have it understood, when there was an available means of improving my condition – this, as Bono might have said, was like choosing to have the flu. From my GP's side of the desk, with ten minutes to diagnose and dispatch me, I must have seemed frustratingly perverse; medical intervention rarely comes without side effects, and it would be a foolish patient who refused life-saving treatment for cancer or diabetes on the grounds that they were afraid of minor discomfort from the side effects. It was even possible that it was my aversion to the idea of medication that was persuading him that my depression could not be all that serious. Halfway home I almost turned back in desperation, almost ran the half-mile back to the surgery to hammer on his door and beg him for the drugs after all, for immediate relief at any price. For a moment I dithered in the street, the desire to slide out from under this present despair pitted against the residual suspicion that I had not been given all the information, that I was merely being processed by a system that was not interested in the details of my experience but simply wanted me shifted from the in-tray to the out-tray as quickly as possible – not the fault of my doctor himself, but of the system as a whole. But I felt convinced that it could not simply be drugs or nothing, just as I felt increasingly sure that there was more to be learned, some deep mystery to be unlocked, about why this kept on happening to me. A small gem of resistance hardened in me; while I still had some will left to me and impetus to try, I determined to research what I could for myself, to experiment on my own mind from within the confines of depression. I could not, I reasoned, get much worse, and if nothing worked, I could always slink back and humbly take the prescription after all.

I did not know what exactly I was hoping to find. In the days when I had been religious, alternative medicine had been viewed askance, treated with a nervous aversion in case it carried the whiff of eastern spirituality. And once I had excised religion from my life, I had no inclination towards fringe versions of it; any philosophy that came dressed in the flourishes of 'spirituality' demanded a step towards the irrational that made me impatient. I did not want anything that would involve chakras or a reverential use of the word 'energy'; I was looking for a treatment that would make logical, empirical sense, in the way that I could understand how and why SSRI antidepressants worked on the brain – but without the side effects. I didn't even know if such a treatment existed, but I dimly remembered having once read an article on how omega 3 oils – the kind found in oily fish – could be effective as mood stabilisers. Clutching this flake of information, I began some preliminary Internet research and ended up at the Brain Bio Centre in Richmond, London, a private outpatient clinic attached to the Institute of Optimum Nutrition founded by the nutritionist Patrick Holford and specialising in the use of nutrition therapy for the treatment of mental illness. The centre claimed to have successfully treated patients suffering from a variety of conditions including depression, bipolar disorder, schizophrenia, Alzheimer's, Attention Deficit Disorder and autism, and after reading Holford's book, *Optimum Nutrition for the Mind*, I felt it seemed plausible enough to investigate further.

Orthomolecular or nutritional medicine works on the premise that brain chemistry can be drastically altered by environmental factors such as chemical pollutants, toxins and the kind of 'affluent malnutrition' prevalent in developed societies, where we may not be starving – quite the reverse – but our heavily processed diet is badly lacking in essential minerals and vitamins. Just as the body needs certain nutrients to function physically – calcium, for example, to build bones – so the biochemical pathways in the brain rely on a balance of vitamins, minerals and amino acids in order to work efficiently. The neurotransmitters that govern mood and motivation – adrenalin, noradrenalin, dopamine and serotonin – are created from amino acids, and a number of key nutrients are essential to this biochemical process, including B vitamins, zinc, magnesium and Essential Fatty Acids (omega 3, 6 and 9). Where conventional psychiatric medicine works by redressing imbalances in brain chemistry through pharmaceutical drugs, nutrition therapy treats deficiencies with naturally derived supplements which do not carry the same risk of addiction or severe side effects, but which work on a similar principle.

I had not expected the science to be so sophisticated. My under-informed assumptions about nutrition therapy were that it would be a matter of telling me to drink green tea and eat more oily fish, so that, arriving at the clinic for my first appointment, I had expected to walk away smug in the knowledge that I was already gleaming with nutritional self-righteousness. It was almost six months since I had given up drinking and, with it, everything else I had once enjoyed, and leaving aside the annoying suspicion that it was this radical abstinence that had precipitated my current bout of depression, I imagined the nutritionists would see me as a model patient. I did, after all, get through an awful lot of soy products.

Instead I was sent off to a lab to have blood, urine and hair samples bagged up and tested for essential mineral and vitamin deficiencies. I also learned that my low-carbohydrate diet, while keeping me from putting on weight, was playing havoc with my blood sugar and was a sure contributor to fatigue and mood swings. Like the connection between drinking and mood, this was so obvious that I should not really have needed an expensive consultation to point it out, but somehow its very obviousness had made me dismiss it. I had always felt, in the gulleys of my depressions, that I could not begin to pull myself out of them through will alone, no matter how widely accepted the notion that a functioning adult should be able to control his or her moods. The idea that I could influence my internal weather through small, practical changes to my lifestyle came as a revelation.

According to David Smith, Professor of Pharmacology at the University of Oxford and Chair of the Scientific Advisory Board for the charity Food for the Brain, there is a degree of scepticism over nutritional medicine among the medical and scientific community, particularly in the arena of mental health. He attributes this view to dated teaching on nutrition in medical degrees and a lack of funding for the kind of large-scale academic studies that would give present research a more solid and widely accepted foundation. 'Until a few years ago, I was a sceptic myself,' explains Professor Smith, whose own research concentrates on the uses of folic acid and B12 supplements in the treatment of cognitive decline and Alzheimer's among older people. 'I thought if you had a balanced diet there was no need for supplements. This is the dominant view among doctors and scientists and I came to the conclusion that it was wrong. "A balanced diet" can mean different things at different stages of life and for different conditions, and the guidelines for daily amounts are completely arbitrary and vary in different countries, so there are no objective criteria. Doctors are only taught about vitamins incidentally, in terms of the diseases caused by severe deficiencies – scurvy or rickets for example – so they are not taught that the brain's biochemical pathways depend on the right levels of vitamins.'

The greatest obstacle to a wider acceptance of nutritional medicine, he explains, is that there are simply not enough clinical trials on a sufficiently large scale and at the moment it is extremely difficult to secure funding to allow such trials to take place. Vitamin supplements are cheap compared with pharmaceutical drugs, a fact which ought to be a bonus but in practice means that the companies which produce quality supplements don't have the kind of money to devote to clinical research that the drug companies can supply, so that unless funding is forthcoming privately or from the government it is hard to see how such research can expand and progress except through small-scale trials. Some more informed doctors may suggest supplements to patients with milder forms of depression, but the lack of extensive clinical trials together with an increasingly litigious public attitude towards the medical profession mean that it would be a very rare doctor who would risk prescribing a patient a supplement programme instead of a course of proven antidepressant medication.

In addition to the lab tests, I had been asked to fill in a highly detailed questionnaire which seemed to cover almost every possible aspect of my mental and physical responses – there were questions about sleep patterns, reactions to stress and to different types of foods and drugs, but others that seemed to me to have nothing to do with mood – questions about sensitivity to light, circulation, whether I tanned easily and whether I was quick or slow to orgasm. Nutrition therapy takes an almost exclusively biochemical approach to mental health (though the centre does recommend talking therapies and regular exercise as supplementary supports) and to a trained nutritionist the answers to all the above questions provide a complete picture of a patient's physical health, which in turn reveals symptoms of underlying deficiencies or allergies that may be affecting mood. Even here the science does not permit a definitive unravelling of cause and effect – strong emotions such as grief or anger are produced by chemical changes in the brain and create a domino effect of chemical changes in their turn (does a low level of serotonin cause depression, or is it the result?) but the treatment offers a programme which can effectively correct the imbalances underlying the depression, often enabling patients to respond better to therapy or to feel better able to manage their situation. I was prescribed an initial daily programme consisting of two high-quality multivitamins, four grammes of omega 3 fish oil, an active B6 and zinc supplement, two grammes of vitamin C and 200 milligrammes of 5-HTP, a substance derived from an African plant, gryffonia, which increases levels of the amino acid tryptophan, a precursor to serotonin. Clinical trials carried out in 2006 by Philip Cowen, Professor of Psychopharmacology at Oxford, suggest that supplementing tryptophan improves serotonin synthesis, boosting levels in the brain in the same way as SSRI antidepressants. One of the most obvious characteristics of depression is the way it inclines you to take the most negative interpretation of any given situation; extraordinary as it may sound, Professor Cowen's research suggests that tryptophan supplements can work to redress that imbalance, actually influencing cognitive processing to take a more positive view. Another study at the University of Basel found that among depressed patients 5-HTP supplements out-performed the leading SSRI antidepressant medication, but with none of the unpleasant side effects associated with the drugs. Given the scientific evidence available for its efficacy and the low cost of 5-HTP compared to drugs, it does seem remarkable that doctors and psychiatrists hardly ever recommend it to patients, and again suggests an institutionalised suspicion of nutritional therapy.

I had my own doubts, but while I waited to see how this treatment programme would take effect, I made an appointment with a psychiatrist. Here, for the first time, my adult life was mapped out in mood swings. He drew a chart where the horizontal axis represented all the years from my first depression and also represented a normal or balanced mood; the vertical axis was calibrated from 0 to +5 and downwards to -5 to represent fluctuating moods up towards the over-energised, over-confident sense of elation I had sometimes experienced and down to the nadir of depression in the other direction. I filled in the major changes in mood I could remember and explained that there were many more, less severe episodes I could not date exactly. When we had finished, the chart looked like a child's drawing of the sea, or a roller coaster. He asked me about my family's psychiatric history, which I had never explored. He also asked me about my reaction to the antidepressant medication I had been prescribed by my GP three years earlier, and when I told him about the agitation, the dreams and the pent-up aggression, he nodded sagely and folded his hands together. Then he asked me what I knew about bipolar disorder. I knew enough to know that it is the present name for manic depression; I also knew that this was what my friend Henry who had committed suicide had suffered, and I was still sure that, since I was not gifted like Henry, I did not have the right to be ill like Henry.

The psychiatrist went on to explain what I had not previously known: that the psychiatric profession now divides bipolar disorder into a number of sub-categories with varying severity of symptoms. What used to be called 'manic depression' as a designation for the more extreme form of the illness, where manic episodes are so severe that they impair the patient's normal functioning and can sometimes be characterised by psychotic or delusional symptoms, is now known as 'Bipolar I'. But there are further categories, Bipolar II and Cyclothymia, in which the patient experiences hypomania, the less severe form of manic behaviour, which does not result in divorce from reality or complete impairment requiring hospitalisation, but which may, nonetheless, lead to behaviour with painful or embarrassing consequences – gleeful overspending, excessive drug or alcohol intake, thrill-seeking and sexual disinhibition. Mood disorders such as bipolar were most commonly first experienced in the late teens or early twenties, often triggered by stressful life events, often (though not always) found in other members of the family and frequently exacerbated in women by childbirth. Many people were not diagnosed with bipolar until their thirties and were often misdiagnosed in the milder, non-psychotic variants because people sought medical help only for the depression and not when they felt excessively well, with the result that they were often prescribed antidepressants which could then precipitate an episode of mania or mixed state. The triggers need not even be negative events, he explained – episodes of hypomania could be ignited by falling in love or a sudden success.

It was as if he were describing me to myself; as if my experience had been cut open, pinned under glass and labelled in all its constituent parts, like a butterfly caught by a collector. He was citing a set of diagnostic criteria from a textbook, yet he seemed to be describing my past as if he had witnessed it. That all these episodes I had considered unique to me, the accidental outcome of circumstances added to my own selfish or thoughtless or idiosyn-cratic behaviour, could have been so clinically and precisely set down in outline by a professional body who had never met me seemed extraordinary, and that my erratic and unpredictable moods could be so easily recognised as a 'condition' was hard to reconcile with my sense of self. I found that I was near to crying, and it surprised me to acknowledge that this was partly out of a sense of relief. Perhaps this diagnosis meant that I was not an alto-gether terrible person! Perhaps there had been instances where

I had genuinely not been in control of my moods and simply been carried by them because I was not able to recognise what was happening. The guilt that had dogged me since that first experience of depression in my teens – the sense that I was, at heart, a bad person and that everything that was wrong with me was in some way a result of turning away from God – was momentarily lifted. I was not a bad person – I was *ill*! It was tempting to see this as my sick-note for everything regrettable I had ever done – it wasn't me, it was the illness!

'It is a kind of disability,' the psychiatrist said, lacing and unlacing his fingers. 'You seem to have a relatively mild form of it, but it is something you will have to learn to live with and manage, in the same way that you would if you had a physical condition such as diabetes.' He went on to talk about medication, and why the most commonly prescribed SSRI antidepressants can be problematic if taken without a mood stabiliser because they can sometimes precipitate a manic or hypomanic episode. Of mood stabilisers I knew only that the most usual was lithium, and what little I had heard of lithium was that it made you fat, shattered your concentration and muffled all your capacity to feel emotion. This is only partly true: in carefully monitored doses, lithium can be highly effective and has restored the possibility of a relatively normal way of life to many thousands of people with the more severe forms of bipolar disorder. But it is also true that, for many people, the longer they stay on lithium, the more severe their condition becomes if they try to come off it, and I was afraid of ending up dependent on something that I might be able to do without. Panicked, I explained my fear of medication and that I was trying out a regime of supplements; to my relief, he said he did not think I appeared to need any kind of mood stabiliser at this stage and went on to outline the positive effects of 'self-management' – regular exercise, diet, particularly a careful regulating of stimulants such as alcohol and caffeine, and cognitive therapy – that would allow me to recognise my 'triggers' and attempt to exert a measure of control over them.

'A lot of people who have it are very high-achievers, you know,' the psychiatrist called cheerfully, as if by way of consolation, as I was on my way out. 'Artists, captains of industry, creative people. Like, you know—' he rummaged for an example and then triumphantly pulled out 'Hemingway!', smiling broadly as if I should be pleased by the comparison. I couldn't help feeling that Hemingway was perhaps not the best example of someone who successfully managed his mood disorder, but I didn't like to argue. 'Thank you,' I said, as if it were a compliment.

About a week after beginning the nutritional supplement programme I had to travel to Edinburgh for work. On my first morning there I woke up in my hotel room and knew immediately that the black mood had lifted, just as I had known two years earlier when the medication had finally taken effect. It was not a grand sense of elation or joy, just a quiet knowledge that, for the first time in months, I was looking at the world with clear eyes, as it really was. Unspectacular, but not catastrophic. I was no longer being crushed. The unfamiliar room was washed with chilly sunlight and it was startling to recall that this was how it felt to be normal. With hours to fill between interviews, I walked through the city in the brittle January air, breath pluming behind me, face slapped raw by the wind. I had dreaded this return to a city that was peopled by memories of some of my most notable romantic triumphs and failures, where I could follow like a heritage trail the streets, bars, cafés, parks and hilltops where I had wept or railed or gazed or made fragile promises to someone or other over the years, places imprinted with the outline of people who had once mattered, people who had once seemed as if they might hold the map of my future, but the light in the sky and the unexpected uprush of lightness in my head and across my chest lent this retracing an air of tender, amused nostalgia. It seemed, to my distinct surprise, that I might be better. I realised that I had not really believed that a cocktail of vitamin supplements bought from a health food shop could make any noticeable impact on my cladding of hopelessness, but despite my lack of faith, a minor miracle had happened.

Feeling better immediately cast a gauze of doubt over my experience with the psychiatrist. Perhaps he had jumped to conclusions, I thought. It was true that I was a little mercurial, a little too intense sometimes, my reactions arguably disproportionate to circumstance, but was this necessarily to be classified as an illness? What had he called it – a *disability*? I did not, drinking coffee in an Edinburgh café while I waited to interview a well-known writer, feel like someone with a disability. But if it kept happening, if it was true that I could not handle disappointment, failure or loss with equanimity, if the ordinary business of living plunged me into pitches of mood so severe that I ended up at the edge of despair every time, could I go on deceiving myself that it would all stop and right itself just as soon as life sorted itself out and delivered a fabulous break, as soon as it stopped being prologue and announced the beginning of the main act? Was it not, perhaps, time to realise that I was the one who would have to make the significant changes rather than waiting for the circumstances to provide them? Perhaps, I reflected, this self-management business might just be part of the process of growing up.

There is a curious wobble of identity that comes with being diagnosed with something as complex as a mood disorder, as with any condition that affects the mind and its ability to perceive and respond to reality, since the mind is where we locate our notion of who we are. To be told that you have a disorder of the spleen would not, however unpleasant, cause you to question your essential character. But we feel – perhaps instinctively, perhaps through conditioning – that the mind is the seat of the self, and that the mark of a civilised adult is the ability to control one's moods and one's reactions, however much we might want to scream and rant and run away. The idea that at times you might not be the master of your own mind is deeply unsettling, yet there is also a temptation to call it in as an excuse. If I accept that some of the more extreme moods I have experienced in adult life were the result of a chemical imbalance prompted by an innate condition that was exacerbated by external events (and drugs and alcohol), is that a way of abdicating responsibility for my actions? Although I have on occasion experienced a sense of being 'possessed' by a mood, either of elation or despair – the sensation that my mind had galloped off beyond my control and that the best I could do was cling on until it slowed down again – I don't think I have ever truly been on the wrong side of reason. I have never been in a position where I lost altogether the ability to make moral choices, so that when I have acted in ways that made me later ashamed, it has always been, ultimately, the result of my decision to act regardless of the consequences. It seemed that it would be disingenuous for me to blame behaviour that was selfish, thoughtless, reckless, aggressive, exhibitionist or dangerous, and which abused the trust and tried the patience of the people who cared about me, on aberrant brain chemistry. Or was it? Could I be excused my worst excesses? Was character – or chemistry – really destiny?

Wanting to learn more about this condition that I felt both was and was not part of me, I visited the Mood Disorder Research Team at the University of Cardiff, the leading research specialists into the causes and nature of bipolar disorder. Here, Professor Nick Craddock and Dr Ian Jones are carrying out the largest study into bipolarity anywhere in the world, with over two thousand participants to date. They are also working on devising a new diagnostic scale to reflect the fact that mood disorders are vastly complex and cover a broad spectrum – some people may experience only brief, mild hypomanic episodes but severe recurring depression, while others may suffer grandiose, delusional manias but only moderate depression – and eventually enable professionals to better tailor treatment to the individual's symptoms rather than relying on standardised treatments that fit the designated existing categories.

One strand of Professor Craddock's research is concerned with what actually takes place in the brain during the mood swings of bipolar disorder. 'It's most helpful to think in terms of the way our mood state is responding all the time to what's going on in the world,' he explained. 'If something good happens, you feel happy, something bad happens, you feel worse – but sometimes anybody can wake up in the morning and feel grumpy or upset for no reason. That's going on all the time – our mood changes partly in response to circumstance and partly of its own accord, but it regulates itself and generally keeps within certain limits. But in somebody with bipolar disorder, whatever does the normal regulation of mood doesn't keep it within normal limits so it either goes to extremes of mood or is fluctuating very rapidly. We know a bit about some of the brain systems that might be involved, but the purpose of the research is to properly pin those down so we can develop treatments that will precisely target what's out of balance and help people to keep their mood within normal limits.'

I felt oddly vindicated, hearing this. It was official: my brain did not know how to operate within normal emotional limits. But where did that leave my sense of moral responsibility? If I had made different decisions in my life, and consequently lived through different experiences, might I have avoided the worst of these mood swings, or were the decisions I made influenced by the fact that I was prone to extremes of behaviour? If, for example, I had remained within the church among people who did not drink to excess, take drugs, spend recklessly or sleep around, who lived a more measured, self-contained life, might I not have exacerbated my hypomanic episodes and not indulged that exuberant, immensely enjoyable sensation of hurtling at speed towards whatever catastrophe beckoned – or would those moods have come anyway, and would the necessity of self-restraint have made things worse? Instinctively I felt that, looking back, the paths I had taken had been directed to some extent by my tendency towards extremes of mood and by a quest for intensely lived moments. But I did not want to accept that I would always be steered by these moods or that they would always hold the greater influence over the way I lived. I could use the nutritional supplements and a carefully managed diet to aid a purely biochemical stability, but I also had to learn how to achieve emotional equilibrium, and for this I turned to Cognitive Behaviour Therapy.

CBT was developed in the 1960s and 1970s as a practical, shorter-term alternative to psychoanalysis, and works on the very simple, almost simplistic, premise that the way we look at the world and ourselves directly colours how we behave and feel. In contrast to traditional forms of analysis, which sift painstakingly, sometimes over the course of years, through early experiences and attempt to recover events perhaps lost in the unconscious, CBT works by identifying negative thought patterns and processes in the present and correcting them through small, practical exercises, so that we begin to counter the feelings of guilt, hopelessness and failure that characterise episodes of depression and to re-learn behaviour that encourages self-confidence and positive interpretations. CBT has been prominently discussed in the British media in the past few years since it remains the only form of therapy to be measured by rigorous scientific studies, which show it to have a significant rate of success – either alone or in conjunction with medication – in lifting sufferers out of depression and preventing recurrence.

I had read about CBT and approached it with curiosity and scepticism; despite all the studies testifying to its success, it seemed to me infected with the language of self-help books. I had lived through enough depressions to know that you don't just make the black weather dissipate with a bit of positive thinking, and the idea of having to do 'homework' exercises, writing down my feelings in a little notebook and confecting counter-statements, made me cringe; it reminded me of youth group camps. This was not how I dealt with the turbulent mass of emotion that gathered in me; what I did was to hoard all the dark and difficult feelings until I had the chance to offload them on someone else, someone invented, who could carry the weight of it through a novel while I looked on, always finding those feelings more manageable when they were being experienced by someone else, even if it was someone I had made up. To take all that emotion and instead process it through bald, anodyne worksheets seemed anathema. Yet I was intrigued: this kind of therapy also promised exactly what I had craved and found missing from my brief experience with the Jungian analyst years before – a practical solution to changing the way I reacted to situations. It might at least be worth a try.

While I waited to shuffle in grinding increments up the five-month NHS waiting list, I found a highly qualified private therapist (possible only because I was writing about the experience for a magazine, which funded the first few sessions) who practised out of an imposing colonnaded house in Harley Street. The downstairs waiting room was furnished like a drawing-room set from a Regency drama, its other inhabitants poised in tailored suits, respectfully avoiding eye-contact and concentrating instead on articles in the copies of *Vogue* or *House and Garden* that lay artfully scattered on the little mahogany occasional tables. Everyone was white and looked as if they belonged to the professional classes; glancing furtively from one to another, I wondered if we were all secretly troubled in the same way. Had all these smart, attractive people considered jumping off a train at one time or another? Beneath the grooming, did they all know how it felt to hate themselves, to be so sunk in despair they had to fight for breath? Had they all sat through a sleepness night in a dark room, silently rocking, afraid they were sliding into madness, or run through city streets at night because they feared they might explode out of their own heads? Or had they come because, within a certain demographic, therapy is fashionable, like a health spa (as long as it costs enough)?

I warmed to the therapist straight away, and this instantly made me want to run for the door. Over the course of the first session, it became abundantly clear that, though I had spent weeks longing for a professional ear to whom I could unburden myself, in practice I was trenchantly resistant to doing so. With every gentle question, I clammed up further, conscious of the absurdity of this transaction reduced to its bald facts: I had just paid a considerable amount of money to invite a stranger to poke around in the most painful and intimate areas of my life, and now that I was expected to play my part, I found I didn't want to tell her anything. I didn't want her to know about me; it was too risky, to hand over so much to another person. And it was not just that I didn't want to let her in or open myself up; I found that I *couldn't* articulate anything difficult or true aloud, I could only do so in writing, so that I was reduced to a bad parody of a teenager, responding with grunts and shrugs and obviously desperate to get away. In part I was afraid of being judged: I wanted this compassionate, fearsomely intelligent woman to think well of me, and how would she be able to do that if I told her the truth – about how I felt about myself as a mother, for example, how fundamentally flawed I believed myself to be in that regard, or about the many ways I would sometimes feel compelled to send myself out of control, and the self-loathing that inevitably followed? I was also terrified of the possibility that I might cry in front of her; so much of my energy over the years had been dedicated to making sure I kept that separate from the rest of the world, I found myself braced against it, all the muscles in my face humming with the tension of making sure it didn't happen, though she placed a box of tissues provocatively on the coffee table between us, as if challenging me to a stand-off. Similarly, the one little exercise she gave me as the week's 'homework' filled me with pulse-racing dread. I had to complete the following three sentences: '*Life is…; I am…; so I…*' I agonised over it all the way home and for the rest of the week, and every time I thought about possible words I would experience a hammering of anxiety and a kind of vertigo. Three words; I couldn't do it. I was furious with myself and sat up long into the night writing lists, but nothing seemed right. I got as far as 'Life is… *shit*', but felt that wouldn't really do. I had written two books and a film as well as ten years' worth of newspaper articles, and yet I could not produce three useful words in a week. Perhaps, I thought glumly, I was not some-one who could be helped by therapy, in the way that there are, apparently, people who just do not respond to antibiotics.

I persisted, and lasted a further three weeks. In part this was because my subsidised sessions ran out and although I could feasi-bly have gone on paying for the therapy myself, there remained a deeply ingrained sense of conscience that still baulked every time at the idea of paying that much money to talk grudgingly about myself for an hour when there were people starving. Even without the starving millions, who were mainly an excuse in the abstract (I did not, on quitting therapy, start sending 130 pounds a week to Oxfam, I'm sorry to admit), it seemed an indulgence I could not justify, especially when it was not as if it was saving my life, when so far I felt I was deliberately sabotaging any good the therapy might potentially do me by my refusal to participate properly. I knew that part of the point of CBT was that the patient has to engage with the therapy and exert themselves to take responsibil-ity for effecting change, but this mode of unpicking thoughts, anatomising and classifying them, sieving them for negative prop-erties, was so far from the way I approached my feelings and responses that I was finding it hard to take my own attempts at the exercises seriously; it seemed so potentially reductive, in a way that, oddly, reducing my emotional life to the interaction of neurotransmitters had not. Even so, I was sorry to give up the therapy, but also mightily relieved; I realised that all along I had not been able to avoid thinking of it, with its writing exercises, as one more form of work, another set of demands being made, one extra reason to become over-stressed and afraid of letting people down. This, too, was an excuse: I ran from a therapist I liked and respected and could, in time, have learned to trust, because some part of me was horrified by the idea of showing too much of myself, letting her get too close or becoming too needy or dependent on her, just as I had from many other relationships. I was almost impressed by the fact that I had sufficient self-knowledge to realise this, though it brought me no nearer to a solution.

I tried again, months later, when the NHS wait finally expired. The appointment, when it arrived, was in a wing of an obscure hospital which sprawled on a hillside above the town where I lived, its buildings Victorian and ominous, lowering over the terraces and railway lines. I had driven past it on occasion and wondered, with only the most cursory curiosity, what went on behind its walls that was different from what happened at the real hospital on the outskirts of the town. Now I understood: though this was not exclusively a psychiatric hospital, much of its space was given over to departments of mental health care and the place had an air of neglect about it, its very ambience a vigorous deterrent. The sensation of entering the dim corridor marked 'Psychological Therapies' could not have been more different from the dainty Harley Street sitting room. There, the starkness of needing help for mental health problems was dressed up with money; that the waiting room had looked like a boutique hotel had distracted us all from what we were doing there, or at least had made it seem like a lifestyle choice. Now, in a narrow, overheated room with peeling walls and the dejected atmosphere of a badly underfunded class-room, I sat opposite a woman who was quietly pulling out small hanks of her own hair while reading a magazine, and a man vigorously rocking back and forth and smiling so hard I could almost hear the muscles in his face straining. He was accompanied by a large woman in a mac who looked as if she were pretending to be somewhere else. The man swung the beam of his smile around the room and fixed it on me; God, I thought, I hope he doesn't try to have a conversation. No – that is disingenuous – what I actually thought was: *I hope the mental patient doesn't talk to me.* And then, for the first time, I understood where I was and what it meant, and was instantly ashamed: I too was now a mental patient, or at least an outpatient in a psychiatric hospital, and immediately I wanted to bolt for the door, or find the person in charge and explain that there had been a terrible administrative error: I was not supposed to be here, my case was different, there had to be some kind of special dispensation. It was exactly how I had felt in the Job Centre all those years ago, and again it both was and wasn't true: I was no different from the other patients in my need of help, but I did possess, through education and support, the potential not to be trapped in this indefinitely. I suspected that some of my fellow patients were not so lucky.

I was dismayed to find myself faced with a male therapist and instantly a whole region of trouble – love, motherhood, sex – was ring-fenced off and declared out of bounds for these sessions; there was no way I wanted to bring any of that into the light for him to examine. It was uncomfortable enough shut away in that small consulting room, through whose grubby net curtains I could see only a slab of wan sky. In the first session he took a detailed history of my depressions and high-voltage moods and then presented me with a collection of leaflets on Managing Bipolar Disorder. I had to write in three separate columns aspects of how I lived and behaved when 'normal', depressed or elated; when I had finished, it sounded as though I had described three different people. I was also to keep a 'mood diary' of how my moods fluctuated between +5 and -5 so that I could track the swings and identify 'triggers'.

Over the next two sessions we examined, with the help of what I considered to be slightly condescending worksheets, different patterns of learned negative responses to situations that may become more acute during episodes of depression and of which we may not even be conscious. Jumping to conclusions based on our own negative feelings; discounting positives and concentrating on negative interpretations; 'personalising' or 'catastrophising'; over-generalising or seeing things only in terms of absolutes; only when I stopped to dissect and analyse these styles of thinking did I realise how much they formed the way I looked at the world, even when I was not depressed.

Here I came up against what I felt to be the fundamental flaw in cognitive therapy: that it asks you to change your thinking, when your thinking might in fact be an accurate response to circumstances. If you are crucified with self-hatred and overwhelmed by hopelessness because you believe yourself to be monstrously fat, even though you are wearing size 10 jeans, or you are afraid to leave the house because you think people are trying to kill you, then this is negative thinking that clearly needs to be corrected and realigned with reality. But if the truth is that you are overwhelmed by hopelessness because you are old or sick or disabled or lonely, or you have lost a job that gave you status and self-esteem, or someone you love has died or betrayed your trust or simply removed themselves from your life, what then? How do you change the way you think about these 'life events', I wondered, when the events them-selves are not going to change, unless you start telling yourself cheery untruths? Few things are more unbearable in the darkness of depression than a well-meaning friend who tries to jolly you along with platitudes about how it will all work out and things aren't as bad as they seem; was I now expected to provide that infu-riating voice in my own ear? I understood the theory: that you learn not to extrapolate absolutes from one particular situation (because one relationship failed does not mean you are unlovable; missing out on a promotion does not mean you are talentless, or that you will *always* be passed over); that you set yourself smaller, incremental goals, so that you can count successes instead of fail-ures; that you learn to separate your sense of self-worth from circumstances that are dependent on others or on events beyond your control. If you can't change the situation, you can at least learn to look at it from a different perspective and adapt your response to it, increasing your sense of control, which seems obvi-ous; perhaps the techniques of cognitive therapy can seem condescending because they are based on common sense, on things we already know in theory. But the problem with depression is that it fogs reason: what if you *can't* talk yourself back to life, if you can't persuade yourself that there is anything worth looking forward to, what then? Who then will persuade you to keep trying, to keep hoping?

I did not get a chance to ask the therapist these questions because I abandoned the therapy abruptly a week later, without having intended to. The dawn had unfolded to reveal a hard, blue autumn sky, high and bright, the first glimpse of sun after days of close, grey weather that had intimated but never quite climaxed in storms; for days I had been feeling a corresponding upswell of that old restless energy – not to its usual degree, because I was still faithfully taking the supplement programme – but enough to have begun a spiral of distressing thoughts. My parents were away in the States, and the sensation of being trapped was always more acute in their absence, implying as it did the greater, permanent absence that awaited me one day; as a result, I had become convinced, to a degree that verged on paranoid, that they were not coming home, that their plane was going to crash, that I was alone in the world. Driving my son to school that bright morning, I was involved in an altercation with a lorry driver who was trying to go the wrong way down a one-way street; during the brief stand-off, his unapologetic disregard for signposts caused something in me to stretch too far and snap with a sharp report – in a white rage I opened my door and screamed out a violent torrent of abuse – if he had descended from his cab at that moment I don't doubt that I would have attempted to hit him. I stood in the road until eventually he backed down and moved his truck, muttering something about mad bitches.

Adrenalised and light-headed, I left my son at school and began the drive to the hospital for my appointment with the therapist; as I neared the turning, I knew that I could not, in this state, spend an hour in that stuffy room with its endlessly re-breathed air, listening to what I found to be mostly platitudes. A sudden inspiration struck: what I needed was to see the sea! Only its vastness and grandeur could correspond in any way with the majestic fury in my head, and with a glorious sense of truancy, I sailed past the road to the hospital and headed out to the dual carriageway for the coast. For the best part of the day I paced up and down the beach, frightening the few scattered birdwatchers along the estuary by roaring into the wind, and by lunchtime all the violence and coiled energy had been dispersed, carried by the waves, and I sat in the lea of the sea wall, under a lukewarm sun, and felt cleansed and calmed. I watched the seagulls and smiled to myself, thinking that I had known, after all, what I best needed; I would not, I was sure, now be feeling such calm and a sense of rightness if I had kept my appointment with the therapist. If I lived beside the sea, I thought fervently, I would never again feel the creeping sense of being possessed, the fear of being alienated from myself; I would always be calm and free, and immediately I started making plans to move to the coast – typical hypomanic train of thought. The healing properties of nature for troubled minds are well-documented, most recently in Richard Mabey's haunting memoir *Nature Cure*, and recent studies have shown that regular walks in the country-side can be as effective as medication in combating symptoms of incipient depression, but my restlessness is always such that even the sea would not be a lasting cure. I would crave the city, the pulse of its energy, and in the city begin to crave the empty horizon again. I have been extremely fortunate in carving out a way of making a living that means no one notices if I take a day without warning to run up and down a beach until I feel less crazy; if I could recommend one self-administered treatment for depression and its corollaries, it would be this freedom to escape the confines we create for ourselves and reconnect with the world around us, to drive straight past the turning we were expected to take and, laugh-ing or roaring into the wind, run to the coast, breathe deeply, skim stones into the glittering waves and allow the sun to burn off every-thing inessential until we discover what is left beneath the parts we unreflectingly continue to play, the expectations we bow to and shrink under.

One final word about therapy: though, for me, it has never been the preferred way to dissect and understand what I feel and why I act or react in particular ways, I have over time absorbed and benefited from many of the basic principles of CBT (mainly through two extremely clear and helpful books, *Overcoming Depression* by Paul Gilbert and *Manage Your Mind* by Gillian Butler and Tony Hope), and I remain firmly convinced of its efficacy either as a supplement or alternative to medication, and equally firmly committed to the campaign for greater investment in psychological therapies so that these can be offered without charge to people seeking help as a real alternative to drug treatment. While I am emphatically not anti-medication – since the licensing of Prozac and other SSRI drugs, these pills have undoubtedly saved many hundreds of thousands of lives, including my own, and vastly improved the quality of life for many sufferers – it does seem that there is widespread anecdotal evidence of antidepressant drugs being prescribed on the most fleeting diagnosis for conditions (including sleep difficulties, bereavement or premenstrual stress) that would once have been expected to resolve naturally or respond well to non-drug treatments. But even here consensus is difficult; many experts agree that antidepressants are too readily prescribed in the developed world without patients being offered or informed about alternatives, but when Professor Gordon Parker of the University of New South Wales published an article in the British Medical Journal in 2007, claiming that the continuing rise in antidepressant prescriptions was due not to a greater prevalence of depressive illness in the population but rather to a lowered diagnostic threshold for depression and clever marketing by pharmaceutical companies, there was an outcry from mental health charities who asserted that it was always better to over-diagnose than to leave people with potentially serious depression untreated.

In addition, in 2002 investigations by the BBC's *Panorama* programme into allegations of serious side effects connected with the commonly prescribed antidepressant Seroxat, including addiction and withdrawal difficulties as well as a rise in rates of self-harm and suicide, suggested that in some cases, particularly among young people, SSRI drugs may cause more problems than they solve, yet the bias in mental health-care research remains in favour of the pharmaceutical companies, so often because they provide the funding for such research. For many people, depression is chronically isolating, often because they do not feel able to discuss it with anyone for fear of stigma or lack of understanding. In our atomised society, the kind of support and pastoral care that might once have been provided by community or religious leaders is often lacking, and the opportunity to talk to a qualified and sympathetic clinical psychologist could make a measurable difference to so many people's lives simply by equipping them with the means to understand and better cope with what is happening to their minds.

6

Faith, Hope and Love

Among my son's storybooks there is one, *The Miraculous Journey of Edward Tulane* by Kate Camillo, which I find almost unbearably poignant. Edward is a supercilious porcelain rabbit whose unfeeling heart is broken and mended over the course of many misfortunes and adventures, teaching him compassion and a capacity for empathy and love that he never possessed when his life was cosseted and easy. Towards the end of the story, Edward finds himself on a shelf in a toy-mender's workshop beside an antique doll who is more than a hundred years old. Edward's hardships and losses have left him embittered and determined never to risk being hurt again; he declares that he is 'done with hope'.

'I don't care if anyone comes for me,' said Edward.

'But that's dreadful,' said the old doll. 'There's no point in going on if you feel that way. No point at all. You must be filled with expectancy. You must be awash in hope. You must wonder who will love you, whom you will love next.'

'I am done with being loved,' Edward told her. 'I'm done with loving. It's too painful.'

'Pish,' said the old doll. 'Where is your courage? …

You disappoint me greatly. If you have no intention of loving or being loved, then the whole journey is pointless. You might as well leap from this shelf right now and let yourself shatter into a million pieces. Get it over with. Get it all over with now.'

'You must be awash in hope.' If depression robs you of hope, then hope must be a ballast against depression. But this is not so easy; when nothing about yourself or your circumstances makes you feel hopeful, hope becomes an act of will rather than a state of mind: a deliberate commitment. I wanted to conclude with an exhortation to anyone who has known what it means to be crushed by the despair of deep depression not to let go of hope, to actively invest in a belief in the future. But hope can also be dangerous: I am persistently reminded of John Cleese's cry of exasperation in Michael Frayn's *Clockwise:* 'It's not the despair, Laura. I can stand the despair. It's the *hope!*'

You know where you are with despair; it doesn't wrong foot you, whereas hope means opening yourself up to the possibility of being disappointed or let down. For a long time I thought hope was all you needed to summon in order to be happy; only recently have I come to understand that acceptance may be just as vital in achieving a kind of peace. But where do you find the balance between acceptance and surrender, between reconciling yourself to your life as it is, even if it is not as you would like it to be, and simply giving up hope of making it better? According to Jung, 'If you sum up what people tell you about their experiences, you can formulate it this way: They came to themselves, they could accept themselves, they were able to become reconciled to themselves, and thus were reconciled to adverse circumstances and events. This is almost like what used to be expressed by saying: He has made his peace with God, he has sacrificed his own will, he has submitted himself to the will of God.'

It is also almost like Reinhold Niebhur's famous Serenity Prayer, so beloved by Alcoholics Anonymous: 'God grant me the serenity to accept the things I cannot change, courage to change the things I can, and the wisdom to know the difference.'

This, in the end, is also the basic tenet of cognitive therapy – except that God is lifted out of the equation, and we must learn to figure out this wisdom, acceptance and courage from our own resources.

More than a year after starting nutrition therapy, I have remained faithful to my regime of supplements and although there have been pitches of mood, often seasonal, their peaks and troughs have been markedly less dramatic. There has not been a recurrence of those crashing, black tides of depression, nor have the upsurges of hypomanic energy swelled into an uncontrollable wave. Though I sometimes experience a sweep of overwhelming melancholy, it is a sensation that remains connected to human emotion rather than the old sense of malevolent possession by a force that could not be fought.

The greatest gift of learning how to stay well has been the revelation of my relationship with my son. Coming out from under the yoke of those black moods, it was as if something was unlocked, and I was astonished to discover the full force of the love I feared myself incapable of feeling; it came into being all at once, as if it had merely been held up in the post, waiting only for me to be restored to myself. My recovery also coincided with his reaching an age where our relationship could be reciprocal, participatory, where he became someone whose company and humour I actively sought and looked forward to, as opposed to the days of his unformed toddlerhood, when entertaining him for a day was often a matter of endurance, and it was gratifying and humbling to see how he blossomed in the light of my newly awakened engagement with life. It was as if we both came to a new kind of consciousness simultaneously; the newness of the companionship we now shared, my delight in being with him, was a little like falling unexpectedly in love.

In the summer of 2006, a few months after I moved shakily back to health, I borrowed a camper van and we drove down to meet friends at an arts festival in Cornwall. After a long, sunlit day filled with music, stories and laughter, my son and I bought pancakes from a little stall and climbed in companionable silence to the top of a hill. Here, as the evening sun slanted golden over the estuary, and music played distantly from behind us as our shadows sloped over the grass, he breathed in deeply, then flung his arms out wide and, turning to me with an expression of pure joy, said fervently, 'Mummy, sometimes I just want to say *thank you* to the world for a lovely day!'

In that moment I had two thoughts. One was that I recognised that surge of feeling. At his age I would already have learned enough in Sunday School to say that I wanted to thank *God* for what I felt: that joyful, awed response to nature and beauty; the awareness of the vibrancy of our own life force and its connection to the world; that passionate, thrumming knowledge of undiluted happiness, of pleasure without guilt, our ability to think and feel and sense and live in a particular moment of time. My son, who had heard very little of formalised religion, felt all this and was moved to thank something greater than himself. Some would call this evidence that the religious impulse is instinctive from child-hood. I would turn the equation around and say that the religious impulse is a name we have invented for this innate, exuberant passion for life.

The second thought was that I wished someone could have told me there would be days like this. In the bleakest moments of the two years after his birth, when I was contemplating jumping from a train, I wish I could have had some idea that the future held golden moments like the one at the top of that hill. Perhaps the essence of learning hope is to believe that life can still deliver these moments, even when they seem more remote than the moon. I have known this passion for life over the years; I have felt it welling up, pure and strong, and I think I have known it more keenly for having brushed up against the possibility of leaving it. When I think of how much I would have missed, had I acted on that impulse, the thought becomes impossible to contemplate, as if someone were threatening to hurt a person I loved. The literature of depression is full of cautionary tales of people who reached the place where it could not be endured shortly before the moment that would have changed everything; the moral, always, is 'don't give up five minutes before the miracle happens.'

I am less turbulent these days, and mostly I am glad to be so. I take my maintenance programme of supplements every day and drink much less, and less often; I try to have a walk or a run outside most days; I am fortunate in being able to structure my work in a way that allows me to manage my own time and try to avoid accepting deadlines or situations that I know will create a degree of stress that I can no longer sustain. With great reluctance, I have turned down jobs that I would have loved because I know I am not yet robust enough to handle levels of stress that I used to find invigorating. This is a question of acceptance: for those of us who are vulnerable to depression, it means learning to be kinder to ourselves, changing our notions of success and failure, reconciling ourselves to scaled-down ambitions. In the worst of it, there may be days when having a bath or walking as far as the end of the street represents a Herculean achievement, even if in the past we have run companies, taught classes, made films or stood for election; on those days, in the furthest reaches of depression, we need to learn to be proud of these small goals instead of measuring ourselves against the person we think we are supposed to be.

Sometimes I am optimistic about what the future holds for me; on other days the prospect of it is frightening, particularly the inevitable future that will one day no longer include my parents and the unconditional love and support they have given me. For now I am much better, but I am not 'cured'; I remain aware of the possibility of its return, of its shadow always hovering at the edges of my line of vision, just out of sight. Perhaps I will be able to keep it at bay for a long time, by recognising it and living in a way that doesn't actively invite it, but I have to acknowledge the probability that prolonged illness, bereavement, heartbreak, perceived or actual failure – however trivial – or perhaps nothing at all, might one day plunge me back into the dark. I live like someone who has built a house on a notorious faultline: every day that passes without incident, I feel as if I have got away with something. But although I will quite probably, at some time, feel again that I would prefer not to go on, I do not think I am likely to spend that coin in my pocket; I have a better grasp now of how to come back from the edge, how to ask for help, and of the reasons to endure.

I am aware, too, that I am probably less fun than I used to be, in one definition of 'fun', now that I have curbed the wild enthusiasm for excess that would sweep other people along in its current. Intensity has been – mostly – sacrificed to moderation and restraint, though if the upsurge of mood is on me and I am away from home, I will occasionally allow myself to hurtle headlong again into the carnival; it cheers my friends to glimpse the person I was, and makes them feel at home, but the price I pay now is high and the pleasure increasingly less worth the bother. Sometimes it seems remarkable that I could have spent the best part of my twenties living like that all the time, or that I would have wanted to. Perhaps this is just an inevitable part of the business of growing up, an achievement our culture whispers to us to defer for as long as possible, and not exclusive to manic depression – the acceptance that, in your thirties, you are no longer in the first act of life, and that while a certain kind of wildness and unpredictability can be sexy in a 22-year-old, it can start to look disturbing ten years later. But the buzz, the energy and disinhibition of hypomania can be addictive; for many years I embraced my mood swings and exulted in their extremes, because the intensity of experience and feeling they unleashed let me know that I was alive, and because what I feared more than anything was an ordinary life, a life without the fierce colours of these moods. I miss it sometimes, that sense of abandonment, of being drenched in feeling so that every mundane task recedes and becomes meaningless in the tsunami of emotion. But I also recognise that this is not a productive way to live, particularly if other people depend on you and your ability to keep a job and pay the mortgage; it is not even, despite my youthful romantic imaginings, the most effective way to create fiction or drama, which come, it turns out, not in great roiling surges of feeling but in steady, painstaking hours at a desk, for which you need to be relatively calm and disciplined (and, generally, sober).

In his 2006 BBC documentary *The Secret Life of the Manic Depressive*, Stephen Fry asked all his interviewees whether, offered a magic button that would take away their mood disorder and allow them a stable, less unpredictable life, they would make the choice to press it. All but one poor woman whose condition was so severe as to have stripped away any semblance of living asserted immediately and emphatically that they would *not*, that their illness had been a gift as well as a curse. Fry himself, despite confessions of suicidal urges and terrible desolation, ends the film by saying, 'I wouldn't have a normal life for all the tea in China.'

There can be something worthwhile in depression if we choose to find it. If we are fortunate, we pass through the dark and emerge altered for the better. My experience of depression, particularly in its increased severity since the birth of my son, has changed me, but I had to learn the significance of those changes. Depression forces a degree of reflection and self-examination for which an untroubled life does not usually provide space. As a result of depression we learn to question our assumptions, our view of ourselves and the way we relate to others, we realign our priorities and reassess what we value and what we aspire to. We have to learn a more realistic assessment of our own limitations, and the grace to live within them. Depression humbles us, and for many of us it is not a bad thing to learn to ask for help, to allow ourselves to be vulnerable and to reach out for a hand to steady us. It teaches us compassion, if we give it the chance. I used to be briskly intolerant of failure, my own and that of others; now I hope I am less judgemental. It has also altered the qualities I value in others and what I look for in someone I might want to share my life with; these days, kindness seems more attractive than charisma. More than anything, I think, it has taught me to love less selfishly, to cling on to a sense of humour and to be profoundly grateful for those fleeting moments of a heightened love of life.

Someone does come for Edward Tulane in the end, of course, once he has let down his defences against the pain of love, because it is a children's story and demands a happy resolution. The little girl who comes is someone special, too, because – the story implies – it takes someone exceptional to love a toy so repeatedly broken and mended, to see beyond all the visible cracks and seams, the clothes patched and worn by experience, and find something of value. Real life does not deliver so reliably. Depressed people are hard to love and require extraordinary patience, just as sometimes it seems impossible to love and be loved from inside the darkest heart of depression. Depression is the loneliest place on earth; no one can reach you there, when you most need to be reached, and even the most steadfast, unswerving love of family and friends must remain an abstract knowledge until you emerge enough to feel again. To believe that life – your life – matters, that what you have to offer is worthwhile, when you are least able to feel it, requires nothing less than faith.

'And now these three remain: faith, hope and love,' says Saint Paul, in his letter to the church at Corinth, quoted at every church wedding you will ever attend. 'But the greatest of these is love.'

I lost – or willingly shook off – an official version of faith, and by a long and often painful route have arrived at another, less doctrinal understanding. The greatest curse of depression is the way it leaches all sense of purpose or value from life; everything you do feels pointless, the forces of history seem stacked against you, everything you once cared about appears to have been devalued or eroded. The world grinds on and your actions are entirely meaningless even to yourself, much less on any larger scale, and so you shut yourself in a room and pull the blankets over your head and wait for the hours unbearably to pass. Pointlessness turns to defeat, and defeat breeds despair. Faith, for me, means insisting on believing that what I do matters in some small way, even when I no longer *feel* that I believe it, in the teeth of that despair.

Recently, as I was travelling to work on a bleak, wet morning in a mood of creeping melancholy, my train was held for a while between stations. From the window I looked out over a vast urban cemetery, empty of living souls except for two elderly nuns tending a grave near the perimeter fence. I watched them as they knelt in the gusting rain, one trimming the borders with a little pair of shears, the other carefully replacing dead flowers with fresh, and my first thought was: *why bother*? Why had they made that journey in such weather, when there was no one to see – not the dead, not God? They were old ladies; it must have cost them a great deal in effort and discomfort, kneeling on the cold ground. Then I understood, with a sudden stab of emotion that I could not quite identify: they had bothered because they believed that it mattered. Perhaps it was the grave of another nun, who had no family to care for it; perhaps they were the only ones who remembered her. Even if no one saw, that small invisible act of love, or thoughtfulness – or loyalty, or duty, or whatever prompted them – was worth the trouble because it connected them to another human being, and thus to the rest of life. And I am glad that they bothered, because it was not, in the end, invisible; *I* saw it, and it reminded me that the value we accord to our own lives is the sum of the value we find in our smallest actions. When you begin to stop caring – when you believe, as depression would have you believe, that nothing is worth the effort – then you stop bothering, and the less you bother, the less reason there seems to carry on. Part of battling depression is holding on to this faith that your life matters, that your smallest gestures can make a difference. This, of course, is the essence of *It's A Wonderful Life*, which, for all its comic angels, has a good humanist moral: you can never know the ripple effect of your own life. If there is one thing I wish I could have said to my friend Henry, had I been given the chance, it is this: *believe that it matters.* The smallest thing, whether for yourself or someone else. When you least feel able to make the effort, do it anyway: walk to the shop and buy some flowers for your kitchen table, even if you feel that every step is going to finish you. Write a letter for Amnesty. Send an email to a friend just to see how they are. Rent a film you love. Remind yourself that there is beauty in the world. Keep bothering. Keep going as if it matters, and trust that one day it will begin to feel like it again.

Hope, too, is a commitment to the future. Though Rebecca Solnit's book *Hope in the Dark* is not about depression but about collective despair and its converse, active political engagement, her words are as pertinent on the individual level as on the global. 'Hopefulness is risky,' she writes, 'because it is, after all, a form of trust, trust in the unknown and the possible, even in discontinuity. To be hopeful is to take on a different persona, one that risks disappointment [and] betrayal.'

And love, what of that? This, too, involves risk. As the old doll wisely says, it requires courage. The only thing I can say for certain about love is that it may not come in the shape you anticipated. When I was younger and more dogmatic about what I wanted from life, I prized the idea of independence so highly that I failed to understand the value of *inter*dependence; illness has forced this recognition on me, against my natural inclination to live as an island, and it has been an important lesson to have learned. The love of my family and friends, especially my parents, shown in practical care and support, brought me through the past five years; without it, I have no doubt that I would not be here. Most people who have passed under the shadow of despair will tell you that it was only love, and a belief in the possibility of love, that kept them from leaping and shattering. In the deepest dark, this is the faith that will keep us alive.

Suggested Reading

Gillian Butler and Tony Hope *Manage Your Mind: The Mental Fitness Guide*, OUP

Paul Gilbert *Overcoming Depression*, Robinson

Patrick Holford *Optimum Nutrition for the Mind*, Piatkus

Oliver James *Affluenza*, Vermilion

Kay Redfield Jamison *An Unquiet Mind*, Picador

Richard Mabey *Nature Cure*, Pimlico

Andrew Solomon *The Noonday Demon*, Vintage

William Styron *Darkness Visible*, Vintage Classics

Lewis Wolpert *Malignant Sadness*, Faber

Elizabeth Wurtzel *Prozac Nation*, Quartet Books

Useful Organisations and Websites

Mind

The National Association for Mental Health

15–19 Broadway

London E15 4BQ

www.mind.org.uk

Info line: 0845 766 0163

The Bipolar Organisation (formerly Manic Depression Fellowship)

MDF The Bipolar Organisation

Castle Works

21 St George's Road

London SE1 6ES

www.mdf.org.uk

Info line: 08456 340540

Charlie Waller Memorial Trust
Organisation founded by the family of Charlie Waller, a successful and popular young advertising executive who suffered undiagnosed bipolar disorder and committed suicide in 1997 at the age of 28. The CWMT works to promote wider understanding of depression and mood disorders and to provide resources.
Mead House
Bradfield
Reading
Berkshire RG7 6HU
www.cwmt.org
Info: 0118 974 5216

American Foundation for Suicide Prevention (online information resource of organisation which also runs campaigns and educational programmes across the US)
www.afsp.org

Students Against Depression (online resource set up by the Charlie Waller Memorial Trust)
www.studentdepression.org

Bullying UK (online resource for children and young people suffering bullying and related problems)
www.bullying.co.uk